DATE			

THE INDUSTRIAL BELT

GARLAND BIBLIOGRAPHIES IN
AMERICAN REGIONAL STUDIES
(General Editor: Kay Mussell)
VOL. 1

GARLAND REFERENCE LIBRARY
OF SOCIAL SCIENCE
VOL. 272

THE INDUSTRIAL BELT
An Annotated Bibliography

Thomas J. Schlereth

GARLAND PUBLISHING, INC. • NEW YORK & LONDON
1987

Library of Congress Cataloging-in-Publication Data

Schlereth, Thomas J.
  The industrial belt.

  (Garland bibliographies in American regional studies ;
v. 1) (Garland reference library of social science ;
v. 272)
  Includes index.
    1. Lake States—Industries—Bibliography. 2. Lake
States—Economic conditions—Bibliography. 3. Lake
States—Social conditions—Bibliography. I. Title.
II. Series. III. Series: Garland reference library of
social science ; v. 272.
Z7165.U6L347 1987   300 s [016.3380977]   86-19438
[HC107.A14]
ISBN 0-8240-8812-3

Printed on acid-free, 250-year-life paper
Manufactured in the United States of America

For

Chad Berry

and

Nila Gerhold

CONTENTS

THE INDUSTRIAL BELT

INTRODUCTION

The work of the bibliographer, like the work of the farmer or
housewife, is never done. Anyone who has ever attempted to survey
a field of scholarly literature recognizes, quite quickly, the
ultimate impossibility of completely doing the task.

This bibliography is, therefore, a selected one. It has no
pretensions to being the definitive assessment of published literature on the American region defined here as the Industrial Belt.
Like other volumes in the Garland Bibliographies in American
Regional Studies series, it does attempt, nonetheless, to provide a
research tool for graduate and undergraduate students, scholars
delving into an unfamiliar field, and librarians attempting to fill
a lacuna in their collections.

Several factors governed the selection of the bibliography's
titles. First, an attempt has been made to include published
scholarship on the geographical region composed of western
Pennsylvania, Ohio, Indiana, Michigan, western New York, and
northern Illinois. With the exceptions of western Pennsylvania and
western New York, this area is also known as the "Northwest
Territory," the "Old Northwest," the "Midwest," or the "Middle
West."

While these terms figure frequently in many of the titles discussed below, another label, "The Industrial Belt," has been chosen
for the bibliography's title. This title reveals an additional
selection principle used in defining the bibliography. Throughout
each of its topical chapters, an emphasis will be found on the
impact of industrialization on a broad range of subjects within a
regional studies perspective.

The urban dimension of this geographic region as it has under-
gone industrialization is a third bibliographic control used
throughout the book. As will be evident, considerable attention is
paid to the major cities of the region such as Pittsburgh, Buffalo,
Cincinnati, Cleveland, Detroit, Grand Rapids, Indianapolis, South
Bend, and Chicago.

Two other criteria will also be evident in the bibliography's
format. One is a deliberate orientation toward published scholarship dealing with the nineteenth and twentieth century history of
the region. A second chronological control is that the scholarly
materials reviewed here are principally works published in the last
two decades.

1

The reader will also discover that the bibliography tends to emphasize monographic literature over serial publications. However, the user can find additional bibliographic information on serial literature in a number of entries within the book. For example, many journals of state historical societies and other regional publications issue annual bibliographies summarizing serial publications in their areas. Such finding aids are noted throughout the bibliography but given particular attention in the first section, "Basic Research Resources."

                    *   *   *   *   *

The purpose of "Basic Research Resources" is to provide the user with an overview of general studies pertinent to understanding the Industrial Belt as a region. This chapter is composed of four types of works: (a) bibliographies and historiographies (for example, Albert H. Greenly, SELECTIVE BIBLIOGRAPHY OF IMPORTANT BOOKS, PAMPHLETS, AND BROADSIDES RELATING TO MICHIGAN HISTORY); (b) regional overviews (for example, Daniel E. Clark, THE MIDDLE WEST IN AMERICAN HISTORY); (c) state surveys (for example, Thomas Cochran, PENNSYLVANIA, A BICENTENNIAL HISTORY); and (d) industrial/urban studies (for example, Warner W. Pflug, A GUIDE TO THE ARCHIVES OF LABOR HISTORY AND URBAN AFFAIRS).

The book's final chapter, "Institutional Resources," provides the user of the bibliography with two types of information. One is a listing of the principal serial publications in this area of regional studies with their publication focus, institutional affiliation, editorial office and address. A second part of this chapter is devoted to important research institutions in the region. Here information is provided on the nature and scope of the research collections (documentary, statistical, and artifactual) available at the institutions. The principal research interest of these institutions and each resource center's address are also given.

Since the topical chapters of the bibliography are extremely broad subject categories, a brief word or two about the subtopics in each of them is in order here. For example, the chapter devoted to "Physical Environment" deals with topics such as the geological and geographical aspects of the region, certain dimensions of its natural history, its archaeology and its natural resources. The chapter on the "Built Environment" encompasses works dealing not only with high-style architecture but also pays attention to vernacular and popular and folk building types. Here the reader will also find references to civic sculpture and public art as well as urban technology and transportation systems.

Understandably the chapter devoted to "Economic Activities" is one of the largest in the book. Included in this chapter are topics such as agriculture, communications, manufacturing, industry, merchandising (wholesale and retail) and a wide variety of commer-

cial activities. Finance and banking are also considered in this
chapter.

The section devoted to "Cultural Expression" is also a
large and diverse topical area. Published scholarship in the
region's literature, fine arts, musical activities, cultural
philanthropy, educational developments, and certain recreational
and popular cultural activities are reviewed.

The chapter on "Politics" attempts to evaluate scholarship
dealing with political activities at the municipal, state and
regional levels. While the legislative and executive branches of
government are a particular focus, some attention is given to
judicial and constitutional questions. As will be evident, there
are numerous cross-references in this section to other parts of
the bibliography, particularly those devoted to ethnic factors and
to rural/urban issues.

While the emphasis within the category titled "Rural/Urban
Issues" is decidedly on urban topics, an attempt has been made to
survey the scholarship of rural life in a region for which rural
history has been an important characteristic. Unfortunately, the
field of rural history is a relatively new one and only beginning
to be fully explored. Rural sociology, a more well-developed field
of study, is given its due where appropriate.

References to important work in the social sciences will also
be found in the chapter devoted to "Social History." Here the
subjects of family, women's and children's histories are
addressed. Social patterns and social structure are also treated
in this chapter. Titles dealing with social mobility and
demographic research are included here too.

              *   *   *   *   *

A final note on the bibliography's organizational format. The
book is designed to enable its users to have ready access to resources on a wide range of topics. In order to accomplish this, a
system of cross-referencing and a tripartite index system has been
devised.

Titles that span two or more topical categories covered by the
bibliography are cross-referenced elsewhere in the book. For example, Harold Gosnell's NEGRO POLITICIANS: THE RISE OF NEGRO
POLITICS IN CHICAGO has entries in "Ethnic and Religious
Factors" (F39) and "Politics" (E56). The title receives its
annotated entry in the section on "Politics" because, in the
judgment of the editor, this is the primary topical focus of
the study. Thus the user of the bibliography will find a clue
to a work's primary topical orientation whenever there is a
complete descriptive annotation. The Proper Name Index lists
the main entries and any cross-reference.

Three types of indexes will be found at the book's conclusion. One is a principal name index that lists all of the authors and co-authors mentioned throughout the bibliography. In this index, as with the others that follow, the reader is directed to the title entry (A1, B2, C3, and so on) rather than the book's pagination. A geographical index is also included so that a reader might pursue titles for a principal city (for example, Cincinnati or Pittsburgh), state (for example, Indiana or Michigan), subregion (for example, western New York or western Pennsylvania) and geographic nomenclature (for example, Midwest).

A third index, devoted to specific subjects in Industrial Belt regional studies. has been devised based upon a wide range of subject categories and topical interests. In this index, for example, an attempt is made to give the reader an orientation to broad subjects such as technology and modernization.

                    *   *   *   *   *

Bibliographic research is invariably a team effort. In compiling this regional study, I have been assisted by many other people. I have made extensive use of the bibliographic labors of librarians, fellow historians, and archivists. I have endeavored to pay my intellectual debts to these scholars in the annotations I have made to those finding aids (particularly Chapter 1) that have been extremely valuable to me in compiling this work.

A special note of thanks must go to Dr. Kay Mussell, general editor for this series in the Garland Bibliographies on American Regional Studies. Dr. Mussell is the conceptual architect of this bibliographic project and has been an invaluable editorial critic and scholarly advisor to my work. Two editors at Garland Publishing, Julia Johnson and Pamela Chergotis, have reviewed the manuscript draft several times and given me invaluable editorial assistance. I am particularly grateful to their careful scrutiny of the text at several stages of its development. I would also like to publicly thank two individuals at the University of Notre Dame who have been involved in this project and, as my dedication suggests, whom I consider co-workers in the enterprise. Special thanks go to Chad Berry, a research assistant who has tirelessly tracked down bibliographic leads, corrected entry citations, and proofread innumerable drafts. Equally indispensable to the publication has been Nila Gerhold, the word processing typist in the Faculty Steno Service of the College of Arts and Letters who has not only put the manuscript through continual revisions but has offered valuable assistance as to its organizational format and visual design.

BASIC RESEARCH RESOURCES

A1. Alvord, Clarence W., ed. THE CENTENNIAL HISTORY OF
     ILLINOIS, 5 vols. Springfield: Illinois Centennial
     Commission, 1918.

     A multi-author text series focused on Illinois politics
     and economic development from statehood (1818) until
     America's entry into World War I. C.W. Alvord's "The
     Illinois Country, 1673-1818" (Volume I) has been reprinted
     by the Loyola University Press in its American West Reprint
     Series in 1965. Volume IV, "The Industrial State, 1870-
     1893," by E.L. Bogart and G.M. Thompson, also contains an
     engaging chapter by Chicago novelist Henry Blake Fuller on
     the development of arts and letters in Illinois.

A2. Ankenbruck, John. TWENTIETH CENTURY OF FORT WAYNE. Fort
     Wayne, IN: Twentieth Century Historical Fort Wayne, Inc.,
     1975.

     A bicentennial project that turns out to have a great
     deal of useful economic and social history included in its
     review of this rail and industrial center.

A3. Bald, Frederick Clever. MICHIGAN IN FOUR CENTURIES,
     Revised Edition. New York: Harper & Row, 1968.

     Good comprehensive bibliography and useful maps.

A4. Baldwin, Leland D. PITTSBURGH: THE STORY OF A CITY,
     1760-1865. Pittsburgh: University of Pittsburgh Press,
     1937 (1970).

     The standard popular history of the city from its days as
     an eighteenth-century outpost of empire to the beginning
     decades of its industrial expansion. Written for the gen-
     eral public, the author occasionally romantically expands
     certain obscure details for dramatic effect. The work
     tells us as much about local history writing in the 1930s
     as it does about Pittsburgh's emergence as a center of
     economic activity in the first half of the nineteenth
     century.

A5. Berquist, James W. "Tracing the Origins of a Midwestern
     Culture: The Case of Central Indiana." INDIANA MAGAZINE
     OF HISTORY 57 (March 1981): 1-32

Uses settlement patterns and linguistic data, particularly materials collected for the Linguistic Atlas of the
North Central States project, to demonstrate that central
Indiana can be regarded as a fairly distinct cultural sub-
area. Useful as a model to investigate Midwest regionalism
on other local levels.

A6. Bingham, Robert W. THE CRADLE OF THE QUEEN CITY: A
     HISTORY OF BUFFALO TO THE INCORPORATION OF THE CITY.
     Buffalo: Buffalo Historical Society, 1931.

     A detailed survey of the "colonial" period of Buffalo's
     history with particular attention to the city's strategic
     importance in transportation development. The major study
     on the pre-1830 city. Includes several useful maps.

A7. Blair, Karen J. "Women's History As Local History." OHIO
     HISTORY 87:4 (1978): 438-443.

     Bibliographical survey of recent publications that
     attempt to place nineteenth-century women in context with
     the social and economic trends that shaped Michigan, Ohio,
     Illinois, and Minnesota.

A8. Brichford, Maynard J., Robert M. Sutton, and Dennis
     F. Walle. MANUSCRIPTS GUIDE TO COLLECTIONS AT THE
     UNIVERSITY OF ILLINOIS AT URBANA-CHAMPAIGN. Urbana-
     Champaign: University of Illinois Press, 1976.

     Finding aid for major research materials housed at the
     University.

A9. Bridges, Roger D. "A Bibliography of Dissertations
     Related to Illinois History, 1884-1976." JOURNAL OF THE
     ILLINOIS STATE HISTORICAL SOCIETY 70:3 (1977): 208-248.

     Includes dissertations by title, author, year, and
     academic institution related to the state's history.

A10. Bridges, Roger D., and Rodney O. Davis. ILLINOIS: ITS
     HISTORY AND LEGACY. St. Louis: River City Publishers,
     1984.

     A multi-author, cross-disciplinary look at the major
     trends in the state's history since 1673. Six of the
     twelve essays focus directly on Chicago architecture,
     ethnicity, crime, politics, and self-identity. Each
     chapter also has a bibliography of the most recent and
     relevant scholarly literature on the topic.

A11. Buck, Solon J., and E.H. Buck. PLANTING OF CIVILIZATION IN
     WESTERN PENNSYLVANIA. Pittsburgh: University of
     Pittsburgh Press, 1939.

Includes extensive use of photographs, contemporary engravings and lithographs, plus a forty-page bibliography. A visual delight coupled with sound scholarship.

A12. Buley, R. Carlyle. THE OLD NORTHWEST, PIONEER PERIOD, 1815-1840. Bloomington: Indiana University Press, 1950, 1984.

A detailed overview, with particular emphasis on Indiana, Illinois, and Ohio, in which Buley sets out to do three things: 1) provide a careful chronology of events of the settlement era, 2) introduce the reader to rich contemporary historical literature of the period, 3) capture something of the attitudes, beliefs, and the way of life--what Timothy Flint called the "material of poetry"--of the time and place.

A13. Burton, William L. "Illinois Manuscript and Archival Collections--A Checklist of Published Guides." JOURNAL OF THE ILLINOIS STATE HISTORICAL SOCIETY 66 (Winter 1973).

Especially valuable guide to materials in state archive depositories.

A14. Clark, Daniel E. THE MIDDLE WEST IN AMERICAN HISTORY. New York: Crowell, 1966.

Originally published as part of Clark's THE WEST IN AMERICAN HISTORY (1937). Particularly strong on the frontier and also represents regionalism theory as applied to historical study in the 1930s. Compare to Jenson's REGIONALISM IN AMERICA (A41).

A15. Cochran, Thomas C. PENNSYLVANIA, A BICENTENNIAL HISTORY. New York: W.W. Norton, 1978.

A model for this bibliography in that much attention is devoted to the state's role in opening up what the author calls "the inland empire of the U.S." Two chapters are devoted to energy and manufacturing in the state's growth. Written by one of the country's outstanding economic historians, the study focuses on the contributions of Pittsburgh and Philadelphia.

A16. Collius, William R. OHIO: THE BUCKEYE STATE. Englewood Cliffs, NJ: Prentice-Hall, 1968.

A standard state history now in its fourth edition.

A17. Condon, George E. CLEVELAND: PRODIGY OF THE WESTERN RESERVE. Tulsa, OK: Continental Heritage, 1979.

Another picture book in the American Portrait Series that attempts to depict the city largely from a "downtown" perspective. Suburbs and neighborhoods receive little attention.

8   BASIC RESEARCH RESOURCES

A18. Dann, John C., and Arlene P. Shy, eds. GUIDE TO MANUSCRIPT
      COLLECTIONS OF THE CLEMENTS LIBRARY. Boston: G.K. Hall,
      1978.

      Definitive finding aid up to time of publication.

A19. DeChambrun, Clara Longworth. CINCINNATI: STORY OF THE
      QUEEN CITY. New York: Scribner's, 1939.

      A romantic survey with particular emphasis on society
      and the arts. Compare to the WPA GUIDE.

A20. Fisk, Arthur M. THE CLARK HISTORICAL COLLECTION WITH A
      LIST OF MICHIGAN IMPRINTS. Mount Pleasant, MI: Central
      Michigan College Press, 1956.

      Bibliographical guide to the Norman E. Clark Collection
      of Michigan History given to the college in 1956.

A21. Fox, Dixon Ryan, ed. SOURCES OF CULTURE IN THE MIDDLE
      WEST: BACKGROUNDS VERSUS FRONTIER. New York:
      Appleton-Century, 1934.

      An early scholarly attempt to define and describe the
      cultural dimensions of an indigenous "Middle West
      Civilization." The topic is explored in three essays, one
      by a political scientist (Benjamin F. Wright) and two by
      historians (Avery Craven and John D. Hicks).

A22. Fuller, Sara, ed. THE OHIO BLACK HISTORY GUIDE. Columbus:
      Ohio Historical Society, 1975.

      See E50.

A23. Geib, George W. INDIANAPOLIS: HOOSIERS' CIRCLE CITY.
      Tulsa, OK: Continental Heritage Press, 1981.

      An upbeat, pictorial celebration of the state capitol
      and its role in Marion County and Midwest. Includes 30
      pages of local corporate advertising.

A24. Ginger, Ray. ALTGELD'S AMERICA, THE LINCOLN IDEAL VERSUS
      CHANGING REALITIES. New York: Funk and Wagnalls, 1958.

      Traces the impact of Lincoln's social and political
      philosophy on the next generation of American reformers
      such as John P. Altgeld, Clarence Darrow, Jane Addams and
      other Chicago intellectuals and writers.

A25. Glazer, Sidney. THE MIDDLE WEST: A STUDY IN PROGRESS.
      New York: Bookman, 1962.

      A short historical survey of the region that sees its
      development as one of ever upward and onward. Largely a
      booster piece, containing little sensitivity to the
      region's historical and contemporary problems.

A26. Goldman, Mark. HIGH HOPES: THE RISE AND DECLINE OF
     BUFFALO, NEW YORK. Albany: State University of New
     York Press, 1983.

     An interpretation of the historical forces--external and
     internal--that have shaped New York's second largest city
     and the eastern anchor of the nation's industrial belt.
     Goldman surveys Buffalo's evolution on the Erie Canal
     through its developments as a major commercial center and
     then its emergence and decline as a significant industrial
     metropolis. Particular emphasis is given to social history
     topics such as work, ethnicity, education, and family and
     community life.

A27. Gray, Ralph D., ed. THE HOOSIER STATE: READINGS IN INDIANA
     HISTORY. VOLUME I. INDIAN PREHISTORY TO 1880. Grand
     Rapids: Eermanns, 1980.

     The seventh set of anthologies of essays and excerpts
     from primary and secondary works about Indiana to appear
     since the first in 1914. For references to the other six
     previous collections, see Howard Peckham's review in the
     INDIANA MAGAZINE OF HISTORY 78 (March 1982).

A28. Gray, Ralph D., ed. THE HOOSIER STATE: READINGS IN
     INDIANA HISTORY. VOLUME II. THE MODERN ERA. Grand
     Rapids: Eermanns, 1980.

     See A27.

A29. Greenly, Albert H. SELECTIVE BIBLIOGRAPHY OF IMPORTANT
     BOOKS, PAMPHLETS, AND BROADSIDES RELATING TO MICHIGAN
     HISTORY. Lunenberg, VT: Stinehour Press, 1958.

     A very limited edition (500 copies) printed of this
     excellent guide to specialized literature on the state.

A30. Gutgesell, Stephen. GUIDE TO OHIO NEWSPAPERS, 1793-1973.
     Columbus: Ohio Historical Society, 1974.

     A valuable compendium listing all the newspapers
     published in the state. Compare to John W. Miller's
     INDIANA NEWSPAPER BIBLIOGRAPHY (A55).

A31. Haller, Stephen E., and Patrick B. Nolan. FIRST STOP FOR
     LOCAL HISTORY RESEARCH: A GUIDE TO COUNTY RECORDS
     PRESERVED AT WRIGHT STATE GREATER MIAMI VALLEY RESEARCH
     CENTER. Dayton, OH: Wright State University, Greater
     Miami Valley Research Center, 1976.

A32. Hansen, Harry, ed. ILLINOIS, A DESCRIPTIVE AND HISTORICAL
     GUIDE. New York: Hastings House, 1974.

     A WPA guide that first appeared in 1939 and was revised
     in 1947. Arranged in the typical format of WPA guides
     with topical treatments from agriculture to theatre, a

section devoted to cities and towns (with Chicago getting the most extensive treatment) and travel tours. The revised edition contains new information on economic and transportation developments. Demographic patterns are surveyed using the most recent census data then available.

A33. Harding, Bruce C. "Sources For Ethnic Studies In Region 5 Archives Branch and Regional Archives Branch--Chicago," ILLINOIS LIBRARIES 57 (March 1975): 184-92.

See E62.

A34. Havighurst, Walter. THE HEARTLAND: OHIO, INDIANA, ILLINOIS. Revised Edition. New York: Harper & Row, 1962, 1974.

This revised edition contains an additional chapter documenting the region's economic diversification, new innovations by state and local governments, and the impact of urban renewal and the Saint Lawrence Seaway. A book in the Regions of America series, Havighurst's treatment is a well-written overview by one of the twentieth-century's outstanding regional historians.

A35. Havighurst, Walter. OHIO, A BICENTENNIAL HISTORY. New York: W.W. Norton, 1976.

An extremely well-written single-volume survey of the state's evolution by one of the Midwest's most prolific and perceptive students of the region. Havighurst gives special emphasis to Ohio's pivotal role in national politics in the nineteenth century and to the state's continually expanding contributions to agriculture, industry, and manufacturing in the twentieth century.

A36. Hinding, Andrea, and Rosemary Richardson. ARCHIVAL AND MANUSCRIPT RESOURCES FOR THE STUDY OF WOMEN'S HISTORY: A BEGINNING. Minneapolis: University of Minnesota Social Welfare History Archives, 1972.

Excellent on Midwest sources.

A37. Hinsdale, Burke Aaron. THE OLD NORTHWEST, WITH A VIEW OF THE THIRTEEN COLONIES AS CONSTITUTED BY THE ROYAL CHARTERS. New York: T. MacConn, 1888.

A representative perception of the region in the late 19th-century.

A38. Hoffmann, John. "The Scope of State History in Michigan Historical Writing." THE OLD NORTHWEST 4 (June 1978): 151-159.

Serves as a good historiographical review of literature published about Michigan in the 1970s.

A39. Honhart, Frederick L., Suzann M. Pyzik, and Saralee R.
      Howard, eds. A GUIDE TO THE MICHIGAN STATE UNIVERSITY
      ARCHIVES AND HISTORICAL COLLECTIONS. East Lansing:
      Michigan State University Archives, 1976.

      Finding aid for both specialized collections such as the
      Land Grant Research Collection and the institution's
      general holdings.

A40. Indiana University Oral History Project. GUIDE TO INDIANA
      UNIVERSITY ORAL HISTORY RESEARCH PROJECT AND RELATED
      STUDIES. Bloomington: Indiana University, 1977.

      Particularly useful for labor history topics.

A41. Jensen, Merrill. REGIONALISM IN AMERICA. Madison:
      University of Wisconsin Press, 1951.

      A survey of historical and social science thinking on
      American regional theory by a historian of colonial America
      who taught for many years at the University of Wisconsin.
      Jensen's argument has several parallels to that of another
      Wisconsin historian, Frederick Jackson Turner, as expounded
      in Turner's THE SIGNIFICANCE OF SECTIONS IN AMERICAN
      HISTORY (New York: H. Holt, 1932). Jensen also reviews
      regional variations in American speech patterns,
      literature, painting, and architecture.

A42. Jensen, Richard. ILLINOIS, A BICENTENNIAL HISTORY. New
      York: W.W. Norton, 1978.

      An attempt to view Illinois as a "microcosm state" where-
      in the economic, political, and social history of the area
      is examined to illuminate the nature of the American
      national character, 1800-1970. Using the explanatory model
      of modernization, Jensen integrates his analysis around
      three different historical patterns that he labels
      "traditional," "modern," and "post-modern." The book has a
      strong Chicago emphasis.

A43. Jordan, Philip D. OHIO COMES OF AGE, 1873-1900. Columbus:
      Ohio State Archaeological and Historical Society, 1943.

      Sees the state's economic expansion, role in national
      politics, and urban growth in the second half of the
      nineteenth century as the crucial watershed in Ohio's
      maturity.

A44. Larned, J.N. THE LITERATURE OF AMERICAN HISTORY: A
      BIBLIOGRAPHICAL GUIDE. Columbia, OH: Long's College
      Book Co., 1953.

      Has a section, "The Middle West and Northwest," that is
      useful on nineteenth-century historical studies of the
      region.

A45. Larson, David R. GUIDE TO MANUSCRIPTS COLLECTIONS AND
      INSTITUTIONAL RECORDS IN OHIO. Columbus: Ohio Society of
      Archivists, 1974.

      Major finding aid to unpublished materials in the state.

A46. Leutz, Andrea, ed. A GUIDE TO MANUSCRIPTS AT THE OHIO
      HISTORICAL SOCIETY. Columbus: Ohio Historical Society,
      1972.

      A basic reference source.

A47. Lubove, Roy, ed. PITTSBURGH. New York: New Viewpoints,
      1976.

      A paperback edition of readings on the city suitable for
      use in teaching a course on Pittsburgh.

A48. Lydeus, Q.Q., ed. THE STORY OF GRAND RAPIDS. Grand
      Rapids: Kregel Publications, 1966.

      A mammoth (682 pages) compendium of local materials;
      strong on the city's important furniture industry.

A49. McKelvey, Blake. ROCHESTER. 3 vols. Cambridge, MA:
      Harvard University Press, 1945.

      A pioneering work in American urban history written by
      one of the first municipally funded city historians.
      Volumes I (The Water-Powered City, 1912-1854) and II (The
      Flower City, 1955-1890) focus on economic life and
      Rochester as a transportation nexus. Volume III (The Quest
      for Quality, 1890-1925) concentrates on a manufacturing
      center's cultural and intellectual life. For insight on
      McKelvey as an urban historian, see his oral history in
      Bruce Stave's THE MAKING OF URBAN HISTORY (New York: Sage
      Publications, 1977), pp. 33-62.

A50. McShane, Stephen G., compiler. GUIDE TO THE COLLECTIONS OF
      THE CALUMET REGIONAL ARCHIVES. Gary, IN: Indiana
      University Northwest, 1984.

      Since 1973, the Calumet Regional Archives has been
      gathering significant records and papers pertaining to
      northwest Indiana. The holdings include minutes, corre-
      spondence, newsletters, photographs, diaries, reports,
      office files, and programs documenting local history.
      Topics include labor history, political history, black
      history, and educational history.

A51. Martin, John B. CALL IT NORTH COUNTRY; THE STORY OF UPPER
      MICHIGAN. New York: A.A. Knopf, 1944.

      One of the best single-volume surveys of a usually
      neglected area of the state.

A52. Mason, Philip P., ed. DIRECTORY OF JEWISH ARCHIVAL
      INSTITUTIONS. Detroit: Wayne State University Press,
      1975.

      See E88.

A53. Mayer, Harold M., and Richard C. Wade. CHICAGO: GROWTH OF
      A METROPOLIS. Chicago: University of Chicago Press,
      1969.

      This book is recognized not only as the most important
      modern historical survey on Chicago but also as a ground-
      breaking work in urban history methodology and pictorial
      as evidence. Almost 1000 photographs and 50 maps are used
      in the book to document and elaborate the argument. Glen
      E. Holt, a research associate of Mayer and Wade, has
      written an interesting article on Chicago's picture
      resources used in researching the book in an article in
      CHICAGO HISTORY I:3 (Spring 1971):158-169.

A54. Miles, William, Compiler. WOMEN'S HISTORY: A GUIDE TO
      UNPUBLISHED RESOURCES IN THE CLARK HISTORICAL LIBRARY.
      Mt. Pleasant, MI: Clark Historical Library, 1976.

      Strongest on Michigan material.

A55. Miller, John C. INDIANA NEWSPAPER BIBLIOGRAPHY.
      Indianapolis: Indiana Historical Society, 1983.

      Arranged by county chapters with towns and cities within
      the county arranged alphabetically, thus bringing together
      newspapers of contiguous communities. Scope runs from 1804
      to 1980.

A56. Murray, John J., ed. HERITAGE OF THE MIDDLE WEST. Norman:
      University of Oklahoma Press, 1958.

      A collection of essays by Midwesterners on Midwesterners,
      generated by the Coe College Conference on the Heritage of
      the Middle West. In addition to treating traditional
      topics such as politics, economics, and ethnicity, the
      anthology contains essays on regional utopian experiments,
      political refugees, philosophy, and higher education.

A57. Murray, Lawrence L. "The Mellon Family: Making and Shaping
      History: A Survey of the Literature." THE WESTERN
      PENNSYLVANIA HISTORICAL MAGAZINE 62 (January 1979):
      61-65.

      Excellent review of studies on the Mellons and their
      historical role in the region.

A58. Odum, Howard W., and Harry E. Moore. AMERICAN REGIONALISM:
      A CULTURAL/HISTORICAL APPROACH TO NATIONAL INDEPENDENCE.
      New York: Henry Holt, 1938.

In spite of its intimidating size, Odum and Moore's classic volume remains the most comprehensive analysis on the subject. The industrial belt is given ample coverage.

A59. Olson, David J., compiler. BIBLIOGRAPHY OF SOURCES RELATING TO WOMEN. East Lansing: Michigan History Division, Michigan Department of State, 1975.

Especially strong on research materials available in the industrial belt region.

A60. Pargellis, Stanley, ed. A MIDWEST BIBLIOGRAPHY. Chicago: The Newberry Library, 1947.

First published as a supplementary number of THE NEWBERRY LIBRARY BULLETIN, the guide serves as an introduction to resources on the region in that major Chicago resource center. Includes sections such as "Fine Presses," "Books of Protest" and an "English Midwest Book Shelf" commonly neglected in other bibliographies.

A61. Peckham, Howard H. INDIANA, A BICENTENNIAL HISTORY. New York: W.W. Norton, 1978.

Commissioned by the American Association for State and Local History as one of the volumes in the series "The State and the Nation," this book turns out to be Howard Peckham's attempt to avoid the tedium of writing another traditional state history and to provide one man's interpretation of what seems distinctive about Indiana. Hoosierism, which Peckham spends an entire chapter defining and which he includes in the title of all the chapters, is put forth as the clue to the state's character.

A62. Pessen, Edward. "Reflections on New York and Its Recent Historians." NEW YORK HISTORY SOCIETY QUARTERLY 63 (1982):145-156.

Stresses new work on the professions, the functions of municipalities, local history, voluntary associations, and the "sociology of politics"; contains an excellent bibliography of current scholarship.

A63. Pflug, Warner W., ed. A GUIDE TO THE ARCHIVES OF LABOR HISTORY AND URBAN AFFAIRS. Detroit: Wayne State University Press, 1974.

See G59.

A64. Pierce, Bessie Louise. A HISTORY OF CHICAGO. 3 vols. New York: A.A. Knopf, 1937.

Without question, the standard text on Chicago history, 1673-1893. Done under the auspices of the University of Chicago's Social Science Research Committee, the three-

volume survey is devoted primarily to economic, political,
and social issues. For a historiographical analysis of its
author, see Perry Duis, "Bessie Louise Pierce, Historian of
Chicago," CHICAGO HISTORY 5:3 (Fall 1976):130-140.

A65. Pierce, Neal R. THE MEGASTATES OF AMERICA: PEOPLE,
      POLITICS, AND POWER IN THE TEN GREAT STATES. New York:
      W.W. Norton, 1972.

      The subtitle of this survey by a Washington-based
      political writer accurately describes its focus.
      "Megastateness," as defined by Pierce, is based upon
      population size and hence five (New York, Pennsylvania,
      Ohio, Michigan, and Illinois) states in his sample are part
      of the Industrial Belt as delineated in this reference
      bibliography. Pierce also seeks to update John Gunther's
      INSIDE U.S.A. (1947) and includes a useful bibliography of
      magazine literature.

A66. Powers, Thomas, and William McWitt. GUIDE TO MANUSCRIPTS
      IN THE BENTLEY HISTORICAL LIBRARY. Ann Arbor:
      University of Michigan Press, 1976.

      Finding aid for one of the region's outstanding research
      institutions.

A67. Quaife, Milo M., and Sidney Glazer. MICHIGAN: FROM
      PRIMITIVE WILDERNESS TO INDUSTRIAL COMMONWEALTH. New
      York: Prentice-Hall, 1948.

      Places the state in the economic context of the
      industrial belt region.

A68. Rimmel, William M. "The Allegheny Story." THE WESTERN
      PENNSYLVANIA HISTORY MAGAZINE 53:3 (1970):237-242.

      Concise survey of the social and economic history of over
      150 years of Allegheny City, Pennsylvania, covering such
      topics as pollution, vandalism, schools, parks, and the
      German quarter, Dutchtown.

A69. Scheiber, Henry N., ed. THE OLD NORTHWEST: STUDIES IN
      REGIONAL HISTORY, 1787-1910. Lincoln: University of
      Nebraska Press, 1969.

      An anthology of previously printed articles on the
      region's social life, agriculture, urbanism, mobility,
      politics, and labor relations. The preface, "On the
      Concepts of Regionalism and the Frontier," is a tidy
      historiographical estimate of the state of these two
      explanatory concepts in the early 1970s.

A70. Schlereth, Thomas J. "Regional Studies In America: The
      Chicago Model." AMERICAN STUDIES INTERNATIONAL 13
      (Autumn 1974): 20-35.

Bibliographical companion to the author's interpretive thesis ("America, 1871-1919: A View From Chicago," AMERICAN STUDIES see H101) of Chicago as a microcosm of urban America in the late nineteenth and early twentieth centuries. Republished in AMERICAN STUDIES: TOPICS AND SOURCES, edited by Robert Walker (Westport, CT: Greenwood Press, 1976), pp. 224-237.

A71. Schlereth, Thomas J. "Regional Studies On The Chicago Model Since 1975." SOURCES FOR AMERICAN STUDIES. Edited by Robert Walker and J.B. Kellog. Westport, CT: Greenwood Press, 1980, pp. 518-532.

Updates the previous bibliographical and historio-graphical review; work in regional social history, architecture, and city planning receives special attention.

A72. Smith, Thomas H., ed. AN OHIO READER: 1750 TO THE CIVIL WAR. Grand Rapids: Eermanns, 1975.

Volume I of a two-volume set of primary resources pertinent to the state's historical development. Includes introductory notes and bibliographic references.

A73. Smith, Thomas H., ed. AN OHIO READER: RECONSTRUCTION TO THE PRESENT. Grand Rapids: Eermanns, 1975.

Volume II.

A74. Stevens, S.K. PENNSYLVANIA: A STUDENT'S GUIDE TO LOCAL HISTORY. New York: Teachers College, Columbia University Press, 1965.

A handbook prepared by the then-Executive Director of the state's Historical and Museum Commission.

A75. Sutton, Robert P. THE PRAIRIE STATE, A DOCUMENTARY HISTORY OF ILLINOIS COLONIAL YEARS TO 1860. Grand Rapids: Eermanns, 1976.

Volume I of a two-volume anthology, this study is organized into two chronological units, the "Formative Period, 8,000 B.C. to 1818" and the "Prairie State, 1818-1860." Each unit is subdivided into topical chapters dealing with the arrivals of the Europeans; the period of French exploration and English control; and the years of territorial government and early statehood. Each chapter consists of what the author calls special accounts (interpretive essays by modern scholars) followed by original narratives (letters, diaries, speeches, travel-ogues).

A76. Sutton, Robert P. THE PRAIRIE STATE, CIVIL WAR TO THE PRESENT. Grand Rapids: Eermanns, 1976.

The companion volume to the author's first anthology of documentation on Illinois development into the twentieth century. Identical in format to Volume one, Sutton divides this work into two chronological units, "The GilJed Age, 1860-1919," and "Modern Illinois, 1920-1975." The first section dealing with the organization of farmers, industrial labor ferment, and progressive reforms, contains more comprehensive data than the second on the modern era. The pattern of special accounts and original narratives initiated in the first volume is repeated here.

A77. Thomson, Peter G. A BIBLIOGRAPHY OF THE STATE OF OHIO. 2 vols. New York: Argonaut Press, 1966.

Reprint of a classic nineteenth-century regional bibliography first issued in 1880.

A78. University of Chicago Library. A PRELIMINARY GUIDE TO MANUSCRIPTS AND ARCHIVES IN THE UNIVERSITY OF CHICAGO LIBRARY. Chicago: University of Chicago: 1973.

Includes sources on literary, religious, and educational history.

A79. Vance, Rubert. "The Region." INTERNATIONAL ENCYCLOPEDIA OF THE SOCIAL SCIENCES. Vol. 13. New York: Macmillan, 1968, pp. 372-382.

Perhaps the best brief introduction to the concept of region that has been done from an American perspective. Offers succinct answers to questions such as: What is a region? What is regionalism?

A80. Waitley, Douglas. PORTRAIT OF THE MIDWEST. New York: Abelard, 1963.

A popular, informed history of Midwest life and letters from "the ice age to the industrial era." Includes several specific chapters on Midwest authors.

A81. Washburn, David E., ed. THE PEOPLES OF PENNSYLVANIA: AN ANNOTATED BIBLIOGRAPHY OF RESOURCE MATERIALS. Pittsburgh: University Center For International Studies, University of Pittsburgh, 1981.

See E121.

A82. Weisenburger, Francis P. OHIO: STUDENT'S GUIDE TO LOCAL HISTORY. New York: Teachers College, Columbia University Press, 1965.

One in a series of fifty handbooks designed to promote the study of local history.

A83. Whipkey, Harry E. GUIDE TO THE MANUSCRIPT GROUPS IN THE PENNSYLVANIA STATE ARCHIVES. Harrisburg: Pennsylvania Historical and Museum Commission, 1976.

Surveys public records of state and provincial
government.

A84. Whipkey, Harry E. GUIDE TO THE RECORD GROUPS IN THE
      PENNSYLVANIA STATE ARCHIVES. Harrisburg: Pennsylvania
      Historical and Museum Commission, 1977.

      In addition to executive, legislative, and judicial
      records, this finding aid surveys holdings in special
      collections such as maps, posters, postcards, photographs
      and films.

A85. Wilkinson, Norman B., Compiler. BIBLIOGRAPHY OF
      PENNSYLVANIA HISTORY. Harrisburg: Pennsylvania
      Historical and Museum Commission, 1957.

      Excellent up to its publication date; includes theses and
      dissertations.

A86. Williams, Peter W. "Religion and the Old Northwest: A
      Bibliography Essay." THE OLD NORTHWEST 5 (Spring
      1979): 37-89.

      See E126.

A87. Writers' Program, Works Projects Administration.
      CINCINNATI: A GUIDE TO THE QUEEN CITY AND ITS NEIGHBORS.
      Cincinnati: Wiesen-Hart Press, 1943.

      Best urban guide to any of the major cities in the in-
      dustrial belt region. Still the best one-volume intro-
      duction to pre-World War II Cincinnati.

A88. Writers' Program, Works Projects Administration. MICHIGAN,
      A GUIDE TO THE WOLVERINE STATE. New York: Oxford
      University Press, 1941.

      WPA guide reprinted by Somerset Publishers in 1973.

A89. Wyman, Walker. "The Old Northwest Bicentennial Histories:
      An Essay Review." PACIFIC NORTHWEST QUARTERLY 72:3
      (1981) 107-110.

      Evaluates eleven volumes in the States and the Nation
      Series published by W.W. Norton and the American
      Association for State and Local History. Provides a quick
      review of those state histories in the industrial belt.

A90. Wynear, Hubomyr R., et al. ETHNIC GROUPS IN OHIO WITH
      SPECIAL EMPHASIS ON CLEVELAND: AN ANNOTATED
      BIBLIOGRAPHICAL GUIDE. Cleveland: Cleveland State
      University Press, 1975.

      See E130.

A91. Yon, Paul D. A GUIDE TO OHIO COUNTRY AND MUNICIPAL RECORDS
      FOR URBAN RESEARCH. Columbus: Ohio Historical Society,
      1972.

      See G90.

A92. Zelinsky, Wilbur. "North America's Vernacular Regions."
      ANNALS OF THE ASSOCIATION OF AMERICAN GEOGRAPHERS 70
      (March 1980): 1-16.

      Classifies various types of American culture areas
      according to vernacular criteria as well as suggests the
      emergence of a "voluntary region" in the U.S.

PHYSICAL ENVIRONMENT

B1. Abbott, Carl. "The Plank Road Enthusiasm in the Antebellum
     Middle West." INDIANA MAGAZINE OF HISTORY 67:2 (1971):
     95-116.

     See I1.

B2. Ballard, Robert M. "Pollution in Lake Erie: 1872-1965."
     SPECIAL LIBRARIES 66:8 (1975): 378-382.

     Reviews the literature and some of the primary sources
     covering the development of pollution in Lake Erie during
     the period discussed.

B3. Bendler, E. Perry. "Exploration for Natural Gas in Ohio."
     INLAND SEAS 18 (Winter 1962): 281-98.

     Describes the nineteenth-century search for new energy
     sources for industrial and domestic uses.

B4. Berry, Fern. "Unchanging Land: The Jack-Pine Plains of
     Michigan." MICHIGAN HISTORY 47 (March 1963): 15-28.

     An ecological analysis of one aspect of the state's
     forest cover.

B5. Bowden, Clyde N., Compiler. CATALOG OF THE INLAND RIVERS
     LIBRARY. Cincinnati: Public Library of Cincinnati and
     Hamilton County, 1968.

     Finding aid to Ohio and inland water navigation.

B6. Bradshaw, James Stanford. "Grand Rapids Furniture
     Beginnings." MICHIGAN HISTORY 52 (Winter 1968): 279-98.

     See C24.

B7. Bretz, J. Harlan. GEOLOGY OF THE CHICAGO REGION. 2 vols.
     Urbana: University of Illinois, 1955.

     The two volumes make up the best geological description
     of Chicago and the area around it. Volume I was intended
     for use in schools and for the layman; Volume II, technical
     in nature, is addressed to geologists and engineers. Both

parts are well illustrated with charts and photographs.
The fifteen color maps that accompany the work are
fundamental to a study of the area.

B8.   Brownell, Joseph W. "The Cultural Midwest." JOURNAL OF
      GEOGRAPHY 39 (February 1960): 81-85.

      Appears to be the first attempt to delineate the outer
      limits of the region in terms of cultural geography;
      explores impact of climate and terrain.

B9.   Cain, Louis P. "Unfouling the Public's Nest: Chicago's
      Sanitary Diversion of Lake Michigan Water." TECHNOLOGY
      AND CULTURE 15 (October 1974): 594-613.

      Summarizes the nineteenth and early twentieth-century
      effort to deal with municipal sanitation and to reverse the
      direction of the Chicago River.

B10. Conzen, Michael P. CHICAGO MAPMAKERS: ESSAYS ON THE RISE
      OF THE CITY'S MAP TRADE. Chicago: The Chicago Map
      Society, 1984.

      Two introductory chapters offer an overview of Chicago's
      evolving map trade in the nineteenth century and an examin-
      ation of the city's earliest manuscript and printed maps
      and their makers. Then, four essays explore the mapmaking
      careers of some of Chicago's most famous nineteenth-century
      cartographers and their firms: Rufus Blanchard, the city's
      first comprehensive map publisher; George F. Cram,
      Blanchard's nephew and a prolific atlas maker; Alfred T.
      Andreas, major figure in county and state atlas publishing;
      and Rand McNally & Co., Chicago's most durable and
      internationally known cartographic firm. Individually and
      collectively, these enterpreneurs developed the aggressive
      Chicago school of cartography, and helped make their city,
      in less than half a century, the map capital of America.
      This collection seeks to throw comparative light on the
      origins and development of commercial mapmaking in an
      "instant city" of the American West.

B11. Cutler, Irving. CHICAGO: METROPOLIS OF THE MID-CONTINENT.
      2nd ed. Chicago: Geographic Society of Chicago, 1976.

      Cutler's account of the city is topical, showing how the
      physical features of the area mixed with the influx of a
      new, varied population, changing transportation technology,
      and a growing, diverse economy. He describes urban growth
      and planning and concludes with lists of historic sites,
      Chicago "firsts," significant dates and selected statis-
      tics. The bibliography is well organized and useful. The
      best short introduction to Chicago.

B12. Davis, Richard C. NORTH AMERICAN FOREST HISTORY: A GUIDE
     TO ARCHIVES AND MANUSCRIPTS IN THE UNITED STATES AND
     CANADA. Santa Barbara, CA: Clio Books, 1977.

     Very useful on Michigan's forest industry.

B13. Dillon, Lowell I., and Edward E. Lyon, eds. INDIANA:
     CROSSROADS OF AMERICA. Dubuque, IA: Kendall/Hunt,
     1978.

     Contains chapters on geology, drainage, streams and
     lakes, weather and climate, vegetation, soils, transpor-
     tation, agriculture, minerals, manufacturing, population,
     and outdoor recreation.

B14. Donnelly, Murray S. "Progress and Problems in
     Environmental Controls With Special Reference to the
     Great Lakes." TRANSACTIONS OF THE ROYAL SOCIETY OF
     CANADA 17 (1979): 187-200.

     Argues that despite greater interest in environmental
     concerns and recent legislation, industries, governments,
     and individuals continue to pollute the water of the
     region.

B15. Engel, J. Ronald. "Social Democracy, the Roots of Ecology,
     and the Preservation of the Indiana Dunes." JOURNAL OF
     FOREST HISTORY 28 (January 1984): 4-13.

     See F26.

B16. Flader, Susan L. "An Ecosystem Perspective on
     Environmental and Social Change in the Great Lakes
     Forest." JOURNAL OF FOREST HISTORY 27 (January 1983):
     34-41.

     Surveys the interrelation of the evolving natural history
     of the forest cover of the Upper Midwest with attention to
     human settlement patterns and economic uses.

B17. Franklin, Kay, and Norma Schaeffer. DUEL FOR THE DUNES:
     LAND USE CONFLICT ON THE SHORES OF LAKE MICHIGAN.
     Urbana: University of Illinois Press, 1983.

     Illuminates the detailed inner workings of government
     decision making on several levels; provides a historical
     overview of the lobbying efforts and the National Park
     Service response. A case study of the ecological movement
     in a sector of the industrial belt.

B18. Goode, John Paul. THE GEOGRAPHIC BACKGROUND OF CHICAGO.
     Chicago: University of Chicago Press, 1926.

     A geography in the conventional sense; that is, not a
     geology but an explanation of how Chicago's situation in
     regard to certain natural features determined aspects of

the city's growth. Among the natural features discussed
are: coal, iron ore, timber, grain and livestock
production, and Chicago's location at the hub of an
important transportation network.

B19. Hart, John Fraser. "Field Patterns in Indiana."
      GEOGRAPHICAL REVIEW 58 (1968): 450-71.

      A classic article that examines field configurations in
      order to demonstrate the surveying techniques and land
      ownership trends.

B20. Holt, Glen E. "Private Plans for Public Spaces: The
      Origins of Chicago's Park System, 1850-1875." CHICAGO
      HISTORY 8 (Fall 1979): 173-84.

      See H62.

B21. Indiana Historical Society. THIS LAND OF OURS: THE
      ACQUISITION AND DISPOSITION OF THE PUBLIC DOMAIN.
      Indianapolis: Indiana Historical Society, 1978.

      Reginald Horsman's highly interpretive historiographical
      essay, "Changing Images of the Public Domain," which was
      first presented at an IHS symposium in 1978, is only one
      of five excellent studies in this volume.

B22. Jakle, John A. IMAGES OF THE OHIO VALLEY. New York:
      Oxford University Press, 1977.

      Summarizes the themes of over 200 travel journals in the
      Midwest for the years between 1740 and 1860, looking at
      what Americans thought the valley to be. The volume
      attempts to answer four questions in this explanation of
      American myth and metaphor, fact and symbol: How was the
      Ohio Valley's early geography organized cognitively by
      those who traveled in the region? What did people think
      they saw? What did they think it meant? What satisfaction
      did they derive from this knowledge?

B23. Jakle, John A. "Salt on the Ohio Valley Frontier,
      1770-1820." ANNALS OF THE ASSOCIATION OF AMERICAN
      GEOGRAPHERS 59 (December 1969): 687-709.

      Surveys the economic importance and geographic
      distribution of mineral deposits in the region's
      settlement, trading, and place-name history.

B24. Jakle, John A. "The American Bison and the Human
      Occupance of the Ohio Valley." PROCEEDINGS OF THE
      AMERICAN PHILOSOPHICAL SOCIETY 112 (August 1968):
      299-306.

      A geographical analysis of the diffusion of the bison and
      the role human settlement played in its changing ecology.

B25. Jones, Cynthia L., and Ronald O. Kapp. "Relationship of
      Bay County Michigan Presettlement Forest Patterns to
      Indian Cultures." MICHIGAN ACADEMICAN 5:1 (1972):
      17-28.

      Examines the type of forest with which the aboriginal
      indians of Michigan interacted. Records of original land
      surveys were used to reconstruct the forest patterns of a
      seven-township area just prior to European settlement in
      the 1850s.

B26. Karpinski, Louis G. BIBLIOGRAPHY OF PRINTED MAPS OF
      MICHIGAN, 1804-1880. Lansing: Michigan Historical
      Commission, 1931.

      Serves as a historical atlas of the state in relation to
      the Great Lakes region. Includes a discusson of Michigan
      maps and mapmakers by William Jenks.

B27. Karrow, Robert W., Jr. CHECKLIST OF PRINTED MAPS OF THE
      MIDDLE WEST TO 1900. 14 Vols. Chicago: The Newberry
      Library, 1983.

      An invaluable 13-volume cartobibliography with an
      additional 14th volume that serves as a subject, author,
      and title index. This reference study is the key resource
      to the published cartography of the region.

B28. Karrow, Robert W., Jr., and David Buisseret. GARDENS OF
      DELIGHT: MAPS AND TRAVEL ACCOUNTS OF ILLINOIS AND THE
      GREAT LAKES FROM THE COLLECTION OF HERMON DUNLAP SMITH.
      Chicago: The Newberry Library, 1984.

      A companion-piece and exhibit catalog to a segment of the
      map collections in the Newberry Library, this text explains
      the source material of the early history of the Midwest in
      general and of early Chicago in particular.

B29. Kingsbury, Robert C. AN ATLAS OF INDIANA. Bloomington:
      Indiana University Dept. of Geography, 1970.

      Best one-volume reference work on the cartography of the
      state.

B30. Lankton, Larry D. "The Machine UNDER the Garden: Rock
      Drills Arrive at the Lake Superior Copper Mines,
      1868-1883. TECHNOLOGY AND CULTURE 24:1 (1983): 1-37.

      The supersession of hand drilling by the pneumatic drill
      greatly increased productivity and lightened the copper
      miner's work. Its adaptation to copper mining, however,
      was far from easy. The Burleigh, a machine drill that had
      proven successful in drilling the Hoosac Tunnel, was tried
      in 1868, but it soon proved too heavy and cumbersome to be
      practical in the different conditions of copper mining.
      For a decade other drills tried and failed. Only with the

introduction of the compact Rand drill around 1883 was the
innovation complete. It was accepted by the miners with
little resistance because it meant higher wages, better
working conditions, and increased employment in the region
as a whole.

B31. Laurent, Jerome K. "Trade, Transport and Technology: The
      American Great Lakes, 1866-1910." JOURNAL OF TRANSPORT
      HISTORY (Great Britain) 4(1) 1983: 1-24.

      See C95.

B32. Lindsey, David. OHIO'S WESTERN RESERVE; STORY OF ITS PLACE
      NAMES. Cleveland: Press of Western Reserve University,
      1955.

      A playful review of a subsection of the state's history,
      particularly the role of New England and New York settlers
      to the area.

B33. Marshall, Douglas W., ed. RESEARCH CATALOG OF MAPS OF
      AMERICA TO 1860 IN THE WILLIAM CLEMENTS LIBRARY. Ann
      Arbor: University of Michigan, 1972.

      Strong on Midwest cartography.

B34. May, George S., and Victor F. Lerner. "Thomas Edison's
      Experimental Work With Michigan Iron Ore." MICHIGAN
      HISTORY 53 (Summer 1969): 109-30.

      Traces the technological history of one of Edison's
      largely unsuccessful inventive undertakings in his program
      of industrial research and development.

B35. Mayer, Harold M. "The Launching of Chicago: The Situation
      and the Site." CHICAGO HISTORY 9 (Summer 1980): 68-79.

      A historical and geographical overview of the factor
      prompting the city's early nineteenth-century growth.

B36. Mayer, Harold M. "Politics and Land Use: The Indiana
      Shoreline of Lake Michigan." ANNALS OF THE ASSOCIATION
      OF AMERICAN GEOGRAPHERS 54 (December 1964): 508-23.

      See F70.

B37. Mayer, Harold M. THE PORT OF CHICAGO AND THE ST. LAWRENCE
      SEAWAY. Chicago: University of Chicago Department of
      Geography Research Paper 49, 1957.

      A view of the impact of the St. Lawrence from the Midwest
      looking eastward. Standard work that has yet to be
      superseded by recent scholarship.

B38. Mayer, Harold M., and Thomas M. Corsi. "The Northeastern
      Ohio Urban Couples." CONTEMPORARY METROPOLITAN AMERICA:

TWENTY GEOGRAPHICAL VIGNETTES. Cambridge, MA: Ballinger, 1976, Vol. 3, pp. 109-179.

Survey of the contemporary economic geography of the region from Youngstown to Cleveland. Bibliography.

B39. Mayfield, Harold. "The Changing Toledo Region--A Naturalist's Point of View." NORTHWEST OHIO QUARTERLY 34 (Spring 1962): 82-106.

A must for those doing research in northwest Ohio and southeastern Michigan, the author first geologically reconstructs the past, when the region was a shallow lake, and then proceeds to discuss the continuing changes in geology and zoology through the present, with estimates for the future.

B40. Nelson, Ronald E. ed. ILLINOIS: LAND AND LIFE IN THE PRAIRIE STATE. Dubuque, IA: Kendall/Hunt, 1978.

In addition to an overview of historical geography of the state, there are useful chapters on farming, mining, manufacturing, and population and social geography. Special attention is paid to the Chicago Metropolitan Area.

B41. Noble, Allen G., and Albert J. Korsek. OHIO--AN AMERICAN HEARTLAND. Columbus: Ohio Division of Geological Survey, 1975.

Compact geographic and geological overview which also situates the state in the wider context of the region.

B42. Peters, Bernard C. "Early Perception of a High Plain in Michigan." ANNALS OF THE ASSOCIATION OF AMERICAN GEOGRAPHERS 62:3 (1972): 57-60.

The "high plain" shown on many early maps of Michigan was not a fanciful creation, but reality as perceived by early travelers. Their perception of a high plain was as much the result of a change in vegetation as of an actual change in land forms.

B43. Peters, Bernard C. "Michigan's Oak Openings: Pioneer Perceptions of A Vegation Landscape." JOURNAL OF FOREST HISTORY 22:1 (1978): 18-23.

Explains why the physical environment of the 1820s in the state's lower peninsula was attractive to the New England and New York farmers.

B44. Peters, Bernard C. "No Trees on the Prairie: Persistence of Error in Landscape Terminology." MICHIGAN HISTORY 54 (Spring 1970): 19-28.

Reviews the influence of the Polk belief that lack of
tree cover indicated poor soil fertility to many early
settlers of the Midwestern prairies.

B45. Peters, Bernard C. "Pioneer Evaluation of the Kalamazoo
      County Landscape." MICHIGAN ACADEMICIAN 3:2 (1970):
      15-26.

      Demonstrates that the pattern of settlement in this
      section of the region was such that the more open the
      landscape, the sooner it was settled, which contradicts
      theories that farmers evaluated quality of soil by the
      vegetation it produced.

B46. Rooney, John. THIS REMARKABLE CONTINENT: AN ATLAS OF THE
      UNITED STATES AND CANADIAN SOCIETY AND CULTURES. College
      Station, TX: Texas A&M University Press, 1982.

      Best cultural atlas produced in this country aspiring to
      cover every important aspect of society and cultures of the
      U.S. and Canada. Includes extensive industrial belt
      material on topics such as land division, structures,
      ethnicity, religion, politics, foodways, and place
      perception. Should be in every regionalist's reference
      library.

B47. Santer, Richard A. MICHIGAN: HEART OF THE GREAT LAKES.
      Dubuque, IA: Kendall/Hunt, 1977.

      Valuable one-volume geographical overview; strong on how
      the state benefits from being central in the Great Lakes
      chain.

B48. Scheiber, Harry N. "State Policy and the Public Domain:
      The Ohio Canal Lands." JOURNAL OF ECONOMIC HISTORY 25
      (March 1965): 86-113.

      Interprets the political debates and economic issues
      surrounding the allocation of Ohio public land for canal
      development in the first half of the nineteenth century.

B49. Schmid, James A. URBAN VEGETATION: A REVIEW AND CHICAGO
      CASE STUDY. Chicago: Department of Geography, University
      of Chicago, 1975.

      A model study describing the physical environment of the
      Chicago area, native vegetation, the effects of urban and
      suburbanization on the native vegetation, and current
      residential landscaping. The actual and potential benefits
      of urban vegetation are assessed. Finally, Chicago's
      situation is set in a broader context of American and West
      European cities.

B50. Schlereth, Thomas J. PAST CITYSCAPES: USES OF CARTOGRAPHY
      IN URBAN HISTORY (Paper 80-1: Newberry Papers in Family
      and Community History). Chicago: The Newberry Library,
      1980.

A survey of the urban map holdings in the Chicago
Historical Society and the Newberry Library. Particular
emphasis is given to the over 900 separate maps that have
been drawn of Chicago for various purposes since the 1830s.

B51. Schlereth, Thomas J. U.S. 40: A ROADSCAPE OF THE AMERICAN
      EXPERIENCE. Indianapolis: Indiana Historical Society,
      1985.

      Examines the cultural role that the National Road and its
      successors (National Old Trails Road, U.S. 40, and
      Interstate 70) have played in Midwest history, particularly
      in Indiana. Makes particular use of extant architecture
      highway patterns, and roadside features to study the
      route's evolution in 1837, 1909, 1925, and 1982. A
      micro-study of an area of U.S. 40 that George Stewart's
      1953 volume on U.S. 40 (see B59) neglected.

B52. Seeney, J. Gray. "Great Lakes Marine Painting of the
      Nineteenth Century: A Michigan Perspective." MICHIGAN
      HISTORY 67:3 (1983): 24-33.

      See H108.

B53. Simonetii, Martha L., compiler. DESCRIPTIVE LIST OF MAP
      COLLECTIONS IN THE PENNSYLVANIA STATE ARCHIVES.
      Harrisburg: Pennsylvania Historical and Museum
      Commission, 1976.

      Best on government-generated cartography.

B54. Sinclair, Robert. THE FACE OF DETROIT: A SPATIAL
      SYNTHESIS. Detroit: Wayne State University, 1970.

      Done for the National Council for Geographic Education,
      U.S. Office of Education, this geography can serve as a
      useful introduction to the city's economic expansion,
      transportation networks, and physical environment.

B55. Sinclair, Robert, and Bryan Thompson. "Detroit and
      Contemporary Metropolitan America." NINETEENTH CENTURY
      INLAND CENTERS AND PORTS. Vol. 3. Cambridge, MA:
      Ballinger, 1976.

      An update in more concise form of Sinclair's earlier
      interpretation, FACE OF DETROIT (1970) (B54).

B56. Sinclair, Robert, and Bryan Thompson. METROPOLITAN
      DETROIT: AN ANATOMY OF SOCIAL CHANGE. Cambridge, MA:
      Ballinger, 1975.

      A brief survey of current trends in demography and social
      and cultural geography; also appears in Ballinger's
      CONTEMPORARY METROPOLITAN AMERICAN series, vol. 3, pp.
      285-354.

B57. Smith, Thomas H. THE MAPPING OF OHIO. Kent: The Kent
      State University Press, 1977.

      Not, as might be implied by the title, a history of
      cartographic efforts in Ohio, but rather an attempt to
      write the history of the state through the unique approach
      of using maps as the primary data. Divided into seven
      topics (for example, "Ohio Country," "Surveying the State,"
      "Mapping the City"), the book also contains a valuable
      appendix that includes bibliography of Ohio county atlases
      and general comprehensive bibliography.

B58. Sommers, Lawrence W. ATLAS OF MICHIGAN. Grand Rapids:
      Eermanns, 1977.

      First such comprehensive publication since 1873. Basic
      organization features the natural environment, people and
      society, history and culture, economy, recreation,
      transportation, and "Michigan Tomorrow." The basic
      reference work.

B59. Stewart, George B. U.S. 40: CROSS SECTION OF UNITED
      STATES OF AMERICA. Boston: Houghton Mifflin, 1953.

      An innovative interpretation of the American landscape
      that is a mixture of travelogue, photograph, caption, and
      essay. Route bisects Ohio, Indiana, Illinois and serves as
      a vital transport corridor in the region. Extremely
      well written.

B60. Stilgoe, John R., Roderick Nash, and Alfred Runte.
      PERCEPTIONS OF THE LANDSCAPE AND ITS PRESERVATION.
      Indianapolis: Indiana Historical Society, 1984.

      In "Mapping Indiana: Nineteenth-Century School Book
      Views," Stilgoe discusses the inadequacies of school maps
      in a well-illustrated article. Roderick Nash, in "The
      Roots of American Environmentalism," explains the birth of
      the conservation movement based on Walter Prescott Webb's
      THE GREAT FRONTIER. Runte begins his discussion with
      William Penn in "Preservation Heritage: The Origins of the
      Park Idea in the United States," and details its
      popularization in Indiana under Colonel Richard Lieber
      early director of the Department of Conservation.

B61. Stimson, George P. "River on a Rampage: An Account of the
      Ohio River Flood of 1937." CINCINNATI HISTORICAL SOCIETY
      BULLETIN 22 (April 1964): 91-109.

      An assessment, in economic and human terms, of the damage
      done by flooding in the Ohio River Valley during the
      Depression.

B62. Tarr, Joel A. TRANSPORTATION, INNOVATION AND CHANGING
     SPATIAL PATTERNS IN PITTSBURGH, 1850-1934. Chicago:
     Public Works Historical Society, 1978.

     Best survey of transportation networks in the area;
     describes evolution of Pittsburgh from walking city to
     streetcar city to motor vehicle city.

B63. Thompson, Betty Flanders. THE SHAPING OF AMERICA'S
     HEARTLAND: THE LANDSCAPE OF THE MIDDLE WEST. Boston:
     Houghton Mifflin, 1977.

     A digest of current understanding of the ecology, botany,
     and geology of the Corn Belt and the Great Lakes States.
     Attention is given to mineral formation as well as
     watercourses but the greatest emphasis is on the
     development of various regional forests (pine, spruce, oak,
     maple). Part of the Naturalist's America book series, the
     volume concludes with an excellent chapter ("Man on the
     Land: A Thumbnail History") on human ecology in the area.

B64. Thompson, Paul W. "A Wet Prairie Community in Ann Arbor,
     Michigan." MICHIGAN ACADEMICIAN 2 (Spring 1970): 87-94.

     Discusses the herbaceous plants and seasonal changes of
     the Ann Arbor prairie tract.

B65. Thrower, Norman J. W. ORIGINAL SURVEY AND LAND
     SUBDIVISION: A COMPARATIVE STUDY OF THE FORM AND EFFECT
     OF CONTRACTING CADASTRAL SURVEYS. Chicago: Rand
     McNally, 1966.

     The most complete analysis of earlier land subdivision in
     Ohio; the standard reference work on the topic.

B66. Vale, Thomas. U.S. 40 TODAY. Madison: University of
     Wisconsin Press, 1984.

     Updates George Stewart's U.S. 40 by visiting each site
     along the transcontinental highway that he did,
     photographing the site, and then analyzing the changes in
     the landscape.

B67. Vernon, Philip H., and Oswald Schmidt. "Metropolitan
     Pittsburgh: Old Trends and New Directions."
     CONTEMPORARY METROPOLITAN AMERICA: TWENTY GEOGRAPHICAL
     VIGNETTES. Cambridge, MA: Ballinger, 1976, Vol. 3, pp.
     1-59.

     Best current survey of the iron city and its changing
     economic geography; includes a good bibliography.

B68. Watts, May Theilgaard. READING THE LANDSCAPE OF AMERICA.
     New York: Collier, 1975.

Although a work that ranges over the natural history of
the entire country, Midwest geology, geography, and botany
are given particular emphasis since the author was an
eminent naturalist for most of her career at the Morton
Arboretum outside of Chicago. Originally published in 1957
as READING THE LANDSCAPE, the present edition is a revised
and expanded treatment wherein Watts, for example,
reconstructs the past from the natural evidence of the
present sand dunes of Indiana, tall grass sod of Illinois,
or forest cover of the Ohio River Valley. A delightful,
witty, engaging tour of the region's landscape.

B69. Williams, E.B. "The Great Lakes in Ancient Times and a
      Glimpse Into the Future." INLAND SEAS 18 (Summer 1962):
      87-95.

Williams explains how the Great Lakes came to be about a
million years ago, when the region was covered by glaciers
as much as six miles thick. Easily understood and very
informative, the author points out that the Great Lakes as
we know them today, are roughly only 3,000 years old.

B70. Zelinsky, Wilbur. CULTURAL GEOGRAPHY OF THE UNITED STATES.
      Englewood Cliffs, NJ: Prentice-Hall, 1973.

A brief volume (164 pages) in the publisher's FOUNDATIONS
OF CULTURAL GEOGRAPHY SERIES, this primer provides a
taxonomy of five major American culture areas divided into
cone, domain, and sphere zones of activity. Within this
comparative classification system, Zelinsky also develops a
fresh theory concerning the emergence of the "voluntary
region" in the United States.

B71. Zunz, Oliver, William Ericson, and Daniel J. Fox.
      "Sampling For A Study of The Population and Land Use of
      Detroit in 1880-1885." SOCIAL SCIENCE HISTORY 1:3
      (1977): 307-332.

Using new sampling techniques, attemps to represent
demographic, ethnic, and occupational structure of Detroit
through an examination of various populations and
neighborhood land use.

ECONOMIC ACTIVITIES

C1. Abbott, Carl. BOOSTERS AND BUSINESSMEN: POPULAR ECONOMIC
     THOUGHT AND URBAN GROWTH IN THE ANTEBELLUM MIDDLE WEST.
     Westport, CT: Greenwood Press, 1981.

     Develops case studies of four key urban centers and their
     "import hinterlands" by way of illustrating how the
     rhetoric of boosterism and the level of entrepreneurial
     ability varied through the area. Centers studied are
     Cincinnati, Indianapolis, Chicago, and Galena. Combines
     manuscript census reforms, city directories, and other
     quantitative data with an analysis of booster literature.

C2. Abbott, Carl. "'Necessary Adjuncts to its Growth': The
     Railroad Suburbs of Chicago, 1854-1875." JOURNAL OF THE
     ILLINOIS STATE HISTORICAL SOCIETY 73:2 (1980): 117-31.

     See G1.

C3. Abbott, Carl. "The Location and External Appearance of
     Mrs. Trollope's Bazaar." JOURNAL OF THE SOCIETY OF
     ARCHITECTURAL HISTORIANS 29:3 (1970): 256-59.

     Describes the building which became a financial failure
     and caused Trollope to return to England from Cincinnati.

C4. Alberts, Robert C. THE GOOD PROVIDER: H.J. HEINZ AND HIS
     57 VARIETIES. Boston: Houghton Mifflin, 1973.

     The first full-scale biography of the founder of
     Pittsburgh's famous food-processing plant; a lively
     narrative that makes extensive use of the detailed diaries
     kept by Heinz.

C5. Armstrong, Louise. WE TOO ARE THE PEOPLE. Boston: Little,
     Brown, 1938.

     See D7.

C6. Asher, Robert. "Painful Memories: The Historical
     Consciousness of Steel Workers and The Steel Strike of
     1919." PENNSYLVANIA HISTORY 45:1 (1978): 61-86.

     Asserts the major reason for lack of strike participation
     by skilled steelworkers in the 1919 strike was their
     recollection of earlier unsuccessful confrontations with
     the steel companies.

33

C7. Babson, Steve. "Pointing the Way: The Role of British and
     Irish Skilled Tradesmen in the Rise of the UAW." DETROIT
     PERSPECTIVE 7 (Spring 1983): 75-96.

     See E7.

C8. Barnes, Joseph W. "Rochester and the Automobile Industry."
     ROCHESTER HSTORY 43:2:3 (1982):1-39.

     Describes how George B. Selden's patent for the first
     automobile in Rochester in 1895 led to a lawsuit by Seldon
     and the Electric Vehicle Company against five defendants,
     including the Ford Company.

C9. Barnhart, John D. VALLEY OF DEMOCRACY: THE FRONTIER VS.
     THE PLANTATION IN THE OHIO VALLEY, 1775-1818.
     Bloomington: Indiana University Press, 1953.

     Barnhart, a student and disciple of F.J. Turner, defends
     his mentor's "frontier thesis" in terms of the economic and
     social development of the Ohio Valley.

C10. Omitted.

C11. Bate, Phyllis A. "The Development of the Iron and Steel
     Industry of the Chicago Industry, 1900-1920." Ph.D.
     dissertation. University of Chicago, 1948.

     Argues that it was Chicago's unique location that caused
     its iron and steel industry to grow and that this growth
     was a vital cause in the overall expansion of the city.
     The location was crucial because it was close both to
     suppliers and the market.

C12. Baughman, James L. "Classes and Company Towns: Legends of
     the 1937 Little Steel Strike." OHIO HISTORY 87:2 (1978):
     175-192.

     Explores the relationship of three Ohio industrial
     communities (Canton, Youngstown, Warren) during the
     labor-management conflict.

C13. Bendler, E. Perry. "Exploration for Natural Gas in Ohio."
     INLAND SEAS 18 (Winter 1962): 281-98.

     See B3.

C14. Bernstein, Barton J. "Walter Reuther and the General
     Motors Strike of 1945-1946." MICHIGAN HISTORY 49:3
     (1965): 260-77.

     Examines the strike that was the first crucial
     confrontation in the postwar battle between the CIO and
     industry.

C15. Berry, Brian J.L., ed. CHICAGO: TRANFORMATIONS OF AN
     URBAN SYSTEM. Cambridge, MA: Ballinger, 1976.

An important, wide-ranging study of population, housing, residential patterns and transportation. The product of team research, the study concludes that "the processes of change described ... unfold in a particular way, reflecting an intricate interweaving of the metabolic rhythms of the growing metropolis with longer term upturns and downswings of the Chicago building cycle and with the unexpected occurrence of a variety of outside shocks. The result is pulsating, reverberating growth and change, beginning in the ways in which new growth is accommodated and ending in the ways in which the costs and benefits filter to the disadvantaged."

C16. Berry, Brian J.L., and Thomas D. Haukin, eds. A
      BIBLIOGRAPHIC GUIDE TO THE ECONOMIC REGIONS OF THE UNITED
      STATES. Chicago: University of Chicago Press, 1963.

      Contains an impressive introduction to regional theory
      and nearly 400 carefully annotated entries of the regional
      concept not only in economics but also in geography,
      regional science, and planning. An indispensable source.

C17. Binder, Frederick Moore. COAL AGE EMPIRE: PENNSYLVANIA
      COAL AND ITS UTILIZATION TO 1860. Harrisburg:
      Pennsylvania Historical Museum Commission, 1974.

      A pioneering treatment of an era in coal mining history
      usually neglected by historians who emphasize post-Civil
      War activities in the industry.

C18. Bogue, Allan G. "Changes in Mechanical and Plant
      Technology: The Corn Belt, 1910-1940." JOURNAL OF
      ECONOMIC HISTORY 43 (1983): 1-25.

      During 1910-40 some changes were occurring in the produc-
      tion practices of the Corn Belt states of Ohio, Illinois,
      and Iowa. Three of the most important were the substitu-
      tion of the tractor for horse power, the introduction of
      hybrid seed corn, and the development of viable mechanical
      picker-huskers for harvesting corn. Examines the back-
      ground of those innovations, evaluates current assumptions,
      presents data concerning the relative per acre savings or
      additional income involved in adoption of such technology,
      and notes the possibility that assumptions about the eco-
      nomic rationality involved in corn improvement research as
      well as the implications of the "dry hole effect" may
      require some revision.

C19. Bogue, Donald J., and Calvin L. Beale. ECONOMIC AREAS OF
      THE UNITED STATES. Glencoe, IL: The Free Press, 1960.

      The authors first divide the nation into five basic eco-
      nomic provinces and then thirteen economic regions--areas
      defined as "clusters of land that are homogeneous in their
      general livelihood and socio-economic characteristics."

The economics of each area is then analyzed. Valuable for the interpretive schema but data is now outdated.

C20. Bollinger, Donna S. "The Iron Riches of Michigan's Upper Penisula." MICHIGAN HISTORY 62:4 (1978): 9-13.

Surveys mining at the state's three iron ranges (Marquette, Menominee, and Gogebic) since the early 1840s.

C21. Borchert, John R. "America's Changing Metropolitan Regions." REGIONS OF THE UNITED STATES. Edited by John Fraser Hart. New York: Harper & Row, 1972, pp. 352-373.

While claiming that the metropolis is still the single most important center of economic organization and cultural diffusion, Borchert sees the regional metropolis decentralizing and dispensing. Excellent maps of banking and migration linkages, changing wholesaling centers, and expanding urban transportation and circulation systems.

C22. Bowman, John D., and Richard H. Keehn. "Agricultural Terms of Trade in Four Midwestern States, 1870-1900." JOURNAL OF ECONOMIC HISTORY 34:3 (1974): 592-609.

Reviews thirty-two indices of purchasing power for farmers in Indiana, Illinois, Iowa and Wisconsin showing improved farm purchasing power over the entire period.

C23. Brophy, Jacqueline. "The Merger of the AFL and the CIO in Michigan." MICHIGAN HISTORY 50:2 (1966): 139-57.

Examines the difficulty that accompanied the merger of these unions in Michigan. In 1957, after two years still brought no constituted organization within the state, nation representatives mediated the struggle and ironed out the obstructions within one month. Gives sketches of Meany and Hoffa.

C24. Bradshaw, James Stanford. "Grand Rapids Furniture Beginnings." MICHIGAN HISTORY 52 (Winter 1968): 279-98.

Reviews the origins of one of the Midwest's major furniture manufacturing centers and its relation to the hardwood forests of Michigan.

C25. Buffa, Dudley W. UNION POWER AND AMERICAN DEMOCRACY: THE UAW AND THE DEMOCRATIC PARTY, 1935-1972. Ann Arbor: University of Michigan Press, 1984.

See F12.

C25A. Bukeley, Peter B. "Agrarian Crisis in Western New York: New Deal Reinforcement of The Farm Depression." NEW YORK HISTORY 59:4 (1978): 391-403.

Argues that the policies of the Agricultural Adjustment

Administration prolonged the farm depression in the region
by seeing the problem as a farm surplus rather than an
oligopoly in the field of distribution.

C26. Bulkley, M. Constance. AGRICULTURAL LABOR: A PRELIMINARY
      GUIDE TO PRIMARY SOURCES. Ithaca, NY: Labor-Management
      Documentation Center, 1975.

      Strong on New York and Pennsylvania data.

C27. Bulkley, M. Constance. A GUIDE TO RECORDS IN THE LABOR-
      MANAGEMENT DOCUMENTATION CENTER. Ithaca, NY: Labor-
      Management Documentation Center, 1963.

      Strong on data relating to collective bargaining agree-
      ments in the industrial belt.

C28. Bulkley, M. Constance. WOMEN AND WORK: A PRELIMINARY GUIDE
      TO PRIMARY SOURCES. Ithaca, NY: Labor-Management
      Documentation Center, 1975.

      A good reference work on women in industrial work.

C29. Omitted.

C30. Burgoyne, Arthur G. THE HOMESTEAD STRIKE OF 1892.
      Pittsburgh: University of Pittsburgh Press, 1979.

      A reprint of the 1893 original volume written by Burgoyne
      in response to demands by Pittsburgh District working men
      for a "correct and impartial" history of the strike. An
      informed and highly accurate report set into historical
      context by an afterword written by David Demarest.

C31. Caress, Richard. "The Terminals of Chicago." NATIONAL
      RAILWAY BULLETIN 45:1 (1980): 27-41.

      See I15.

C32. Carr, Lowell J., and James E. Sterner. WILLOW RUN: A STUDY
      OF INDUSTRIALIZATION AND CULTURAL INADEQUACY. New York:
      Harper and Row, 1952.

      See D32.

C33. Chazanof, William. WELCH'S GRAPE JUICE: FROM CORPORATION
      TO CO-OPERATIVE. Syracuse: Syracuse University Press,
      1977.

      First-rate business history of an important company in
      upstate New York. Especially insightful on the religious
      idealism and business acumen of Charles E. Welch, the
      firm's founder.

C34. Clive, Alan. STATE OF WAR: MICHIGAN IN WORLD WAR II. Ann
      Arbor: The University of Michigan Press, 1979.

      See D37.

C35.   Cochran, Thomas C. PENNSYLVANIA, A BICENTENNIAL HISTORY.
       New York: W.W. Norton, 1978.

       See A15.

C36.   Cohen, Steven R. "Steel Workers Rethink the Homestead
       Strike of 1892." PENNSYLVANIA HISTORY 48:2 (1981):
       155-177.

       Based upon field notes of 145 interviews conducted by
       John A. Fitey as part of the famous Pittsburgh Survey of
       1909.

C37.   Cooke, Patricia. "The Erie Canal: American History Through
       Folklore." NEW YORK FOLKLORE 5:3/4 (1979): 155-167.

       Recounts folktales about construction, grand opening
       boats, canal life, and outlaws during its heyday in the
       nineteenth century.

C38.   Corplan Associates. TECHNOLOGICAL CHANGE, ITS IMPACT ON
       INDUSTRY IN METROPOLITAN CHICAGO, A REPORT. Chicago:
       Privately published, 1964.

       An important series of economic reports describing the
       impact of technological change on electronics, metal work-
       ing, office industry, primary metals, chemical industries,
       printing and publishing, with sections on industries of the
       future, a summary of contemporary needs, and a course of
       suggested action.

C39.   Cotrin, George B. "Strikebreakers, Evictions and Violence:
       Industrial Conflict in the Hooking Valley, 1884-1885.
       OHIO HISTORY 87:2 (1978): 140-150.

       Examines the absence of direct violence against immigrant
       strikebreakers and the forms it took against coal company
       properties in the nine-month strike.

C40.   Cowles, Karen. "The Industrialization of Duquesne and the
       Circulation of Elites, 1891-1933." THE WESTERN
       PENNSYLVANIA HISTORICAL MAGAZINE 62 (January 1979): 1-17.

       See D41.

C41.   Crockett, Norman L. THE WOOLEN INDUSTRY OF THE MIDWEST.
       Lexington: University Press of Kentucky, 1970.

       Focuses on the business history from 1860 to 1920 of
       the multi-faceted industry that "processes various
       fleeces into different types of yarn and cloth."
       Although a brief book, all facets of woolen mills are
       discussed: assembling of "new wool" and a labor force
       to work it, production techniques, credit arrangements,
       marketing, changes in fashions, and the impact of
       ready-made clothing.

C42. Cutler, Irving. CHICAGO: METROPOLIS OF THE MID-CONTINENT,
      2nd ed. Chicago: Geographic Society of Chicago, 1976.

      See B11.

C43. David, Donald R. "The Price of Conspicious Production: The
      Detroit Elite and the Automobile Industry, 1900-1933."
      JOURNAL OF SOCIAL HISTORY 16: (1982): 21-46.

      Describes how Detroit's old families were eclipsed by a
      new elite who gain their status, power and wealth from
      automobile manufacturing.

C44. David, Henry. THE HISTORY OF THE HAYMARKET AFFAIR. New
      York: Russell and Russell, 1958.

      A standard historical account of the 1886 bombing and
      aftermath.

C45. Davis, C.M. "The Cities and Towns of the High Plains of
      Michigan." GEOGRAPHICAL REVIEW 28 (1938): 664-73.

      Explains how both settlement and communication patterns
      were produced by the lumbering activity in the region and
      how towns grew and declined with lumbering activity.

C46. Detroit Public Library. THE AUTOMOTIVE HISTORY COLLECTION
      OF THE DETROIT PUBLIC LIBRARY: A SIMPLIFIED GUIDE TO ITS
      HOLDINGS. Boston: G.K. Hall, 1966.

      Has data on the social impact of the car culture.

C47. Dickerson, Dennis C. "The Black Church in Industrializing
      Western Pennsylvania, 1870-1950." THE WESTERN
      PENNSYLVANIA HISTORICAL MAGAZINE 64 (October 1981):
      329-344.

      See E33.

C48. Dorson, Richard M. LAND OF THE MILLRATS. Cambridge:
      Harvard University Press, 1981.

      See G14.

C49. Downard, William L. THE CINCINNATI BREWING INDUSTRY: A
      SOCIAL AND ECONOMIC HISTORY. Athens: Ohio University
      Press, 1973.

      Concentrates on the industry's peak years (1840-1920) for
      both activity and interest in brewing in the city, particu-
      larly among its large German population. Extensive use
      made of local Brewery Workers Unions' records in the
      Cincinnati Historical Society.

C50. Draine, Edwin H. IMPORT TRAFFIC OF CHICAGO AND ITS
      HINTERLAND. Chicago: Department of Geography, University
      of Chicago, 1963.

      A detailed geographical study of the traffic of goods
      through the city, how they move, their value, their source,
      and their destination.

C51. Duggan, Edward P. "Machines, Markets, and Labor: The
      Carriage and Wagon Industry in Late Nineteenth-Century
      Cincinnati." BUSINESS HISTORY REVIEW 51:3 (1977):
      308-325.

      Tests H.J. Habakkuk's labor supply hypothesis which
      asserts that a labor shortage stimulates rapid technologi-
      cal change.

C52. Duncan, Otis Dudley, et al. METROPOLIS AND REGION.
      Baltimore: The Johns Hopkins Press, 1960.

      Uses the insights of human ecologists such as Robert Park
      and R.D. McKenzie and the work of political scientists to
      probe the economic structure and function of metropolitan
      communities and their relationships to surrounding regions.
      Especially good on Chicago, Cleveland, Indianapolis,
      Detroit, Pittsburgh and their hinterlands. Parallels
      Perloff's REGIONS, RESOURCES, AND ECONOMIC GROWTH (C120).

C53. Eggert, Gerald G. STEELMASTERS AND LABOR REFORM,
      1886-1927. Pittsburgh: University of Pittsburgh Press,
      1981.

      A study of the steel industry's labor relations through
      the biography of William Brown Dickson, first vice-
      president of United States Steel. Eggert sees Dickson
      in the larger history of American management, as an
      actor in the conflicts between steelmen and bankers, compe-
      tition and cooperation, production and marketing,
      efficiency and predictability.

C54. Farrell, Richard T. "Cincinnati, 1800-1830: Economic
      Development Through Trade and Industry." OHIO HISTORY
      77:4 (1968): 111-29.

      Discusses the boosterism that transformed the frontier
      town into a city with almost 25,000 people, as well as the
      diversification from agriculture to manufacturing,
      because of demands of the War of 1812.

C55. Filante, Ronald W. "A Note on the Economic Viability of
      the Erie Canal, 1825-1860." BUSINESS HISTORY REVIEW
      48:1 (1974): 95-102.

      Compares canal freight shipments, composition, and
      destinations before and after the 1830s, an era of intense
      railroad competition.

C56. Fisher, James S., Dean M. Hanink, and James O. Wheeler.
      INDUSTRIAL VOCATION ANALYSIS: A BIBLIOGRAPHY, 1966-1979.
      Athens, GA: University of Georgia Department of
      Geography Bibliography No. 7, 1979.

      Contains over 1,200 entries arranged by studies on
      locational analyses, systematic analyses, and regional
      studies. A vital source for the cities of the industrial
      belt.

C57. Folmar, John N., and Ivan W. Sanders. "Some Reflections on
      Railroad Development in Western Pennsylvania." THE
      WESTERN PENNSYLVANIA HISTORICAL MAGAZINE 65 (1982):
      363-371.

      Depicts western Pennsylvania railroading during 1846-1952
      as a microcosm of the evolution of locomotives, the devel-
      opment of a national rail network and the change from
      frontier life to urbanization in the U.S.

C58. Gandre, Donald A. "Recent Changes in the Flow of Iron Ore
      on the Great Lakes." INLAND SEAS 27:4 (1971): 247-259.

      Analyzes changes in shipments and receipts, 1920-1970,
      with special attention to the use of the St. Lawrence
      Seaway.

C59. Garreau, Joel. "The Foundry." THE NINE NATIONS OF NORTH
      AMERICA. Boston: Houghton Mifflin, 1981, pp. 49-97.

      Written in the interpretive reporting tradition of John
      Gunther's INSIDE U.S.A., Garreau, a Washington Post editor,
      attempts to re-draw the North American continent with its
      regional capitals, networks of power and influence, and
      perceptions of the other eight "nations" (for example,
      Dixie, Mexamerica, New England, The Breadbasket). "The
      Foundry" is defined as the industrial nation of the
      Northeast plus the area that this bibliography identifies
      as the Industrial Belt. A contemporary overview that is
      short on history and long on prediction of future demo-
      graphic and economic decline for the region, the essay
      tends to repeat clichés that may prove quite dated in the
      future.

C60. Gates, Paul W. THE ILLINOIS CENTRAL AND ITS COLONIZATION
      WORK. Cambridge: Harvard University Press, 1934.

      Still the standard discussion of a major Midwestern
      railroad as real estate agent and town planner/developer.

C61. Gedics, Al. "Ethnicity, Class Solidarity and Labor
      Radicalism Among Finnish Immigrants in Michigan Copper
      Country." POLITICS AND SOCIETY 7:2 (1977): 127-156.

      See E52.

C62. Goldman, Mark. HIGH HOPES: THE RISE AND DECLINE OF
      BUFFALO, NEW YORK. Albany: State University of New York
      Press, 1983.

      See A26.

C63. Grant, H. Roger. A HISTORY OF THE CHICAGO GREAT WESTERN
      RAILROAD COMPANY. DeKalb: Northern Illinois University
      Press, 1984.

      The book explores the history of the mediocre CGW, from
      its beginnings relatively late, in 1885, to its merger
      with its giant competitor, the Chicago & North Western, in
      1968.

C64. Gutman, Herbert G. "Reconstruction in Ohio: Negroes in the
      Hocking Valley Coal Mines in 1873 and 1874." LABOR
      HISTORY 3:3 (1962): 243-64.

      Explores the event that brought large numbers of blacks
      into the coal mines.

C65. Hacker, Louis M. THE WORLD OF ANDREW CARNEGIE, 1865-1901.
      Philadelphia: J.B. Lippincott, 1968.

      Uses Carnegie as an ideal or representative type to
      explain "why this country, a young developing nation at the
      outset of the Civil War (1861), became the mightiest
      industrial power in the world in less than forty years."

C66. Haeger, John Denis. THE INVESTMENT FRONTIER: NEW YORK
      BUSINESSMEN AND THE ECONOMIC DEVELOPMENT OF THE OLD
      NORTHWEST. Albany: State University of New York Press,
      1981.

      Seeks to demonstrate Easterners' effects (particularly
      those of Arthur Bronson and Charles Butler) on the economic
      expansion of the West, and to offer a critique of arguments
      advanced by those historians who have stressed the negative
      impact of nonresident speculators in the region.

C67. Hannon, Joan Underhill. "City Size and Ethnic
      Discrimination: Michigan Agricultural Implements and
      Iron Working Industries." JOURNAL OF ECONOMIC HISTORY
      42:4 (1982): 825-845.

      Argues that discrimination in hiring made it more diffi-
      cult for immigrants to break into small-city labor forces
      thus keeping them concentrated in large cities where they
      continued to experience less occupational mobility.

C68. Hannon, Joan Underhill. "Ethnic Discrimination in a 19th
      Century Mining District: Michigan Copper Mines, 1888."
      EXPLORATIONS IN ECONOMIC HISTORY 19:1 (1982): 28-50.

      See E61.

C69. Hantley, Joseph R. THE ECONOMIC EFFECTS OF OHIO RIVER
      NAVIGATION. Bloomington: Indiana University Press,
      1959.

      Valuable monograph with special emphasis on
      nineteenth-century economic activity.

C70. Hardeman, Nicholas P. SHUCKS, SHOCKS, AND HOMINY: CORN AS
      A WAY OF LIFE IN PIONEER AMERICA. Baton Rouge: Louisiana
      State University Press, 1981.

      A lively social history of the king of American agricul-
      ture from colonial Jamestown to contemporary Midwestern
      agribusiness; replaces Dorothy Gile's SINGING VALLEYS: THE
      STORY OF CORN as the definitive work.

C71. Hardin, Thomas L. "The National Road in Illinois."
      JOURNAL OF THE ILLINOIS STATE HISTORICAL SOCIETY 60
      (Spring 1967): 5-22.

      See I35.

C72. Hart, John Fraser. "The Middle West." REGIONS OF THE
      UNITED STATES. Edited by John Fraser Hart. New York:
      Harper & Row, 1972, pp. 258-282.

      Reviews the economic and political history of the region
      and sees a century of rural stability (1860-1960) producing
      a pecuniary value system associated with the family farm
      ideology. Notes how manufacturing in the western sector
      remains agriculturally oriented, with the automobile indus-
      try more important in the east. Shows how the metropolitan
      Democratic vote is balanced by a Republican tradition in
      rural areas.

C73. Havinghurst, Walter. OHIO, A BICENTENNIAL HISTORY. New
      York: W.W. Norton, 1976.

      See A35.

C74. Hazard, John L. MICHIGAN'S COMMERCE AND COMMERCIAL POLICY
      STUDY. East Lansing: Michigan State University, 1965.

      Focuses on international business practices and trends in
      the state. Prepared by the International Business
      Management Division of Research in the Michigan State
      Graduate School of Business Administration.

C75. Henderson, James M., and Anne O. Krueger. NATIONAL GROWTH
      AND ECONOMIC CHANGE IN THE UPPER MIDWEST. Minneapolis:
      University of Minnesota Press, 1965.

      Prepared as the final report of the Upper Midwest
      Economic Study (UMES) research program, this volume
      emphasizes the future directions and regional growth
      opportunities as envisioned by planners, economists, and

social scientists in the mid-1960s. The analysts devote
considerable space to the continuing role of manufacturing,
mineral resources, and transportation in the area's economy
as well as the recent impact of service and government
factors.

C76. Henley, Ronald L., and Carl F. Ojala. "The Beet Sugar
Industry of Michigan: A Geographical Analysis." MICHIGAN
ACADEMICIAN 6:3 (1974): 321-32.

Chronicles the historical development of the industry, as
well as the events that have caused wide fluctuations in
it.

C77. Hessen, Robert. STEEL TITAN: THE LIFE OF CHARLES M.
SCHWAB. New York: Oxford University Press, 1975.

First biography of the most atypical, least orthodox
of American tycoons of the industrial belt. Corrects
several myths and misconceptions about Carnegie, the
Carnegie Steel Company, and Schwab's contribution (with the
development of Bethlehem beam) to industrial construction
technology.

C78. Holt, Glen E. "The Birth of Chicago: An Examination of
Economic Parentage." JOURNAL OF THE ILLINOIS STATE
HISTORICAL SOCIETY 76:2 (1983): 82-94.

Prior to 1850, the growth of Chicago was determined by
the federal government, the state of Illinois, and outside
capital. The establishment of Fort Dearborn in 1803
created the town and catalyzed the growth of its meat-
packing industry. State construction of the Illinois and
Michigan Canal, beginning in 1836, encouraged rapid
expansion. Improvement of Chicago's harbor by the Army
Corps of Engineers established Chicago's regional and
national goals, encouraging the local populace to seek
additional assistance for expansion of transportation and
manufacturing facilities. As the commerce of the Great
Lakes and the Midwest, tied to the financial health of the
East, increased, Chicago became the primary connection
between the regions, leading it to host the River and
Harbor Convention of 1847.

C79. Howard, Robert P. ILLINOIS, A HISTORY OF THE PRAIRIE
STATE. Grand Rapids: Eermanns, 1972.

A massive (626 pages) single volume survey that serves as
the best source on Illinois history in the twentieth century. Howard pays particular attention to the state's
agriculture and to its role as a multi-faceted depot in the
nation's transportation nexus. Written by a CHICAGO
TRIBUNE political and legislative correspondent who covered
the Springfield beat for over 25 years, the book was
compiled to celebrate the sesquicentennial of Illinois in
1968 and to update the five-volume centennial history of
1918.

C80. Hunter, Louis C. STEAMBOATS ON THE WESTERN RIVER: AN
      ECONOMIC AND TECHNICAL HISTORY. Cambridge: Harvard
      University Press, 1949.

      Standard work on the topic by a master economic historian
      with broad expertise in the history of technology and
      hydraulics.

C81. Ingham, John N. THE IRON BARONS: A SOCIAL ANALYSIS OF AN
      AMERICAN URBAN ELITE, 1965-1974. Westport, CT: Greenwood
      Press, 1978.

      Attempts to trace through their ancestors and descendants
      the social relationships of 907 men in the iron and steel
      industry, particulary those concentrated in cities such as
      Pittsburgh, Youngstown, and Cleveland. Ingham concludes
      that urban elites, as represented in his sample, tended to
      live in homogeneous neighborhoods; belong to or sought to
      belong to, similar social clubs; and, especially among
      those labeled "core" families in the upper-class structure,
      to marry endogamously.

C82. Innes, Lowell. PITTSBURGH GLASS 1797-1891: A HISTORY AND
      GUIDE FOR COLLECTORS. Boston: Houghton Mifflin, 1976.

      More than a typical collector's manual; rather a solid
      economic history divided into two parts: a) the milieu in
      which glass factories were established and flourished; b)
      specific production methods and designs of glass products.

C83. Jensen, Richard. ILLINOIS, A BICENTENNIAL HISTORY. New
      York: W.W. Norton, 1978.

      See A42.

C84. Jeuch, John E., and Boris Emmet. CATALOGUES AND COUNTERS:
      A HISTORY OF SEARS, ROEBUCK & COMPANY. Chicago:
      University of Chicago Press, 1950.

      A model business history; best book on the firm but needs
      updating for the last thirty years. Excellent
      bibliography.

C85. Jones, Robert L. A HISTORY OF AGRICULTURE IN OHIO TO 1880.
      Kent: Kent State University Press, 1983.

      A detailed economic history using ample statistical data;
      should be read in conjunction with Wheeler McMillen's OHIO
      FARM (G49).

C86. Karlowicz, Titus M. "Notes on the Columbian Exposition's
      Manufactures and Liberal Arts Building." JOURNAL OF
      SOCIAL ARCHITECTURAL HISTORIANS 33 (October 1974):
      214-18.

      See I49.

C87. Katz, Michael B., and Mark J. Stern. "Gentility, Class,
      and Industrial Capitalism: Erie County, New York,
      1855-1915." AMERICAN QUARTERLY 33:1 (1981): 63-92.

      SEE D86.

C88. Keeran, Roger. THE COMMUNIST PARTY AND THE AUTO WORKERS
      UNIONS. Bloomington: Indiana University Press, 1980.

      See F55.

C89. Keil, Harnut, and John B. Jantz, eds. GERMAN WORKERS IN
      INDUSTRIAL CHICAGO, 1850-1910: A COMPARATIVE PERSPECTIVE.
      DeKalb: Northern Illinois University Press, 1983.

      See G39.

C90. Klingamann, David C., and Richard K. Vedder, eds. ESSAYS IN
      NINETEENTH CENTURY ECONOMIC HISTORY: THE OLD NORTHWEST.
      Athens: Ohio University Press, 1975.

      Attempts to fill the void in American economic history
      (the editors see the Old Northwest as "a relatively neglec-
      ted region") via a series of econometric studies that deal
      with population, agriculture, wealth, banking, and trans-
      portation. Almost a quarter of the book is devoted to the
      issue of the railroads and to Midwestern development during
      the period 1870-1890.

C91. Korson, George G., ed. COAL DUST ON THE FIDDLE: SONGS AND
      STORIES OF THE BITUMINOUS INDUSTRY. Philadelphia:
      University of Pennsylvania Press, 1943.

      See G44.

C92. Lankton, Larry D. "The Machine UNDER the Garden: Rock
      Drills Arrive at the Lake Superior Copper Mines,
      1868-1883." TECHNOLOGY AND CULTURE 24:1 (1983): 1-37.

      See B30.

C93. Lansky, Lewis. "Buffalo and the Great Depression." In AN
      AMERICAN HISTORIAN: ESSAYS TO HONOR SELIG ADLER. Edited
      by Milton Pleur. Buffalo: State University of New York,
      1980, pp. 204-213.

      Surveys the various attempts--private and later
      municipal--to cope with unemployment and the economic
      slump.

C94. Larson, John Lauritz, and David G. Vanderstel. "Agent of
      Empire: William Conner on the Indiana Frontier, 1800-
      1855." INDIANA MAGAZINE OF HISTORY 80:4 (December 1984):
      301-328.

      This article examines the life of the fur trader who, as
      a representative of commercial America, eventually made it

big on the central Indiana frontier and helped transform
the wilderness into civilization. Also includes a brief
history of William's father, Richard, and his western
migrations.

C95. Laurent, Jerome K. "Trade, Transport and Technology: The
      American Great Lakes, 1866-1910." JOURNAL OF TRANSPORT
      HISTORY (Great Britain) 4:1 (1983): 1-24.

      Changes in water transport on the Great Lakes strongly
      influenced economic development in the Midwest during 1866-
      1910. Two of the most important changes were improvements
      in key connecting channels and major harbors, and the
      building and employment of larger vessels that were rela-
      tively inexpensive to operate. Improvements in vessels
      occurred later and more slowly than did improvements in
      channels and harbor facilities; many small, older vessels
      were improved rather than replaced immediately by the new
      ships. Based on manuscripts in the U.S. Engineer Offices
      and on published sources.

C96. Lee, James H. "The Ohio Agricultural Commission,
      1913-1915." OHIO HISTORY 79 (Summer-Autumn 1970):
      219-30.

      See G46.

C97. Lewis, David L. THE PUBLIC IMAGE OF HENRY FORD: AN
      AMERICAN FOLK HERO AND HIS COMPANY. Detroit: Wayne State
      University Press, 1976.

      Has produced the most detailed (598 pages) account to
      date of any American business firm's advertising and public
      relations program; assuredly supersedes this aspect of
      Ford's story as portaryed in Allan Nevins' three-volume
      biography. Fails to be critical of the company's PR work
      or to test its image against other scholarship on the
      firm and its founder.

C98. Lindsey, Almont. THE PULLMAN STRIKE: THE STORY OF A UNIQUE
      EXPERIMENT AND OF A GREAT LABOR UPHEAVAL. Chicago:
      University of Chicago Press, 1942.

      The definitive study on the labor crisis in which strands
      of economic, social, constitutional, business, and politi-
      cal history are woven. Should be read in concert with
      Buder's PULLMAN (1967) (D26) for an updated bibliography.

C99. Longini, Arthur. REGION OF OPPORTUNITY. Pittsburgh:
      Pittsburgh and Lake Erie Railroad Co., 1961.

      A mammoth, four-volume study designed "to delineate the
      prospects for economic group growth of particular indus-
      tries in the Pittsburgh-Youngstown area." Reviews economic
      status of 249 industries and their potential for expan-
      sion.

C100. Lurie, Jonathan. THE CHICAGO BOARD OF TRADE: 1859-1905;
       THE DYNAMICS OF SELF-REGULATION. Urbana: University of
       Illinois Press, 1979.

       An attempt to show, on the local level, the development
       of self-regulating forces in business during the nineteenth
       century. Examines various court cases involving the Board
       as well as relates the institution to the growth of Chicago
       as a grain and manufacturing center.

C101. McDonald, Forest. INSULL. Chicago: University of Chicago
       Press, 1962.

       The definitive biography of Samuel Insull (1859-1938), an
       early key figure in the business of centralized electric
       supply across the Midwest, who worked out a widely copied
       model of nationwide product distribution. McDonald sees
       Insull as a pre-Henry Ford proponent of mass-production and
       "natural monopoly," a progenitor of rural electrification,
       a developer of marketing securities leading to gigantic
       corporations, and an inventor of public relations tech-
       niques linking him to P.T. Barnum and Madison Avenue.

C102. McKenney, Ruth. INDUSTRIAL VALLEY. New York: Harcourt,
       Brace, 1939.

       Sound economic overview of industrialization in the major
       urban centers of the Ohio River Valley up to the Great
       Depression.

C103. McLear, Patrick E. "William Butler Ogden: A Chicago
       Promoter In the Speculative Era and the Panic of 1837."
       JOURNAL OF THE ILLINOIS STATE HISTORICAL SOCIETY 70:4
       (1977): 289-291.

       Claims Ogden was "Chicago's most important nineteenth-
       century business leader."

C104. Maizlish, Stephen E. THE TRIUMPH OF SECTIONALISM: THE
       TRANSFORMATION OF OHIO POLITICS, 1844-1856. Kent: Kent
       State University Press, 1983.

       See F66.

C105. Marshall, James R., and George W. Dowdall. "Employment and
       Mental Hospitalization: The Case of Buffalo, New York:
       1914-1955." SOCIAL FORCES 60:3 (1982): 843-853.

       Explores the connection between employment trends and
       hospital admissions, using employment data for the Buffalo
       area and admissions to the only major public psychiatric
       hospital in the area during the time examined.

C106. Maxwell, Margaret F. "James Clements of Ann Arbor: A
       Nineteenth-Century Entrepreneur." MICHIGAN HISTORY 62:1
       (1978): 16-30.

Traces the exploits of a Brooklyn gas engineer who went to Ann Arbor to oversee the change from kerosene lamps with gas lamps on the city's streets, soon became interested in politics, and amassed a fortune with his investments in midwestern gas companies.

C106A. May, George S. A MOST UNIQUE MACHINE: THE MICHIGAN ORIGINS OF THE AMERICAN AUTOMOBILE INDUSTRY. Grand Rapids: Eermanns, 1975.

A collective biography, both of the pioneering individuals who tried to build cars and of the companies they, their friends, and other investors created. Beginning at the time of the Chicago World's Fair in 1893 and ending for all practical purposes with the formation of General Motors in 1909, the book contributes more in the way of data than analysis.

C107. May, George S., and Victor F. Lerner. "Thomas Edison's Experimental Work with Michigan Iron Ore." MICHIGAN HISTORY 53 (Summer 1969): 109-30.

See B34.

C108. Mayer, Harold M. "The Launching of Chicago: The Situation and the Site." CHICAGO HISTORY 9 (Summer 1980): 68-79.

See B35.

C109. Meakin, Alexander. "Four Long and One Short: A History of the Great Lakes Towing Company." INLAND SEAS 31:1 (1975): 14-33.

This article gives the corporate history of the firm from 1901 to 1918.

C110. Meier, August, and Elliot Rudwick. BLACK DETROIT AND THE RISE OF THE UAW. New York: Oxford University Press, 1979.

See E89.

C111. Miller, E. Willard. "Connersville Beehive Coke Region, A Declining Mineral Economy." ECONOMIC GEOGRAPHIC 29 (1953): 144-58.

Examines a region delimited by the area of the Pittsburgh coal bed in Fayette and Westmoreland counties. The rise and decline of the mining industry in the region are explained.

C112. Miller, E. Willard. MANUFACTURING: A STUDY OF INDUSTRIAL LOCATION. University Park: Pennsylvania State University Press, 1977.

A standard economic geography with good survey material on the industrial belt's manufacturing areas, particularly in New York and Pennsylvania.

C113. Miller, Ernest C. THIS WAS EARLY OIL. Harrisburg:
       Pennsylvania Historical and Museum Commission, 1968.

       A collection of nineteenth-century documents from Western
       Pennsylvania sources. Should be read in concert with Paul
       H. Giddens' two volumes--THE BEGINNINGS OF THE PETROLEUM
       INDUSTRY (1941) and PENNSYLVANIA PETROLEUM, 1750-1872
       (1947)--which were also published by the Historical
       Commission.

C114. Mohl, Raymond A. "The Great Steel Strike of 1919 in Gary,
       Indiana: Working-Class Radicalism or Trade Union
       Militancy?" MID-AMERICA 63:1 (1981): 36-52.

       Argues that despite the claims of steel industry execu-
       tives, the majority of the Gary steel strikers were not
       Bolsheviks but workers in search of better wages, shorter
       hours, and improved working conditions.

C115. Morgan, Iwan. "Fort Wayne and the Great Depression: The
       New Deal Years, 1933-1940." INDIANA MAGAZINE OF HISTORY
       80:4 (December 1984): 348-378.

       See G53.

C116. Murray, John J., ed. HERITAGE OF THE MIDDLE WEST. Norman:
       University of Oklahoma Press, 1958.

       See A56.

C117. Nevins, Allan. FORD. 3 vols. New York: Scribner's,
       1954-63.

       Business history, multi-volume style, as done in the
       post-World War II era. Focuses on the corporation as an
       institution.

C118. Nye, David E. HENRY FORD: "IGNORANT IDEALIST." Port
       Washington, NY: Kennikat Press, 1979.

       A valuable counterpoint to the Nevins three-volume
       corporate biography in that it explores two basic themes:
       the world's view of Ford and Ford's view of the world.
       Central to the interpretation is Nye's contention that
       Ford, "an ignorant idealist," was a quasi-utopian in the
       spirit of an individual such as the novelist Henry Olerick
       who published A CITYLESS AND A COUNTRYLESS WORLD in 1893.

C119. O'Day, Laura. "Buffalo as a Flour-Milling Center."
       ECONOMIC GEOGRAPHY 8 (1932): 81-93.

       Buffalo's regional leadership in the milling industry is
       explained by two principal factors: 1) its location at the
       eastern end of Lake Erie and thus its role as a natural
       break-in-bulk point; and 2) its position as a logical
       distribution center for the large eastern flour market.

C120. Perloff, Harvey, et al. REGIONS, RESOURCES, AND ECONOMIC
      GROWTH. Baltimore: The Johns Hopkins Press, 1960.

      Larger multi-state units are identified and analyzed in
      this companion volume to Duncan's METROPOLIS AND REGION
      (C52). Especially useful on the theoretical perspectives
      of how a region grows and expands--an argument summarized
      in Perloff's HOW A REGION GROWS: AREA DEVELOPMENT IN THE
      U.S. ECONOMY (New York: Committee for Economic Development,
      1963).

C121. Philips, Clifton. INDIANA IN TRANSITION, THE EMERGENCE OF
      AN INDUSTRIAL COMMONWEALTH, 1880-1920. Indianapolis:
      Indiana Historical Bureau and Indiana Historical Society,
      1968.

      Key overview assessing Indiana's early role in the
      formation of the industrial belt. Good bibliography.

C122. Piertak, Paul. BUFFALO, ROCHESTER & PITTSBURGH RAILWAY.
      North Boston, NY: Privately published, 1979.

      A good historical narrative (supported by ample photog-
      raphy and cartography) of one of the industrial belt's sub-
      regional transportation networks. A valuable vignette of
      railroads, coal, and travel in western Pennsylvania and
      western New York in the early years of the twentieth cen-
      tury.

C123. Powell, H. Benjamin. "The Pennsylvania Anthracite
      Industry, 1769-1976." PENNSYLVANIA HISTORY 47:1 (1980):
      3-28.

      Excellent overview that contrasts the agrarian-mercantile
      age (1769-1850) with the age of industry (1850-1914) with
      the age of managerial economy (1914-1980).

C124. Quaite, Milo M., and Sidney Glazer. MICHIGAN: FROM
      PRIMITIVE WILDERNESS TO INDUSTRIAL COMMONWEALTH. New
      York: Prentice-Hall, 1948.

      See A67.

C125. Raucher, Alan R. "Paul G. Hoffman, Studebaker, and the Car
      Culture. INDIANA MAGAZINE OF HISTORY 1983 79(3):
      209-230.

      During his long association with the manufacture and
      sales of automobiles--including his presidency of
      Studebaker--Paul G. Hoffman participated in many activities
      whose goal was to promote the increased use of the car by
      Americans. Among these activities were his advocacy of
      safer roads, a campaign for automobile safety, a drive
      against drunk drivers, and the promotion of more economical
      and efficient engines. His desire for improved fuel
      efficiency and safety was reflected in the 1939 Studebaker
      Champion. Hoffman always believed that the car was impor-
      tant to the American public.

C126. Roberts, Warren E. "The Tools Used in Building Log Houses
       in Indiana." PIONEER AMERICA 9 (July 1977): 30-61.

       See I75.

C127. Rodgers, Allan. "The Iron and Steel Industry of the
       Mahoning and Shenango Valleys." ECONOMIC GEOGRAPHY 28
       (1952), 331-42.

       Focus on steel fabrication, industrial diversification,
       and new industry development in these two river valleys in
       northeastern Ohio and northwestern Pennsylvania. Sees
       Youngstown, Ohio, as the industrial core city in the sub-
       region.

C128. Rose, Dan. ENERGY TRANSITION AND THE LOCAL COMMUNITY: A
       THEORY OF SOCIETY APPLIED TO HAZELTON, PENNSYLVANIA.
       Philadelphia: University of Pennsylvania Press, 1981.

       Provides an ethnographic study of how this Pennsylvania
       community, once dependent upon the now largely exhausted
       anthracite industry, responded to the challenges caused by
       economic dislocation.

C129. Rose, William Ganson. CLEVELAND, THE MAKING OF A CITY.
       New York: World Publishing Co., 1950.

       A gigantic (1270 pages) economic study of Cleveland
       commerce from founding in 1796 to 1940. Has a superb index
       and an appendix listing Greater Cleveland Manufacturers.

C130. Salvatore, Nick. "Railroad Workers and the Great Strike of
       1877: The View From a Small Midwest City (Terre Haute)."
       LABOR HISTORY 21:4 (1980): 522-45.

       Examines the unique Terre Haute Strike as an example of
       the transition to industrial capitalism. Good background
       on the city.

C131. Sawyer, Alvah L. A HISTORY OF THE NORTHERN PENINSULA AND
       ITS PEOPLE: ITS MINING, LUMBERING AND AGRICULTURAL
       INTERESTS. 3 vols. Chicago: Lewis Publishing Co.,
       1911.

       A compendium of data on a region of Michigan all too
       often neglected by students of the state's economy.

C132. Schatz, Ronald W. THE ELECTRICAL WORKERS: A HISTORY OF
       LABOR AT GENERAL ELECTRIC AND WESTINGHOUSE, 1923-1960.
       Urbana: University of Illinois Press, 1983.

       Attempts to explain the rise and decline of militant
       unionism among electrical workers in industrial belt cities
       such as Erie and Pittsburgh.

C133. Scheiber, Harry N. OHIO CANAL ERA: A CASE STUDY OF
GOVERNMENT AND THE ECONOMY, 1820-1861. Athens: Ohio
University Press, 1968.

See F86.

C134. Scheiber, Henry N., ed. THE OLD NORTHWEST: STUDIES IN
REGIONAL HISTORY, 1787-1910. Lincoln: University of
Nebraska Press, 1969.

See A69.

C135. Scheiber, Harry N. "Urban Rivalry and Internal
Improvements in the Old Northwest, 1820-1860." OHIO
HISTORY 71 (October 1962): 227-39.

See G70.

C136. Schenker, Eric, Harold Mayer, and Harry C. Brockel. THE
GREAT LAKES TRANSPORTATION SYSTEM. Madison: University
of Wisconsin, 1976.

Most useful for its thorough bibliographies at the end of
each chapter.

C137. Schlereth, Thomas J. "Big Money and High Culture: The
Commercial Club of Chicago and Charles L. Hutchinson."
GREAT LAKES REVIEW: A JOURNAL OF MIDWEST CULTURE 3:2
(Summer 1976): 15-27.

Explores, using the career of a wealthy Chicago businessman and Board of Trade member, the interrelation between
cultural philanthropy and second-generation wealth.
Hutchinson's involvement with the city's Art Institute is
stressed.

C138. Schlereth, Thomas J. "Mail-order Catalogs As Resources In
American Cultural Studies." PROSPECTS: AN ANNUAL JOURNAL
OF AMERICAN CULTURAL STUDIES (1981): 141-161.

See G72.

C139. Schneirov, Richard. "Chicago's Great Upheaval of 1877."
CHICAGO HISTORY 9 (Spring 1980): 2-17.

Overview of the railroad strikes and labor unrest in the
city during 1877.

C140. Scholo, David E. HIRED HANDS AND PLOWBOYS: FARM LABOR IN
THE MIDWEST, 1816-1860. Urbana: University of Illinois
Press, 1976.

A brillant reconstruction of early nineteenth-century
farm life, particularly in Illinois, from the perspective
of the hired man, boy, and girl. Monitors Midwest farming
practices during the shift from frontier subsistence

economy of 1815 to more sophisticated, large scale farming of 1860. Superb economic history, written with an informed social history perspective.

C141. Shade, William Gerald. BANKS OR NO BANKS: THE MONEY ISSUE IN WESTERN POLITICS, 1832-1865. Detroit: Wayne State University Press, 1972.

Using the five states of the old Northwest as a data base, Shade develops six topics: the bipartisan effort to increase banks and capital in the 1830s; the impact of the panic of 1837; the hard-money revulsion against banks as a result of the 1830s depression; rise of free banking in the 1850s, its nationalization in the 1860s, and the key role Westerners played in national currency legislation.

C142. Shepherd, Rebecca A. "Restless Americans: The Geographic Mobility of Farm Laborers in the Old Midwest, 1850-1870." OHIO HISTORY 89:1 (1980): 25-45.

See G77.

C143. Shergold, Peter R. "Wage Rates in Pittsburgh During The Depression of 1908." JOURNAL OF AMERICAN STUDIES 9:2 (1975):163-188.

Assesses statistical and qualitative evidences to explain the phenomenon of wage rates declining less drastically in Pittsburgh during 1908 than in earlier recessions of considerable greater severity.

C144. Shergold, Peter R. WORKING-CLASS LIFE: THE "AMERICAN STANDARD" IN COMPARATIVE PERSPECTIVE, 1899-1913. Pittsburgh: University of Pittsburgh Press, 1982.

See D130.

C145. Solomon, Ezra, and Zarko G. Bilbija. METROPOLITAN CHICAGO: AN ECONOMIC ANALYSIS. Glencoe, IL: Free Press, 1960 (1959).

This book investigates the economics of the Chicago metropolitan area in terms of the major variables used in modern economic analysis. It presents specially prepared estimates of the size and structure of the area's population, labor force, employment, output, income, expenditures and saving.

C146. Speiss, Phillip D., II. "Exhibitions and Expositions in 19th Century Cincinnati." CINCINNATI HISTORICAL SOCIETY BULLETIN 28 (Fall 1970): 171-92.

See H111.

C147.   Stimson, George P. "River on a Rampage: An Account of the
        Ohio River Flood of 1937." CINCINNATI HISTORICAL SOCIETY
        BULLETIN 22 (April 1964): 91-109.

        See B61.

C148.   Stover, John F. HISTORY OF THE ILLINOIS CENTRAL RAILROAD.
        New York: Macmillan, 1975.

        A masterful synthesis in which the IC, one of the
        region's major rail carriers out of Chicago, is evaluated
        in the broad context of region, nation, and the entire
        transportation industry.

C149.   Strassman, W. Paul. RISK AND TECHNOLOGICAL INNOVATION:
        AMERICAN MANUFACTURING METHODS IN THE NINETEENTH CENTURY.
        Ithaca: Cornell University Press, 1959.

        Considers technological breakthroughs in industrial ıs-
        cities such as Pittsburgh.

C150.   Tarbell, Ida. THE HISTORY OF THE STANDARD OIL COMPANY.
        New York: McClure Phillips, 1904.

        A classic muckraker text on the petroleum industry with
        its corporate and commercial base largely centered in Ohio
        and Western Pennsylvania.

C151.   Tarr, Joel A., and Denise DiPasquale. "The Mill Town In
        The Industrial City: Pittsburgh's Hazelwood." URBANISM
        PAST AND PRESENT 7:1 (1982): 1-14.

        See D134.

C152.   Tarr, Joel A. "The Chicago Anti-Department Store Crusade
        of 1897: A Case Study in Urban Commercial Development."
        JOURNAL OF THE STATE HISTORICAL SOCIETY 64 (Summer 1971):
        161-72.

        The article examines the opposition to department stores
        in the central business districts of which they became
        part. The author pinpoints this opposition from three
        groups: small and middle-sized retail merchants outside
        the CBD, real estate people with holdings outside the CBD,
        and labor unions that objected to department store labor
        policies.

C152A. Tebbel, John William. AN AMERICAN DYNASTY: THE STORY OF
        THE McCORMICKS, MEDILLS, AND PATTERSONS. Garden City,
        NY: Doubleday, 1947.

        A popular study in collective biography which cuts across
        the Chicago region's journalism, agricultural machinery
        industry, and real estate history.

C153.   Tebbel, John William. THE MARSHALL FIELDS: A STUDY IN
        WEALTH. New York: E.P. Dutton, 1947.

        A popular account of the men who have borne the name
        Marshall Field; provides considerable information on the
        family mercantile business but needs revision for the
        activities of Field Enterprises in the recent decades.

C154.   Torrey, Kate Douglas. "Visions of a Western Lowell:
        Cannelton, Indiana, 1847-1851." INDIANA MAGAZINE OF
        HISTORY 73:4 (1977): 276-304.

        Examines the planning and boosterism that went into Ohio
        River-bank town.

C155.   Tully, Judy Corder, Elton F. Jackson, and Richard F.
        Curtis. "Trends in Occupational Mobility in
        Indianapolis." SOCIAL FORCES 49 (December 1970): 186-99.

        See D136.

C156.   Twyman, Robert W. HISTORY OF MARSHALL FIELD AND COMPANY,
        1852-1906. Philadelphia: University of Pennsylvania
        Press, 1954.

        A detailed, corporate history of one of the Midwest's
        giant merchandising operations. In an analysis of both the
        retail and wholesale trades of the Field enterprises,
        Twyman traces the department store's commercial expansion
        from a series of short-lived partnerships in the dry-goods
        business to a multi-million dollar company by the 1890s.

C157.   Waggoner, Madeline S. THE LONG HAUL WEST: THE GREAT CANAL
        ERA, 1817-1850. New York: Putnam, 1958.

        Particularly strong on upper New York state and the
        development of the Erie Canal, an economic history that
        emphasizes the business import of the canals and the
        culture they helped to create along their routes.

C158.   Wall, Joseph Frazier. ANDREW CARNEGIE. Oxford, England:
        Oxford University Press, 1970.

        A detailed analytical biography that supplies not only
        extensive business information on the rise of this colorful
        entrepreneur, but also a good understanding of the iron and
        steel industry.

C159.   Walsh, Margeret. THE RISE OF THE MIDWEST MEAT PACKING
        INDUSTRY. Lexington: University Press of Kentucky,
        1982.

        A monographic analysis of how one of the region's key
        forms of agricultural processing grew from an economic
        activity involving the individual hinterland farmer and his
        herd of razorbacks in the 1840s to the business.

oligarchies represented by Armour, Swift, and other large
meat packing corporations by the 1880s.

C160.   Warren, Kenneth. THE AMERICAN STEEL INDUSTRY: 1850-1970; A
        GEOGRAPHICAL INTERPRETATION. Oxford: Clarendon Press,
        1973.

        Excellent economic history; a standard reference.

C161.   Waters, Mary. ILLINOIS IN THE SECOND WORLD WAR. 2 vols.
        Springfield, IL: Illinois Historical Library, 1951.

        Volume I, subtitled "Operation Home Front," is partic-
        ularly strong on the techniques of civilian defense,
        mobilization and the status of education during the WW II
        years. Volume II, devoted to "The Production Front,"
        chronicles the roles that industry, transportation, organ-
        ized labor, and agriculture played in the war effort.
        Wartime labor disputes and debate over wage stabilization
        practices are particularly well covered.

C162.   Weber, Michael P. SOCIAL CHANGE IN AN INDUSTRIAL TOWN:
        PATTERNS OF PROGRESS IN WARREN, PENNSYLVANIA, FROM THE
        CIVIL WAR TO WORLD WAR I. University Park: Pennsylvania
        State University Press, 1976.

        See D139.

C163.   Wendt, Lloyd, and Herman Kogan. GIVE THE LADY WHAT SHE
        WANTS. Chicago: Rand McNally and Company, 1952.

        A more anecdotal and journalistic study of Chicago's
        Marshall Field than Robert Twyman's standard reference,
        HISTORY OF THE MARSHALL FIELD COMPANY (1954). Particular
        emphasis is given to Field's cultivation of the woman
        consumer through the use of extensive newspaper advertis-
        ing, delivery services, and in-store amenities such as tea-
        rooms, stenographic services, children's playrooms,
        customer libraries, and telephone facilities.

C164.   Whitaker, James W., ed. FARMING IN THE MIDWEST, 1840-1900.
        Washington: The Agricultural History Society, 1974.

        A symposium of papers with useful essays on history of
        public lands research, rural settlement patterns, corn and
        wheat economies, commodities exchanges, tenant farming, and
        farm mortgaging practices. While nineteenth century farm-
        ing in the Industrial Belt region is treated in many of the
        book's articles, the general typical orientation of the
        volume is toward agricultural history in Iowa, Kansas and
        Nebraska.

C165.   White, Langdon. "The Iron and Steel Industry of the
        Pittsburgh District." ECONOMIC GEOGRAPHY 4 (1928):
        115-59.

Explains the concentration of industry in this region by
1) its proximity to good coking coal, 2) to the lower
lake ports, 3) its strategic location with respect to the
great steel markets, 4) the tendency of great steel concerns to remain where they have large amounts of capital
invested, 5) favorable rail rates for steel shipment and
6) excellent water and railroad transport available.

C166. Williamson, Harold F., and Arnold Daum. THE AMERICAN
       PETROLEUM INDUSTRY: THE AGE OF ILLUMINATION, 1859-1899.
       Evanston: Northwestern University Press, 1959.

       A thorough monograph with abundant details on the period
       as well as notes and bibliography to assist in further
       reading. Particularly strong with the impact of the
       Pennsylvania oilfields in their heyday.

C167. Williamson, Sammuel H. "The Growth of The Great Lakes as a
       Major Transportation Resource, 1870-1911." RESEARCH IN
       ECONOMIC HISTORY 2 (1977): 173-248.

       Presents annual data on the major commodities carried on
       the Great Lakes, showing that the annual amount of trade
       carried increased from 6 million to more than 80 million or
       1300 percent during the period studied.

C168. Winters, Donald L. "Agricultural Tenancy in the
       Nineteenth-Century Middle West: The Historiographical
       Debate." INDIANA MAGAZINE OF HISTORY 78:2 (1982): 128-
       153.

       See G88.

C169. Zunz, Oliver. THE CHANGING FACE OF INEQUALITY:
       URBANIZATION, INDUSTRIALIZATION, AND IMMIGRANTS IN
       DETROIT, 1880-1920. Chicago: University of Chicago
       Press, 1983.

       See G91.

SOCIAL HISTORY

D1. Abbott, Edith. TENEMENTS OF CHICAGO, 1908-1935. Chicago:
     University of Chicago Press, 1936.

     Perceptive early analysis of the relationship between
     housing and urban problems; a landmark document in Chicago
     social work.

D2. Omitted.

D3. Agocs, Carol. "Who's In On The American Dream? Ethnic
     Representation in Suburban Opportunity Structures in
     Metropolitan Detroit, 1940-1970." ETHNIC GROUPS 4:4
     (1982): 239-254.

     Argues that ethnic suburbanization is more strongly
     related to income mobility than occupational mobility.
     Blacks and Mexicans are exceptions to this general trend.

D4. Alexander, June Grautin. "Staying Together: Chain
     Migration and Patterns of Slovak Settlement in Pittsburgh
     Prior To World War I." JOURNAL OF AMERICAN ETHNIC
     HISTORY 1:1 (1981): 56-83.

     See E2.

D5. Anderson, Nels. THE HOBO: THE SOCIOLOGY OF THE HOMELESS
     MAN. Chicago: University of Chicago Press, 1923.

     Another classic of the Chicago School of Sociology and
     its approach to studying urban problems using the city as
     its laboratory.

D6. Angus, David I. "The Politics of Progressive School
     Reform: Grand Rapids, 1900-1910." MICHIGAN ACADEMICIAN
     14:3 (1982): 239-58.

     See F5.

D7. Armstrong, Louise. WE TOO ARE THE PEOPLE. Boston: Little,
     Brown, 1938.

     Comprehensive survey of unemployment in Michigan during
     the 1930s Depression with particular emphasis on the social
     implications of public relief and unemployment.

D8. Arnold, Eleanor, ed. FEEDING OUR FAMILIES: MEMORIES OF
     HOOSIER HOMEMAKERS. Indianapolis: Indiana Extension
     Homemakers Association, 1983.

     The book's basis is an oral history project with 243
     interviews from seventy-two Indiana counties; these inter-
     views describe everyday life during the period 1890-1930
     from the woman's perspective. The book is the first of a
     planned series under the subtitle, MEMORIES OF HOOSIER
     HOMEMAKERS.

D9. Asbury, Charles. "A Comparison of a Riot in Ancient Rome
     and the Detroit Riot of 1967." MICHIGAN ACADEMICIAN 2:1
     (Summer 1969): 23-38.

     Explores the striking similarities between contemporary
     and ancient rioting.

D10. Aschenbrenner, Joyce. LIFELINES: BLACK FAMILIES IN
     CHICAGO. New York: Holt, 1975.

     A contemporary estimate of family structure.

D11. Atherton, Lewis. MAIN STREET ON THE MIDDLE BORDER.
     Bloomington: Indiana University Press, 1954.

     A lyrical, amusing, whimsical assessment of the Mid-
     western "country town" in life and literature that also
     serves as cultural and economic history of this local
     institution. Based on extensive journalistic, scholarly,
     and literary sources, this is truly one of the region's
     outstanding evocations of vernacular thought and culture.
     A delightful and insightful book, whose dedication is to a
     furniture-music-grocery store.

D12. Babson, Steve. "Pointing the Way: The Role of British and
     Irish Skilled Tradesmen in the Rise of the UAW." DETROIT
     PERSPECTIVE 7 (Spring 1983): 75-96.

     See E7.

D13. Bahr, Howard M., and Alexander Bracken. "The Middletown of
     Yore: Population, Persistence, Migration and
     Stratification." RURAL SOCIOLOGY 48 (1983):120-132.

     Shows that pre-industrial Munice, Indiana, experienced
     rapid growth and high population turnover during 1860-80,
     that wealth was concentrated in the hands of a small elite,
     and that the percentage of the population owning real
     estate decreased during 1850-70.

D14. Bahr, Howard M. "Shifts in the Denominational Demography
     of Middletown, 1924-1977." JOURNAL FOR SCIENTIFIC STUDY
     OF RELIGION 21:2 (1982): 99-114.

Discusses the social status and denominational cleavage between "Northern" and "Southern" Protestants, the convergence between Catholics and Protestants in Muncie, Indiana.

D15. Bakerman, Jane S. "When God Looks Down, It's the Bottom--Tony Morrison's Images of the Midwest." JOURNAL OF REGIONAL CULTURES 2:1 (Spring/Summer 1982): 24-32.

See H9.

D16. Barrows, Robert G. "Hurryin' Hoosiers and the American 'Pattern': Geographic Mobility in Indianapolis and Urban North America." SOCIAL SCIENCE HISTORY 5:2 (1981): 197-222.

Sees Indianapolis as an exception to Stephan Thernstorm's postulations and utility of using the term "pattern" to describe geographic mobility.

D17. Bauman, John F. "Ethnic Adaption In A Southwestern Pennsylvania Coal Patch." JOURNAL OF ETHNIC STUDIES 7:3 (1979): 1-23.

See E11.

D18. Baylen, Joseph O. "A Victorian's 'Crusade' in Chicago, 1893-1894." JOURNAL OF AMERICAN HISTORY 51 (December 1964): 418-34.

See E12.

D19. Beijbom, Ulf. SWEDES IN CHICAGO: A DEMOGRAPHIC AND SOCIAL STUDY OF THE 1846-1880 IMMIGRATION. Stockholm: Laromedeisforlager, 1971.

See E13.

D20. Bigham, Darrel E. "Family Structure of Germans and Blacks in Evansville and Vanderburg County, Indiana in 1880: A Comparative Study." THE OLD NORTHWEST 7:3 (1981): 255-275.

Title aptly describes the focus of a case study that concludes that social and economic circumstances, rather than family conditions, were the basis for differences between black and white families.

D21. Blee, Kathleen. "Family Ties and Class Conflict: The Politics of Immigrant Communities in the Great Lakes Region, 1890-1920." SOCIAL PROBLEMS 31 (February 1984): 311-21.

Challenges the traditional view that families react to, rather than influence, political organization, comparing

the role of the family in six industrial communities in the
Great Lakes region at the turn of the century. Finds that
families play an important role in creating stable working-
class cultural organizations, and that family bonds and
imagery provide a mechanism for political recruitment into
both right-wing and left-wing movements.

D22. Bodnar, John, Michael Weber, and Roger Simon.
      "Migration, Kinship, and Urban Adjustment: Blacks and
      Poles in Pittsburgh, 1900-1930." JOURNAL OF AMERICAN
      HISTORY 66:3 (1979): 548-565.

      Using oral history interviews the authors compare the two
      groups as to their migration experiences, socialization
      practices, and occupational mobility patterns.

D23. Bogue, Donald J. SKID ROW IN AMERICAN CITIES. Chicago:
      Community and Family Study Center at University of
      Chicago, 1963.

      A detailed sociological study which includes information
      on several industrial belt cities, especially Chicago.

D24. Bowly, Devereux. THE POORHOUSE: SUBSIDIZED HOUSING IN
      CHICAGO, 1895-1976. Carbondale: Southern Illinois
      University Press, 1978.

      See I9.

D25. Bray, Robert. "Robert Herrick, A Chicago Trio." THE OLD
      NORTHWEST 1:1 (1975): 63-84.

      See H11.

D26. Buder, Stanley. PULLMAN: AN EXPERIMENT IN INDUSTRIAL ORDER
      AND COMMUNITY PLANNING, 1880-1930. New York: Oxford
      University Press, 1967.

      Attempts to explain the social and economic factors that
      led to Pullman Strike of 1894. A careful analysis of the
      ethnic composition of the model town's inhabitants and the
      community planning concepts to which they were subjected by
      George Pullman. Best study to date on the pre-1894 model
      railroad community.

D27. Burg, David F. CHICAGO'S WHITE CITY OF 1893. Lexington:
      University Press of Kentucky, 1976.

      See H14.

D28. Butera, Ronald J. "A Settlement House and The Urban
      Challenge: Kingsley House in Pittsburgh, Pennsylvania,
      1893-1920." THE WESTERN PENNSYLVANIA HISTORICAL
      MAGAZINE 66 (January 1983): 24-47.

      See G7.

D29. Byington, Margaret F. HOMESTEAD: THE HOUSEHOLDS OF A MILL
     TOWN. Pittsburgh: University of Pittsburgh Center For
     International Studies, 1974 (1910).

     Part of the Pittsburgh Survey, a series of investigative
     volumes on urban social conditions in western Pennsylvania
     in the early twentieth century, this study focuses on the
     mill community that was the scene of the famous strike of
     1892. Unlike the other volumes of the survey that dealt
     with particular subjects such as wages, housing, sani-
     tation, or particular ethnic-cultural groups, the Byington
     social survey brings many facets of urban-industrial life
     into a single context. Urban historian Samuel P. Hayes
     provides a detailed introductory essay and critique to one
     of the major published primary sources of industrial belt
     history.

D30. Caplow, Theodore. "Christmas Gifts and Kin Networks."
     AMERICAN SOCIOLOGICAL REVIEW 47:3 (1982): 383-392.

     Explores ritualized gift-giving in Muncie, Indiana, and
     finds it to be primarily a way of reinforcing social
     relationships that are highly valued but often insecure.

D31. Caplow, Theodore. MIDDLETOWN FAMILIES: FIFTY YEARS OF
     CHANGE AND CONTINUITY. Minneapolis: University of
     Minneapolis Press, 1982.

     A follow-up sociological analysis of Muncie, Indiana, in
     the 1970s based on the earlier investigations by Robert and
     Helen Lynd published as MIDDLETOWN (1924) and MIDDLETOWN IN
     TRANSITION (1936), this Middletown III project finds more
     continuity than change in the general social ambience of
     the town.

D32. Carr, Lowell J., and James E. Sterner. WILLOW RUN: A
     STUDY OF INDUSTRIALIZATION AND CULTURAL INADEQUACY. New
     York: Harper & Row, 1952.

     A sociological analysis emphasizing poor working and
     living conditions at a wartime airplane factory near
     Detroit.

D33. Carson, Mina J. "Agnes Hamilton of Fort Wayne: The
     Education of a Christian Settlement Worker." INDIANA
     MAGAZINE OF HISTORY 80 (March 1984): 1-34.

     A thorough examination of the settlement worker who went
     from Hull House to the Lighthouse Settlement in
     Philadelphia. Also explores her sister Alice's life and
     the influence of Christian Socialism upon both.

D34. Carter, William. MIDDLE WEST COUNTRY. Boston: Houghton
     Mifflin, 1975.

Primarily a photo-text book wherein the author mixes, not
always successfully, personal narrative and social analysis. Striking photography and an imaginative bibliography.

D35. Chambers, Clarke. PAUL U. KELLOGG AND THE SURVEY: VOICES
      FOR SOCIAL WELFARE AND SOCIAL JUSTICE. Minneapolis:
      University of Minnestoa Press, 1971.

      An excellent biography of a dedicated social reformer,
      Paul Kellogg (1897-1958) and his crusading journal, THE
      PITTSBURGH SURVEY. Demonstrates how Kellogg set the tone
      for a generation of social work journalism and helped
      transform the field. Kellogg contributed to the pro-
      fession's shift from its traditional attachment to adminis-
      trative philanthropy to its contemporary, professional
      concern for the social and economic dilemmas of industrial
      poverty.

D36. Choldin, Harvey M., and Claudine Hanson. "Status Shifts
      Within The City." AMERICAN SOCIOLOGICAL REVIEW 47:1
      (1982): 129-141.

      An analysis of changing status over a thirty-year period
      among neighborhoods in Chicago. Hypotheses regarding the
      effects on status, race composition, and housing are
      tested.

D37. Clive, Alan. STATE OF WAR: MICHIGAN IN WORLD WAR II. Ann
      Arbor: The University of Michigan Press, 1979.

      Sees Michigan as a representative window on the war
      experience which heretofore has largely been studied only
      on the national level. In seven nicely balanced chapters
      dealing with business, workers, communities, race, Southern
      white migrants, women and youth, and victory and recon-
      version, Clive probes the interaction of the forces of
      change and continuity set in motion by the need to meet the
      production challenge of the war.

D38. Cohen, Ronald D., and Raymond A. Mohl. THE PARADOX OF
      PROGRESSIVE EDUCATION: THE GARY PLAN AND URBAN SCHOOLING.
      Port Washington, NY: Kennikat Press, 1979.

      A segment of local history as well as an exploration of
      the general character of educational change in the early
      twentieth century via one of its most celebrated institu-
      tions. The paradox of the plan is depicted by considering
      its primary promoters: the conservative William
      A. Wirt, Gary Superintendent of Schools, and the social
      democrat, Alice Barrows.

D39. Cooke, Patricia. "The Erie Canal: American History Through
      Folklore." NEW YORK FOLKLORE 5:3/4 (1979): 155-167.

      See C37.

D40. Costin, Lela B. TWO SISTERS FOR SOCIAL JUSTICE: A
      BIOGRAPHY OF GRACE AND EDITH ABBOTT. Urbana: University
      of Illinois Press, 1983.

      This dual biography traces the relationship and achieve-
      ments of Grace (the activist) and Edith (the scholar)
      Abbott in the area of social justice. Costin notes that
      the sisters/partners were, unlike Addams, professional
      experts who sought to challenge the traditional views
      toward women during the first four decades of the twentieth
      century.

D41. Cowles, Karen. "The Industrialization of Duquesne and the
      Circulation of Elites, 1891-1933." THE WESTERN
      PENNSYLVANIA HISTORICAL MAGAZINE 62 (January 1979):
      1-17.

      Applying Vilfredo Pareto's theory of dual elites
      (rentiers vs. speculators), the author examines economic
      elites in the small city of Duquesne, located twelve miles
      up the Monongahela River from Pittsburgh, and sees their
      movement as indicative of the industrialization process in
      mill towns. Also explores the interaction of community
      politics and industrial growth.

D42. Cox, Kevin. "Housing Tenure and Neighborhood Activities."
      URBAN AFFAIRS QUARTERLY 18 (1982): 107-129.

      Neighborhood activism in advanced capitalistic societies
      is thought to be due to home ownership and homeowners'
      concern over the home as a major investment. However, a
      survey of both activists and nonactivists in the Columbus,
      Ohio, area suggests that neighborhood activism is due to
      cost barriers to relocation.

D43. Cremin, Lawrence. THE TRANSFORMATION OF THE SCHOOL.
      New York: A. A. Knopf, 1961.

      A major study in the history of American education in
      which two transplanted New Englanders--Francis Parker
      (1837-1902) and John Dewey (1859-1952)--are seen as the
      major forces behind the progressive education movement
      in Chicago.

D44. Davis, Allen F. SPEARHEADS FOR REFORM: THE SOCIAL
      SETTLEMENTS AND THE PROGRESSIVE MOVEMENT, 1890-1914. New
      York: Oxford University Press, 1967.

      Davis concentrates on the people involved in the settle-
      ment house movement, their thoughts, their problems, and
      their influence on the community. Evidence and examples
      are drawn from Boston, New York, and Chicago.

D45. Davis, Donald F. "The City Remodelled: The Limits of
      Automotive Industry Leadership In Detroit, 1910-1919."
      SOCIAL HISTORY 13 (1980): 451-486.

      See F21.

D46. Davis, James E. "New Aspects of Men and New Forms of
     Society: The Old Northwest, 1790-1820." JOURNAL OF THE
     ILLINOIS STATE HISTORICAL SOCIETY 69:3 (1979): 164-172.

     Argues that two traits--republicanism and creativity--
     characterized the settlers to the region during the
     National Era. Traits resulted from selective migration,
     diverse origins of migration, abundant land, scarce labor
     and low economic thresholds.

D47. Demarest, David P., ed. FROM THESE HILLS, FROM THESE
     VALLEYS: SELECTED FICTION ABOUT WESTERN PENNSYLVANIA.
     Pittsburgh: University of Pittsburgh Press, 1976.

     See H24.

D48. DeVries, James E. RACE AND KINSHIP IN A MIDWESTERN TOWN:
     THE BLACK EXPERIENCE IN MONROE, MICHIGAN, 1900-1915.
     Urbana: University of Illinois Press, 1984.

     See E32.

D49. Diner, Steven J. "Chicago Social Workers and Blacks in the
     Progressive Era." SOCIAL SERVICE REVIEW 44:4 (1970):
     393-410.

     Explores the relationship between social workers and
     blacks in Chicago between 1900 and 1920, when leading
     social workers discovered many similarities between poor
     blacks and poor immigrants, although researchers were
     intrigued by the unique problems faced by blacks because of
     discrimination.

D50. Duis, Perry R. THE SALOON: PUBLIC DRINKING IN CHICAGO AND
     BOSTON, 1880-1920. Urbana: University of Illinois
     Press, 1984.

     This study explores drinking itself, comparing and con-
     strasting Chicago's numerous saloons to Boston's few and
     tightly regulated ones.

D51. Duis, Perry R. "Whose City? Public and Private Places in
     Nineteenth-Century Chicago." CHICAGO HISTORY 12 (1983):
     Part I (2-27); Part II (2-23).

     See G15.

D52. Duncan, Hugh D. CULTURE AND DEMOCRACY: THE STRUGGLE FOR
     FORM IN SOCIETY AND ARCHITECTURE IN CHICAGO AND THE
     MIDDLE WEST DURING THE LIFE AND TIMES OF LOUIS H.
     SULLIVAN. Totowa, NJ: Bedminster Press, 1965.

     See H31.

D53. Eckert, Kathryn. "Midwestern Resort Architecture: Earl H.
     Mead in Harbor Springs." MICHIGAN HISTORY 63:1 (1979):
     10-20.

     See I28.

D54. Esslinger, Dean R. IMMIGRANTS AND THE CITY: ETHNICITY AND
      MOBILITY IN A NINETEENTH CENTURY MIDWESTERN COMMUNITY.
      Port Washington, NY: Kennikat Press, 1975.

      See E39.

D55. Eversole, Theodore W. "The Cincinnati Union Bethel: The
      Coming of Age of the Settlement Idea in Cincinnati."
      CINCINNATI HISTORICAL SOCIETY BULLETIN 32 (Spring-Summer
      1974): 47-59.

      Evaluates the development of social settlement work in
      the city's early twentieth-century history.

D56. Fairbanks, Robert B. "Housing the City: The Better
      Housing League and Cincinnati, 1916-1939." OHIO HISTORY
      89:2 (1980): 157-180.

      See I30.

D57. Farris, Robert E. CHICAGO SOCIOLOGY, 1920-1932. San
      Francisco: Chandler, 1967.

      Discusses the extensive urban research in early sociology
      generated by the University of Chicago.

D58. Fish, John Hall. BLACK POWER/WHITE CONTROL. Princeton:
      Princeton University Press, 1973.

      Argues that a set of dualistic and contending forces
      characterized late 1960s' white-black relations: inte-
      gration versus revolution, politics versus culture,
      planning versus participation. These forces are examined
      in a detached account of the evaluation of an indigenous
      urban project known as the Temporary Woodlawn Organization
      and its successes and failures against the Chicago
      Democratic Machine.

D59. Flanagan, John T. "A Decade of Middlewestern
      Autobiography." CENTENNIAL REVIEW 26:2 (1982):
      115-133.

      See H37.

D60. Gerber, David A. BLACK OHIO AND THE COLOR LINE, 1860-1915.
      Urbana: University of Illinois Press, 1976.

      Bridges the usual gap in black historiography dealing
      with the period between the Reconstruction years and the
      Jim Crow era. Describes an old and a new leadership among
      blacks contending for allegiance; the former stressing
      individual development, the latter attempting to foster
      group action. Should serve as a model for state studies of
      the black populace in other parts of the region.

D61. Gitlin, Todd, and Nanci Hollander. UPTOWN: POOR WHITES IN
      CHICAGO. New York: Harper, 1970.

      Taped interviews with transplanted Appalachian whites in
      Chicago.

D62. Grabowski, John J. "From Progressive To Patrician: George
      Bellamy and Hiram House Social Settlement, 1896-1914."
      OHIO HISTORY 87:1 (1978): 37-52.

      Traces the early history of Cleveland's first social
      settlement through the changing attitudes of its founder
      and first director.

D63. Graham, James Q., Jr. "Family and Fertility in Rural Ohio:
      Wood County, Ohio, in 1860." JOURNAL OF FAMILY HISTORY
      8:3 (1983): 262-278.

      See G26.

D64. Grant, William R. "Community Control vs. School
      Integration--the Case of Detroit." THE PUBLIC INTEREST
      24 (Summer 1971): 62-79.

      Argues that Detroit's decentralization program is just as
      important as New York's; the issue was whether community
      control was compatible with racial integration. The
      answer, the author says, is no.

D65. Hall, Bradley. "Elites and Spatial Change in Pittsburgh:
      Minersville As A Case Study." PENNSYLVANIA HISTORY
      48:4 (1981): 311-334.

      Analyzes the manner in which successive generations of
      Pittsburgh elites contributed to spatial and social
      differentiation within the city. The first generation
      held community-oriented values while successive
      elites embraced private ones.

D66. Haller, Mark H. "Organized Crime in Urban Society: Chicago
      in the Twentieth Century." JOURNAL OF SOCIAL HISTORY 5:2
      (1971-72): 210-34.

      Examines the social worlds within which the criminals
      operated, the diverse patterns by which different ethnic
      groups became involved in organized criminal activities,
      and the broad and pervasive economic impact of organized
      crime in urban neighborhoods.

D67. Hampsten, Elizabeth. READ THIS ONLY TO YOURSELF: THE
      PRIVATE WRITINGS OF MIDWESTERN WOMEN, 1880-1910.
      Bloomington: Indiana University Press, 1982.

      Evaluates this genre of women's history primarily from
      the point of view of a literary critic rather than of a

social historian. Makes useful comparisons to men writers
and their verbal interpretation of the frontier
experience.

D68. Harring, Sidney L. "Class Conflict and the Suppression of
      Tramps in Buffalo, 1892-1894." LAW AND SOCIETY REVIEW
      11:5 (1977): 873-911.

      Analyzes the origins, scope, and context of the state's
      Tramp Act (1885) focusing on its enforcement in Buffalo in
      1894.

D69. Hartman, Grover L. "The Hoosier Sunday School: A Potent
      Religious Cultural Force." INDIANA MAGAZINE OF HISTORY
      78:3 (1982): 215-241.

      A survey of the founding, growth, and decline of the
      Sunday School movement from the early nineteenth century to
      present. Concludes that at its height the movement pro-
      vided much adult education and standard behavioral norms
      for a society of disparate social groups.

D70. Hatcher, Harlan. THE WESTERN RESERVE: THE STORY OF NEW
      CONNECTICUT IN OHIO. Indianapolis: Bobbs-Merrill, 1949.

      Deals with that area of northeastern Ohio which was a
      "reserve" of Connecticut until 1800. Emphasizes the
      unique mixture of old New England stock and later European
      immigrant culture in that part of the industrial belt.

D71. Havinghurst, Robert J., and Hugh G. Morgan. THE SOCIAL
      HISTORY OF A WAR-BOOM COMMUNITY. New York: Longmans,
      1951.

      Describes the impact of social change on Seneca,
      Illinois, during World War II, when that small town became
      an important center of armaments manufacturing.

D72. Heinz, John P., and Edward O. Laumann. CHICAGO LAWYERS:
      THE SOCIAL STRUCTURE OF THE BAR. New York: Russell Sage
      Foundation and American Bar Foundation, 1982.

      Analyzes lawyers' roles in client relations, describes
      lawyers' social background, social values, and career
      mobility as well as their networks of associations, organi-
      zations, and political activities.

D73. Herrick, Mary. THE CHICAGO SCHOOLS: A SOCIAL AND A
      POLITICAL HISTORY. Beverly Hills: Sage Publications,
      1971.

      Most comprehensive treatment to date of the political
      conflicts, personalities, and interworkings of a major
      Midwestern urban school system.

D74. Hilliard, Celia. "'Rent Reasonable to Right Parties': Gold
      Coast Apartment Buildings 1906-1929." CHICAGO HISTORY 8
      (Summer 1979): 66-77.

      See I37.

D75. Hinding, Andrea, and Rosemary Richardson. ARCHIVAL AND
      MANUSCRIPT RESOURCES FOR THE STUDY OF WOMEN'S HISTORY: A
      BEGINNING. Minneapolis: University of Minnesota Social
      Welfare History Archives, 1972.

      See A36.

D76. Hogeland, Ronald W. "Coeducation of the Sexes at Oberlin
      College: A Study of Social Ideas in Mid-Nineteenth
      Century America." JOURNAL OF SOCIAL HISTORY 6 (Winter
      1972-73): 160-76.

      See H61.

D77. Holbrook, Stewart W. THE YANKEE EXODUS: AN ACCOUNT OF
      MIGRATION FROM NEW ENGLAND. Seattle: University of
      Washington Press, 1950.

      See E68.

D78. Horowitz, Helen Lefkowitz. CULTURE AND THE CITY: CULTURAL
      PHILANTHROPY IN CHICAGO FROM THE 1880S TO 1917.
      Lexington: University Press of Kentucky, 1976.

      A study of some of the major cultural institutions of the
      city, centering on the Art Institute. She argues that the
      institutions were largely organized, sustained, and
      controlled by a group of businessmen who served, with
      considerable overlapping, on their boards of trustees.
      Their trustees had turned to cultural philanthropy not so
      much to satisfy personal aesthetics or scholarly yearnings
      as to accomplish social goals. Disturbed by social forces,
      they could not control and filled with idealistic notions
      of culture, these businessmen saw in the museum, the
      library, the symphony orchestra, and the university a way
      to purify their city and to generate a civic renaissance.

D79. Hoyt, Homer. ONE HUNDRED YEARS OF LAND VALUES IN CHICAGO:
      THE RELATIONSHIP OF CHICAGO TO THE RISE IN ITS LAND
      VALUES, 1830-1933. Chicago: University of Chicago
      Press, 1933.

      A pioneering correlation of detailed real estate history,
      urban geographical expansion, architectural development,
      and social structure. Unfortunately nothing like it exists
      for the last fifty years of the city's growth.

D80. Hugill, Peter J. "Houses in Cazenovia: The Effects of Time
      and Class." LANDSCAPE 24:2 (1980): 10-15.

      See I43.

D81. Hutton, Graham. MIDWEST AT NOON. Chicago: University of
     Chicago Press, 1946.

     A personal reflection on the cultural meaning of the
     Midwest by a transplanted English writer living in the
     region for five years. Aspiring to do for twentieth-
     century America (from the vantage point of the Midwest)
     what James Bryce did for the nineteenth-century, Hutton
     attempts to show, with a bit of help from Emerson's ENGLISH
     TRAITS, how much alike are "the Midwesterners of today and
     the Britishers of yesterday." Not a scholarly book, the
     volume is, however, helpful in evoking the sense of Anglo-
     American relations at the close of WW II in a region
     periodically prone to Anglophobia.

D82. Ingham, John N. THE IRON BARONS: A SOCIAL ANALYSIS OF AN
     AMERICAN URBAN ELITE, 1965-1974. Westport, CT:
     Greenwood Press, 1978.

     See C81.

D83. Jakle, John A. "The American Bison and the Human
     Occupance of the Ohio Valley." PROCEEDINGS OF THE
     AMERICAN PHILOSOPHICAL SOCIETY 112 (August 1968):
     299-306.

     See B24.

D84. Jenkins, William D. "The Ku Klux Klan in Youngstown,
     Ohio: Moral Reform in The Twenties." HISTORIAN 4:1
     (1978): 76-93.

     Explains rapid growth of the KKK in this industrial belt
     city not on the grounds of nativism or racial or religious
     prejudice but for moral reform of the lower classes.

D85. Katz, Michael B., and Mark J. Stern. "Fertility, Class,
     and Industrial Capitalism: Erie County, New York,
     1855-1915." AMERICAN QUARTERLY 33:1 (1981): 63-92.

     Of the various factors considered--birthplace, urban-
     rural differences, ethnicity, economic factors--class is
     shown to be the most significant independent influence on
     fertility patterns.

D86. Katz, Michael B., and Mark J. Stern. "Migration and the
     Social Order in Erie County, New York, 1855." JOURNAL OF
     INTER-DISCIPLINARY HISTORY 8:4 (1978): 659-701.

     Illustrates a new statistical method for calculating
     persistence (the proportion of population remaining in a
     given place) for Buffalo and Erie counties using the New
     York State census of 1855.

D87. Kaufman, Martin, and Leslie L. Hanawalt. "Body Snatching
     in the Midwest." MICHIGAN HISTORY 55 (Spring 1971):
     23-40.

The authors focus upon the grisly, yet widespread nineteenth-century practice of grave robbing, due in large part, the authors hold, to the unwillingness of the public and the legislators to legalize body donation for cadaver research in medical schools.

D88. Kern, Richard. FINDLAY COLLEGE: THE FIRST HUNDRED YEARS. Findlay: Findlay College, 1984.

See E77.

D89. Kleinberg, Susan J. "Death and the Working Class." JOURNAL OF POPULAR CULTURE 11:1 (1977): 193-209.

Explores attitudes toward death in their social and economic context among working class residents of Pittsburgh during the 1890s.

D90. Kleinberg, Susan J. "Technology and Women's Work: The Lives of Working Class Women in Pittsburgh, 1870-1900." DYNAMOS AND VIRGINS REVISITED. Edited by Martha Trescott. Metuchen, NJ: Scarecrow Press, 1979, pp. 185-204.

See G42.

D91. Knoke, David. "Political Mobilization by Voluntary Associates." JOURNAL OF POLITICAL AND MILITARY SOCIOLOGY 10:2 (1982): 171-182.

See F58.

D92. Kornblum, William. BLUE COLLAR COMMUNITY. Chicago: University of Chicago Press, 1974.

Careful case study of ethnic and political life in south Chicago neighborhoods.

D93. Kornhauser, Arthur. DETROIT AS THE PEOPLE SEE IT. Detroit: Wayne State University Press, 1952.

Typical field survey of local social attitudes in one of the industrial belt's major cities.

D94. Lane, James B. "CITY OF THE CENTURY" A HISTORY OF GARY, INDIANA. Bloomington: Indiana University Press, 1978.

A personal but professional account that attempts to explain the impact of specific historical factors, diverse loyalties, contrary goals, and numerous conflicts on a city that the author sees as never quite able to overcome its original nineteenth-century frontier town character.

D95. Larson, John Lauritz, and David G. Vanderstel. "Agent of Empire: William Conner on the Indiana Frontier,

1800-1855." INDIANA MAGAZINE OF HISTORY 80:4 (December
1984): 301-328.

See C94.

D96. Leggett, John C. "Class Consciousness and Politics in
     Detroit: A Study in Change." MICHIGAN HISTORY 48
     (December 1964): 289-314.

     Explores the changing character of social stratification
     as it has affected the development of working class
     consciousness in the city from 1900 to 1960.

D97. LeMasters, E. F. BLUE-COLLAR ARISTOCRATS: LIFE STYLES AT A
     WORKING CLASS TAVERN. Madison: University of Wisconsin
     Press, 1975.

     Focuses primarily on this social institution's role in
     twentieth century culture; should be read along with Perry
     Duis's historical study of THE SALOON (1984) (D50).

D98. Levstik, Frank B. "Life Among the Lowly: An Early View of
     An Ohio Poor House." OHIO HISTORY 88:1 (1979): 84-88.

     Analysis of letter to the state's governor in 1858
     describing conditions in a county poor house.

D99. Lindsey, Almont. THE PULLMAN STRIKE: THE STORY OF A UNIQUE
     EXPERIMENT AND OF A GREAT LABOR UPHEAVAL. Chicago:
     University of Chicago Press, 1942.

     See C98.

D100. Lissak, Rivka. "Myth and Reality: The Pattern of
      Relationship Between the Hull House Circle and the 'New
      Immigrants' On Chicago's West Side." JOURNAL OF AMERICAN
      ETHNIC HISTORY 2 (1983): 21-50.

      See E85.

D101. Lyford, Joseph P. THE TALK IN VANDALIA. Santa Barbara,
      CA: Center For The Study of Democratic Institutions,
      1962.

      Under the auspices of the Center and the Fund for the
      Republic, political journalist Lyford conducted revealing
      taped interviews with the residents of Vandalia, Illinois,
      a place that aptly represented "small town Midwest
      America." He hoped to do for this community what the Lynds
      had done for Muncie, Indiana; he did not.

D102. McCarthy, Kathleen. NOBLESSE OBLIGE: CHARITY AND CULTURAL
      PHILANTHROPHY IN CHICAGO, 1849-1929. Chicago: University
      of Chicago Press, 1982.

An examination of the social structure that sponsored
activities such as family welfare, medical charities, and
cultural institutions.

D103.   McClymer, John F. "The Pittsburgh Survey, 1907-1914:
         Forging an Ideology in the Steel District." PENNSYLVANIA
         HISTORY 41:3 (1974): 169-186.

         A concise summary of the survey made by social scientists
         who thought it possible to measure the effects of industri-
         alization and to suggest viable remedies. Surveys of other
         cities in the industrial belt were modelled on this classic
         effort.

D104.   Marshall, James R., and George W. Dowdall. "Employment and
         Mental Hospitalization: The Case of Buffalo, New York:
         1914-1955." SOCIAL FORCES 60:3 (1982): 843-853.

         See C105.

D105.   Mayer, John A. "Relief Systems and Social Control: The
         Case of Chicago, 1890-1910." THE OLD NORTHWEST 6:3
         (1980): 217-244.

         Maintains that contrary to the dominant view in the
         literature of social welfare which asserts that welfare
         institutions were used by the upper and middle classes as a
         form of social control, the attempted regulation of the
         lower class was not effective because there were many
         alternative relief systems available.

D106.   Miles, William, compiler. WOMEN'S HISTORY: A GUIDE TO
         UNPUBLISHED RESOURCES IN THE CLARK HISTORICAL LIBRARY.
         Mt. Pleasant, MI: Clark Historical Library, 1976.

         See A54.

D107.   Miller, Zane L. BOSS COX'S CINCINNATI URBAN POLITICS IN
         THE PROGRESSIVE ERA. New York: Oxford University Press,
         1968.

         See F71A.

D108.   Modell, John. "Family and Fertility on the Indiana
         Frontier, 1820." AMERICAN QUARTERLY 23 (December 1971):
         615-34.

         The author's findings agree with those of Jack E. Eblen,
         who found that families, and not single, unattached males,
         were predominant on the frontier. Also discusses the
         families' size and composition. Well-documented with
         charts and tables.

D109.   Monkkonen, Eric H. THE DANGEROUS CLASS: CRIME AND POVERTY
         IN COLUMBUS, OHIO, 1885-1960. Cambridge: Harvard
         University Press, 1975.

Suggests, on the basis of research for a twenty-five year
period in a medium-sized city, that not only did a "dangerous class," as defined by nineteenth-century reformers,
probably not exist in Columbus, but also that the relationship between poverty and criminal behavior was tenuous at
best. Concludes that crime and poverty rates did not
increase with the urbanization and industrialization of the
city.

D110. Motz, Marilyn F. TRUE SISTERHOOD: MICHIGAN WOMEN AND THEIR
       KIN, 1820-1920. Albany: State University of New York
       Press, 1982.

Investigates the familial relationships among women in
nineteenth-century Michigan and the correspondence networks
and support systems they established among their peers.

D111. Murray, John J., ed. HERITAGE OF THE MIDDLE WEST.
       Norman: University of Oklahoma Press, 1958.

See A56.

D112. Nelli, Humbert S. ITALIANS IN CHICAGO: A STUDY IN ETHNIC
       MOBILITY, 1880-1930. New York: Oxford University Press,
       1970.

See E93.

D113. Nelson, Otto M. "The Chicago Relief and Aid Society,
       1850-1874." JOURNAL OF THE ILLINOIS STATE HISTORICAL
       SOCIETY 59 (Spring 1966): 48-68.

Analyses the organizational structure and social
philosophy of an early private welfare agency in Chicago.

D114. Olson, David J., compiler. BIBLIOGRAPHY OF SOURCES
       RELATING TO WOMEN. East Lansing: Michigan History
       Division, Michigan Deptartment of State, 1975.

See A59.

D115. Parkerson, Donald H. "How Mobile Were Nineteenth-Century
       Americans?" HISTORICAL METHODS 15:3 (1982): 99-109.

A detailed methodological analysis of census data for New
York State concluding that mobility in this region had two
characteristics: the migration was first from countryside
to city but once in the city, people tended to stay in one
location.

D116. Parot, Joseph. "Ethnic versus Black Metropolis: The
       Origins of Polish-Black Housing Tensions in Chicago."
       POLISH AMERICAN STUDIES 29 (Spring-Autumn 1972): 5-33.

See E96.

D117. Peterson, Jon A. "From Social Settlement to Social Agency:
       Settlement Work in Columbus, Ohio, 1898-1958." SOCIAL
       SERVICE REVIEW 39 (June 1965): 191-208.

       Summarizes the professionalization of social work from
       neighborhood settlement origins to its incorporation into
       the city's social welfare bureaucracy.

D118. Pickar, Madge, and R. Carlyle Buley. THE MIDWEST PIONEER:
       HIS ILLS, CURES AND DOCTORS. New York: Henry Schuman,
       1976.

       See G62.

D119. Prosser, Daniel J. "Chicago and the Bungalow Boom of the
       1920s." CHICAGO HISTORY 10 (Summer 1981): 86-95.

       See I71.

D120. Quandt, Jean B. FROM SMALL TOWN TO GREAT COMMUNITY: THE
       SOCIAL THOUGHT OF PROGRESSIVE INTELLECTUALS. New
       Brunswick: Rutgers University Press, 1970.

       Argues that many Midwestern urban reformers such as Jane
       Addams and Frederic Howe brought their small town
       perspective to their attempt to change big city social
       problems. A model American Studies approach that deals
       with nine American intellectuals.

D121. Quantic, Diane Dufva, and Wayne C. Rohrer. "Growing Up in
       the Middle West as Reflected in Sociological and Literary
       Words." JOURNAL OF REGIONAL CULTURES 2:1 (Spring/Summer
       1982): 6-15.

       The authors compare the observations of novelists and
       sociologists on growing up in the midwest and find that
       both disciplines reflect "similar attitudes and incidents
       in rural and urban Middle Western settings."

D122. Rose, Dan. ENERGY TRANSITION AND THE LOCAL COMMUNITY:
       A THEORY OF SOCIETY APPLIED TO HAZELTON, PENNSYLVANIA.
       Philadelphia: University of Pennsylvania Press, 1981.

       See C128.

D123. Scheiber, Henry N., ed. THE OLD NORTHWEST: STUDIES IN
       REGIONAL HISTORY, 1787-1910. Lincoln: University of
       Nebraska Press, 1969.

       See A69.

D124. Schlereth, Thomas J. "Regional Studies On The Chicago
       Model Since 1975." SOURCES FOR AMERICAN STUDIES.
       Westport, CT: Greenwood Press, 1980, pp. 518-532.

       See A71.

D125. Schneider, John C. "Urbanization and the Maintenance of
       Order: Detroit, 1824-1847." MICHIGAN HISTORY 60:3
       (1976): 260-81.

       See G74.

D126. Schneirov, Richard. "Chicago's Great Upheaval of 1877."
       CHICAGO HISTORY 9 (Spring 1980): 2-17.

       See C139.

D127. Scriabine, Christine. "Upton Sinclair and the Writing of
       THE JUNGLE." CHICAGO HISTORY 10:1 (1981): 26-37.

       See H107.

D128. Sehr, Timothy J. "Three Gilded Age Suburbs of
       Indianapolis: Irvington, Brightwood, and Woodruff Place,"
       INDIANA MAGAZINE OF HISTORY 77 (December: 1981):
       305-332.

       Traces the ability of groups to create distinctive
       communities with a city and the consequent socioeconomic
       segregation of urban space that resulted in Indiana's
       capitol city. Shows how the early histories of three
       suburbs illustrate different views of the suburban ideal in
       the Midwest.

D129. Sennett, Richard. FAMILIES AGAINST THE CITY: MIDDLE CLASS
       HOMES OF INDUSTRIAL CHICAGO, 1872-1890. New York:
       Cambridge, MA: Harvard University Press, 1970.

       Discusses middle-class families in the last third of the
       19th century. The book has received strong criticism; see
       the review by Perry R. Duis in AMERICAN JOURNAL OF
       SOCIOLOGY (March 1971).

D130. Shergold, Peter R. WORKING-CLASS LIFE: THE "AMERICAN
       STANDARD" IN COMPARATIVE PERSPECTIVE, 1899-1913.
       Pittsburgh: University of Pittsburgh Press, 1982.

       An empirical comparison of the working-class standard of
       living in Pittsburgh and Birmingham, England, that argues
       Americans may have been better paid but that they were
       saddled with higher costs of food, shelter and clothing.
       Sees a two-tiered working class composed of an "aristoc-
       racy of labor" (skilled workers) and unskilled workers
       (blacks and new immigrants).

D131. Smith, Thomas V., and Leonard White. CHICAGO: AN
       EXPERIMENT IN SOCIAL SCIENCE RESEARCH. Chicago:
       University of Chicago Press, 1929.

       One of the first social theory assessments of Chicago's
       social theorists; compare to later studies by Farris
       (CHICAGO SOCIOLOGY) (D57) and Short (SOCIAL FABRIC OF THE
       METROPOLIS, Chicago: University of Chicago Press, 1971).

D132.   Suskind, Richard. "Chicago's Bloody Haymarket Riot--First
        Anarchist Drama--Evoked Loud Demands, Law-and-Order."
        SMITHSONIAN 2 (October 1971): 52-59.

        Reviews the responses of Chicago's economic and social
        elite to strengthen the city's police force and to
        establish arsenals as deterrents to public disorder.

D133.   Suttles, Gerald D. THE SOCIAL ORDER OF THE SLUM:
        ETHNICITY AND TERRITORY IN THE INNER CITY. Chicago:
        University of Chicago Press, 1968.

        Examines the struggles within and among four West Side
        Chicago groups: Blacks, Puerto Ricans, Mexicans, and
        Italians.

D134.   Tarr, Joel A., and Denise DiPasquale. "The Mill Town in
        The Industrial City: Pittsburgh's Hazelwood." URBANISM
        PAST AND PRESENT 7:1 (1982): 1-14.

        Focuses on this industrial belt neighborhood during two
        eras of its history in relation to the city of Pittsburgh:
        1870-1920 when it was dominated by two major employers--
        Jones and Laughlin Steel and the Baltimore and Ohio RR--
        and the town maintained its independence of Pittsburgh;
        and the 1920-1950 period when its two employers declined
        and Hazelwood was transformed from an autonomous city into
        a neighborhood of Pittsburgh.

D135.   Thrasher, Frederic Milton. THE GANG: A STUDY OF 1,313
        GANGS IN CHICAGO. Chicago: University of Chicago Press,
        1927, 1938.

        Thrasher's study of youth gangs is a standard work in the
        University of Chicago Sociological Series. He gives a
        thorough description of gang life and the urban gang
        environment. Chapters are devoted to the relation of the
        gang to politics and crime. The bibliography, though
        limited to work prior to 1938, is comprehensive.

D136.   Tully, Judy Corder, Elton F. Jackson, and Richard F.
        Curtis. "Trends in Occupational Mobility in
        Indianapolis." SOCIAL FORCES 49 (December 1970): 186-99.

        Intergenerational occupational mobility patterns measured
        from survey data collected in Indianapolis in 1966 and 1968
        were compared to patterns present in Rogoff's 1910 and 1940
        marriage license data. The following moderate differences
        appeared between the 1966-68 and the earlier data: (1) the
        proportion of people moving out of their original stratum
        remained about the same, but among the movers upward
        mobility became more common and downward mobility less
        common; (2) the linear dependence of a son's occupation on
        father's occupation increased, mainly due to a higher level
        of dependence for men under 24 years of age in 1966-68; (3)
        the 1966-68 mobility process, compared to the 1940 process,

tended to produce an upgrading within both manual and
nonmanual categories.

D137. Wade, Louise. GRAHAM TAYLOR: PIONEER FOR SOCIAL JUSTICE.
       Chicago: University of Chicago Press, 1964.

       See G81.

D138. Weber, Michael P. "Residential and Occupational Patterns
       of Ethnic Minorites in Nineteenth-Century Pittsburgh."
       PENNSYLVANIA HISTORY 44:4 (1977): 317-334.

       See E122.

D139. Weber, Michael P. SOCIAL CHANGE IN AN INDUSTRIAL TOWN:
       PATTERNS OF PROGRESS IN WARREN, PENNSYLVANIA, FROM THE
       CIVIL WAR TO WORLD WAR I. University Park: Pennsylvania
       State University Press, 1976.

       A case study of social mobility of native and foreign-
       born laborers modelled after Stephan Thernstrom's POVERTY
       AND PROGRESS.

D140. Wheeler, James O., and Stanley D. Brunn. "An Agricultural
       Ghetto: Negroes in Cass County, Michigan, 1845-1968."
       GEOGRAPHICAL REVIEW 59 (July 1969): 317-29.

       See E124.

D141. Whitaker, F.M. "Ohio WCTU and the Prohibition Amendment
       Campaign of 1883." OHIO HISTORY 83:2 (1974): 85-102.

       See F115.

D142. Williams, Kenny J., and Bernard Duffey, eds. CHICAGO'S
       PUBLIC WITS: A CHAPTER IN THE AMERICAN COMIC SPIRIT.
       Baton Rouge: Louisiana State University Press, 1983.

       See H119.

D143. Wilson, Ben C. "Idlewood, Michigan, 1912-1930: Growth of
       One of America's Oldest Black Resorts." JOURNAL OF
       REGIONAL CULTURES 2:1 (Spring/Summer 1982): 56-70.

       See H121.

D144. Wood, Arthur Evans. HAMTRAMCK: A SOCIOLOGICAL STUDY OF A
       POLISH-AMERICAN COMMUNITY. New Haven: Yale University
       Press, 1955.

       A somewhat dated but still interesting study of Detroit's
       Polonia with some attention to religious factors.

D145. Zorbough, Harvey. GOLD COAST AND SLUM, A SOCIOLOGICAL
       STUDY OF CHICAGO'S NEAR NORTH SIDE. Chicago: University
       of Chicago Press, 1929.

A classic of the Chicago School of Sociology; much
imitated by researchers in other industrial belt cities
with similar social and economic stratifications in their
populations.

ETHNIC/RELIGIOUS FACTORS

E1. Agocs, Carol. "Who's In On the American Dream? Ethnic
    Representation in Suburban Opportunity Structures in
    Metropolitan Detroit, 1940-1970." ETHNIC GROUPS 4:4
    (1982): 239-254.

    See D3.

E2. Alexander, June Grautin. "Staying Together: Chain
    Migration and Patterns of Slovak Settlement in Pittsburgh
    Prior To World War I." JOURNAL OF AMERICAN ETHNIC
    HISTORY 1:1 (1981): 56-83.

    Presents a case study examining the movement of Slovak
    immigrants into the city and the subsequent emergence of
    Slovak settlement and cultural areas. The author
    illustrates different forms of chain migration--by village,
    village clusters, and regions--and concludes that previous
    critics of the chain migration thesis have defined its
    scope too narrowly.

E3. Allswang, John. A HOUSE FOR ALL PEOPLES: ETHNIC POLITICS
    IN CHICAGO, 1890-1936. Lexington: University Press of
    Kentucky, 1971.

    Argues that the impact of the ethnic vote became much
    greater in this period of Chicago's history. This is
    particularly true of the years after WW I when masses of
    immigrants become citizens and registered to vote for the
    first time. By the election of 1932 a clear pattern of
    ethnic support for the Democratic Party had developed.
    "The ethnics entered the Democracy because their support
    was sufficiently reciprocated to make it reasonable for
    them to do so."

E4. Allswang, John M. "The Chicago Negro Voter and the
    Democratic Consensus: A Case Study, 1918-1936." JOURNAL
    OF THE ILLINOIS HISTORICAL SOCIETY 60:2 (1967): 145-75.

    Examines black voting behavior that ultimately was
    reluctant to join in on the "Swing" to the Roosevelt
    Coalition until well into the 1930s.

E5. Anderson, James M. "The Development and Conceptualization
    of Ethnic Studies in Michigan." ETHNIC FORUM 1:2 (1981):
    23-28.

Describes the surge of interest in the topic of ethnicity in ethnically diverse Michigan since 1969, with special attention to the foundation of the Detroit Area Inter-Ethnic Studies Association, The Michigan Ethnic Heritage Studies Center, and the Ethnic Studies Bill of 1974.

E6. Arndt, Karl John Richard. "The Indiana Decade of George Rapp's Harmony Society: 1814-1824." PROCEEDINGS OF THE AMERICAN ANTIQUARIAN SOCIETY 80 (October 1970): 299-323.

Focuses on the Rappite migration from western Pennsylvania to southern Indiana and the establishment of an early nineteenth-century utopian community theme.

E7. Babson, Steve. "Pointing the Way: The Role of British and Irish Skilled Tradesmen in the Rise of the UAW." DETROIT PERSPECTIVE 7 (Spring 1983): 75-96.

Demonstrates the importance of two particular ethnic and occupational cadres in organizing and promoting union-ization among Midwestern auto workers.

E8. Bahr, Howard M. "Shifts in the Denominational Demography of Middletown, 1924-1977." JOURNAL FOR SCIENTIFIC STUDY OF RELIGION 21:2 (1982): 99-114.

See D14.

E9. Bakerman, Jane S. "When God Looks Down, It's the Bottom--Tony Morrison's Images of the Midwest." JOURNAL OF REGIONAL CULTURES 2:1 (Spring/Summer 1982): 24-32.

See H9.

E10. Barclay, Norgan J. "Changing Images of Toledo's Polish Community," NORTHWEST OHIO QUARTERLY 44:3 (1972): 64-71.

Explains that Toledo press coverage contributed to the development of diverse myths and images concerning the city's large Polish community.

E11. Bauman, John F. "Ethnic Adaption In A Southwestern Pennsylvania Coal Patch." JOURNAL OF ETHNIC STUDIES 7:3 (1979): 1-23.

Focuses on the mining community of Daisytown, Pennsylvania, and the mobility patterns of the eastern and southern Europeans who migrated there and attained social and economic stability in spite of strikes, evictions, and mine town living.

E12. Baylen, Joseph O. "A Victorian's 'Crusade' in Chicago, 1893-1894." JOURNAL OF AMERICAN HISTORY 51 (December 1964): 418-34.

A detailed analysis of the visit of William T. Stead, British evangelist and social reformer, to Chicago and the genesis of his book, IF CHRIST CAME TO CHICAGO (1894).

E13. Beijbom, Ulf. SWEDES IN CHICAGO: A DEMOGRAPHIC AND SOCIAL STUDY OF THE 1846-1880 IMMIGRATION. Stockholm: Laromedeisforlager, 1971.

A model empirical study done from both sides of the Atlantic; translated by Donald Brown.

E14. Berwanger, Eugene. THE FRONTIER AGAINST SLAVERY: WESTERN ANTI-NEGRO PREJUDICE AND THE SLAVERY EXTENSION CONTROVERSY. Urbana: University of Illinois Press, 1967.

A detailed examination of the anti-black feeling on the pre-Civil War frontier, especially in the Old Northwest. The author finds that Negro prejudice and anti-slavery were far from mutually exclusive.

E15. Bigham, Darrel E. "Family Structure of Germans and Blacks in Evansville and Vanderburg County, Indiana in 1880: A Comparative Study." THE OLD NORTHWEST 7:3 (1981): 255-275.

See D20.

E16. Bigham, Darrel E. "The Black Family in Evansville and Vanderburg County, Indiana: A 1900 Postscript." INDIANA MAGAZINE OF HISTORY 78:2 (1982): 154-69.

Argues that post-Civil War black families were not unorganized, and that the urban experience, not the heritage of slavery, was the determinant of the late nineteenth-century black life.

E17. Bjorklund, Ilaine U. "Ideology and Culture as Exemplified in Southwest Michigan." ANNALS OF THE ASSOCIATION OF AMERICAN GEOGRAPHERS 54 (1964): 227-41.

Provides a detailed examination of immigration patterns into an important Dutch-American region; a cultural geography that concentrates on Kalamazoo and its hinterland.

E18. Blee, Kathleen. "Family Tied and Class Conflict: The Politics of Immigrant Communities in the Great Lakes Region, 1890-1920." SOCIAL PROBLEMS 31 (February 1984): 311-21.

See D21.

E19. Bodnar, John, Michael Weber, and Roger Simon. "Migration, Kinship, and Urban Adjustment: Blacks and Poles in

Pittsburgh, 1900-1930." JOURNAL OF AMERICAN HISTORY 66:3 (1979): 548-565.

See D22.

E20. Bodnar, John, Roger Simon, and Michael P. Weber. LIVES OF THEIR OWN: BLACKS, ITALIANS, AND POLES IN PITTSBURGH, 1900-1060. Urbana: University of Illinois Press, 1982.

Uses an "interactional framework" to observe the interplay of traditional life-style (pre-migration culture), urban structure, industrial employment opportunity, and discrimination in determining the separate lives of black, Italian, and Polish working-class families.

E21. Bridges, Roger D., and Rodney O. Davis. ILLINOIS: ITS HISTORY AND LEGACY. St. Louis: River City Publishers, 1984.

See A10.

E22. Buder, Stanley. PULLMAN: AN EXPERIMENT IN INDUSTRIAL ORDER AND COMMUNITY PLANNING, 1880-1930. New York: Oxford University Press, 1967.

See D26.

E23. Bulmer, Martin. "Charles E. Johnson, Robert E. Park, and the Research Methods of the Chicago Commission of Race Relations, 1919-22: An Early Experiment in Applied Social Research." ETHNIC AND RACIAL STUDIES 4:3 (1981): 289-306.

Explains just how THE NEGRO IN CHICAGO (Chicago: University of Chicago Press, 1922) came to be carried out and discusses the originality of this early experiment in social research.

E24. Buni, Andrew. ROBERT L. VANN OF THE PITTSBURGH COURIER: POLITICS AND BLACK JOURNALISM. Pittsburgh: University of Pittsburgh Press, 1974.

See F13.

E25. Buroker, Robert L. "From Voluntary Association to Welfare State: The Illinois Immigrant's Protective League, 1908-1926. JOURNAL OF AMERICAN HISTORY 58 (December 1971): 643-60.

Describes the transition from private to public sector involvement in the handling of immigrant issues in the state.

E26. Cardenas, Gilbert. "Who Are The Midwestern Chicanos? Implications For Chicano Studies." AZTLAN 7:2 (1976): 141-152.

Attempts to provide a theoretical framework for the study of the Midwest Chicano experience beyond what is used in studies of Chicano life in the American Southwest. Chicano life in the American Southwest.

E27. Clayton, Horace R., and St. Clair Drake. BLACK METROPOLIS. New York: Harcourt Brace, 1945; Harper Torch Edition, 1962.

Especially strong on the social and economic factors that forged the "black belts" on Chicago's south and west sides.

E28. Clive, Alan. STATE OF WAR: MIGHIGAN IN WORLD WAR II. Ann Arbor: The University of Michigan Press, 1979.

See D37.

E29. Cotter, John V., and Larry L. Patrick. "Disease and Ethnicity in an Urban Environment." ANNALS OF THE ASSOCIATION OF AMERICAN GEOGRAPHERS 71:1 (1981): 40-49.

Impact of the cholera epidemic that struck Buffalo, New York, in 1844 was not uniformly felt, for ethnicity, socio-economic status and geographical and physical factors all influenced its diffusion.

E30. Cubun, Larry. "A Strategy for Racial Peace: Negro Leadership in Cleveland, 1900-1919." PHYLON (1967): 299-311.

The author maintains that the lack of black unrest was due to the peace that had characterized the city's race relations up to WWI. When tensions arose later, black leaders outside Cleveland were confused about local blacks who called their city a "Negro Eden"; those outside did not understand the long history of peace.

E31. Cutler, Irving. CHICAGO: METROPOLIS OF THE MID-CONTINENT. 2nd ed. Chicago: Geographic Society of Chicago, 1976.

See B11.

E32. DeVries, James E. RACE AND KINSHIP IN A MIDWESTERN TOWN: THE BLACK EXPERIENCE IN MONROE, MICHIGAN, 1900-1915. Urbana: University of Illinois Press, 1984.

The author shows how kinship was the only way that the small group of blacks (16 of 6,893 people in 1910) in Monroe could cope with the racism that permeated daily life. DeVries argues that "Monroe was not an atypical situation in the American black experience in the Midwest," despite the small amount of blacks.

E33. Dickerson, Dennis C. "The Black Church in Industrializing
      Western Pennsylvania, 1870-1950." THE WESTERN
      PENNSYLVANIA HISTORICAL MAGAZINE 64 (October 1981):
      329-344.

      Demonstrates how industrialists in the Pittsburgh area
      supported black churches that espoused the work ethic and
      preached thrift and sobriety to workers.

E34. Diner, Steven J. "Chicago Social Workers and Blacks in the
      Progressive Era." SOCIAL SERVICE REVIEW 44:4 (1970):
      393-410.

      See D49.

E35. Dunbar, Willis F., and William G. Shade. "The Black Man
      Gains the Vote: The Centennial of 'Impartial Suffrage' in
      Michigan." MICHIGAN HISTORY 56:1 (1972): 42-57.

      See F23.

E36. Edmunds, Arthur J. DAY BREAKERS: THE STORY OF THE URBAN
      LEAGUE OF PITTSBURGH, THE FIRST SIXTY-FIVE YEARS.
      Pittsburgh: Urban League of Pittsburgh, 1983.

      Particularly insightful on the League's early role in
      addressing the needs of the black immigrant to the city
      since 1918, when Pittsburgh's black population grew at an
      annual rate of nearly 45 percent for several years.

E37. Elazar, Daniel J. CITIES OF THE PRAIRIE: THE METROPOLITAN
      FRONTIER AND AMERICAN POLITICS. New York: Basic Books,
      Inc., 1970.

      See G19.

E38. Engelmann, Larry D. "Billy Sunday: 'God, You've Got A Job
      on Your Hands in Detroit.'" MICHIGAN HISTORY 55 (Spring
      1971): 1-22.

      Discusses the Midwestern evangelist's crusades in
      Detroit.

E39. Esslinger, Dean R. IMMIGRANTS AND THE CITY: ETHNICITY AND
      MOBILITY IN A NINETEENTH CENTURY MIDWESTERN COMMUNITY.
      Port Washington, NY: Kennikat Press, 1975.

      Examines the geographic, residential, and occupational
      mobility of the varied immigrant groups which appeared in
      South Bend, Indiana, over the mid-nineteenth century.

E40. Eversole, Theodore W. "The Cincinnati Union Bethel: The
      Coming of Age of the Settlement Idea in Cincinnati."

CINCINNATI HISTORICAL SOCIETY BULLETIN 32 (Spring-Summer 1974): 47-59.

See D55.

E41. Exoo, Calvin. "Ethnic Culture and Political Language in Two American Cities." JOURNAL OF ETHNIC STUDIES 11:2 (1983): 79-105.

Analysis of public political discourse in two cities with contrasting ethnic compositions--Gary, Indiana, and Rockford Illinois--suggesting that the "ways of thinking... and believing" reflected in the discourse of each city match some cultural features associated with the cities' dominant ethnic groups. While Gary appears "parochial, paternalistic, and fatalistic" in its political discourse, Rockford's ethnics are "universalistic, autonomous, and interested in politics as a moral enterprise." Based on items in the ROCKFORD MORNING STAR and GARY POST-TRIBUNE, and other sources.

E42. Fanning, Charles. FINLEY PETER DUNNE AND MR. DOOLEY: THE CHICAGO YEARS. Lexington: University Press of Kentucky, 1978.

See F28.

E43. Fanning, Charles. "The Short Sad Career of Mr. Dooley in Chicago." ETHNICITY 8:2 (1981): 169-188.

Analyzes Finley Peter Dunne's evaluation of Chicago's Irish neighborhoods, concentrating on local ethnic concerns.

E44. Findlay, James. DWIGHT MOODY: AMERICAN EVANGELIST, 1837-1899. Chicago: University of Chicago Press, 1969.

The most complete and well-balanced assessment of one of the Midwest's most successful urban evangelists. Moody's role as a social reformer is also emphasized.

E45. Fish, John Hall. BLACK POWER/WHITE CONTROL. Princeton: Princeton University Press, 1973.

See D58.

E46. Fish, Lydia Marie. "Roman Catholicism As Folk Religion in Buffalo." INDIANA FOLKLORE 9:2 (1976): 165-174.

Argues that folk religion practiced by ethnic groups within the Catholic Church in Buffalo, New York, stems from its origins in tradition-oriented rural Europe and basic ignorance of church tenets.

E47. Flanagan, Maureen A. "The Ethnic Entry into Chicago
      Politics: The United Societies for Local Self-Government
      and the Reform Charter of 1907." JOURNAL OF THE ILLINOIS
      STATE HISTORICAL SOCIETY 75:1 (1982): 2-14.

      Examines the history surrounding Chicago's problems with
      liquor regulation, which began in 1905 and caused an
      immense popular uproar. This led to the formation of the
      United Societies, and gave ethnics considerable political
      power.

E48. Flanagan, John T., ed. AMERICA IS WEST: AN ANTHOLOGY OF
      MIDDLE-WESTERN LIFE AND LITERATURE. Minneapolis:
      University of Minnesota Press, 1945.

      See H38.

E49. Fogarty, Robert. THE RIGHTEOUS REMNANT: THE HOUSE OF
      DAVID. Kent: Kent State University Press, 1981.

      The first scholarly, in-depth account of the rise and
      decline of an important Benton Harbor, Michigan, religious
      community founded in 1903, its prophet (the Shiloh), its
      theological and social underpinnings, and its tensions with
      the outside world. Although Fogarty did not have access to
      the sect's official records, his account provides a basic
      chronology of the group's activities on which further
      research can be done.

E50. Fuller, Sara, ed. THE OHIO BLACK HISTORY GUIDE.
      Columbus: Ohio Historical Society, 1975.

      Surveys the research holdings pertinent to black history
      in two hundred Ohio Institutions, as well as in the Library
      of Congress, The National Archives, Howard University and
      other sites. Sections of the GUIDE are devoted to books,
      pamphlets, articles, newspapers, doctoral dissertations,
      masters theses, manuscript collections, federal, state,
      county, and municipal records, and audio-visual materials.

E51. Funchion, Michael F. "Irish Nationalist and Chicago
      Politics in the 1880s." EIRE-IRELAND 10:2 (1975):
      3-18.

      See F35.

E52. Gedics, Al. "Ethnicity, Class Solidarity and Labor
      Radicalism Among Finnish Immigrants in Michigan Copper
      Country." POLITICS AND SOCIETY 7:2 (1977): 127-156.

      Case study of class consciousness that also examines the
      antecedents of labor radicalism among the Finnish miners
      during 1890-1920.

E53.   Gerber, David A. "Cutting Out Shylock: Elite
       Anti-Semitism and the Quest For Moral Order In the
       Mid-Nineteenth-Century Americal Marketplace." JOURNAL OF
       AMERICAN HISTORY 69:3 (1982): 615-637.

       Using ethnic stereotypes as a basis for assumptions about
       Jewish moral character and business practices, the
       Protestant commercial elite in Buffalo, New York--
       particularly its credit investors--produced a secretive
       and deceptive image of Jewish businesses in the city. The
       effect was denial of credit to Jewish firms.

E54.   Gerber, David A. BLACK OHIO AND THE COLOR LINE, 1860-1915.
       Urbana: University of Illinois Press, 1976.

       See D60.

E55.   Gitlin, Todd, and Nanci Hollander. UPTOWN: POOR WHITES IN
       CHICAGO. New York: Harper, 1970.

       See D61.

E56.   Gosnell, Harold F. NEGRO POLITICIANS: THE RISE OF NEGRO
       POLITICS IN CHICAGO. Chicago: University of Chicago
       Press, 1935, 1967.

       See F39.

E57.   Gottfried, Alex. BOSS CERMAK OF CHICAGO: A STUDY OF
       POLITICAL LEADERSHIP. Seattle: University of Washington
       Press, 1962.

       See F40.

E58.   Griffin, William W. "The Political Realignment of Black
       Voters in Indianapolis, 1924." INDIANA MAGAZINE OF
       HISTORY 79:2 (1983): 133-166.

       See F41.

E59.   Groh, George W. THE BLACK MIGRATION: THE JOURNEY TO URBAN
       AMERICA. New York: Weybright and Tallen, 1972.

       See G27.

E60.   Hannon, Joan Underhill. "City Size and Ethnic
       Discrimination: Michigan Agricultural Implements and
       Iron Working Industries, 1890." JOURNAL OF ECONOMIC
       HISTORY 42:4 (1982): 825-845.

       See C67.

E61. Hannon, Joan Underhill. "Ethnic Discrimination in a 19th
      Century Mining District: Michigan Copper Mines, 1888."
      EXPLORATIONS IN ECONOMIC HISTORY 19:1 (1982): 28-50.

      A careful study of regional wage discrimination.

E62. Harding, Bruce C. "Sources For Ethnic Studies In Region 5
      Archives Branch and Regional Archives Branch--Chicago."
      ILLINOIS LIBRARIES 57 (March 1975): 184-92.

      Describes records for ethnic study in all areas of the
      industrial belt except western New York.

E63. ter Harmsel, Larry. "Dutch Language Remnants in Holland,
      Michigan." JOURNAL OF REGIONAL CULTURES 2:1 (Spring/
      Summer 1982): 71-77.

      See H53.

E64. Hartman, Grover L. "The Hoosier Sunday School: A Potent
      Religious Cultural Force." INDIANA MAGAZINE OF HISTORY
      78:3 (1982): 215-241.

      See D69.

E65. Hatcher, Harlan. THE WESTERN RESERVE: THE STORY OF NEW
      CONNECTICUT IN OHIO. Indianapolis: Bobbs-Merrill, 1949.

      See D70.

E66. Hesslink, George K. BLACK NEIGHBORS: NEGROES IN A NORTHERN
      RURAL COMMUNITY. Indianapolis: Bobbs-Merrill, 1974.

      See G29.

E67. Hirsch, Arnold R. MAKING THE SECOND GHETTO: RACE AND
      HOUSING IN CHICAGO, 1940-1960. Cambridge, England:
      Cambridge University Press, 1983.

      See G30.

E68. Holbrook, Stewart W. THE YANKEE EXODUS: AN ACCOUNT OF
      MIGRATION FROM NEW ENGLAND. Seattle: University of
      Washington Press, 1950.

      Traces migration patterns and cultural achievements of
      New Englanders on the Midwest and Western landscape in the
      nineteenth century. Mostly a descriptive narrative with
      little attempt to analyze why the immigrants chose the
      areas they did. For example, neglects to explain who went
      to rural environments and who preferred the city. Still
      the best single volume survey of this transcontinental
      story.

E69. Holli, Melvin G., and Peter d' A. Jones, eds. THE ETHNIC
     FRONTIER: ESSAYS IN THE HISTORY OF GROUP SURVIVAL IN
     CHICAGO AND THE MIDWEST. Grand Rapids: Eermanns, 1977.

     An important collection of essays dealing with Chicago's
     multi-ethnic background, housing, ethnic leaders, Jews,
     Poles, Blacks, and Mexicans.

E70. Homel, Michael W. DOWN FROM EQUALITY: BLACK CHICAGOANS
     AND THE CHICAGO PUBLIC SCHOOLS, 1920-41. Urbana:
     University of Illinois Press, 1984.

     The book emphasizes lack of black equality in the schools
     by focusing on different aspects (facilities, appropria-
     tions, home, community, and classrooms), and shows that
     "black experiences with the public schools heightened their
     sensitivity to racial injustice and stimulated civic action
     that promoted group solidarity and tried to improve black
     lives."

E71. Jackson, Kenneth T. THE KU KLUX KLAN IN THE CITY,
     1915-1930. New York: Oxford University Press, 1967.

     Finds the impact of the KKK to be much more widespread in
     northern urban areas that was previously thought. Excel-
     lent on the major role that the Klan played in Indiana,
     especially in cities such as Fort Wayne. Maintains that
     the Klan's greatest urban strength was during the 1920s.

E72. Jackson, W. Sherman. "Emancipation, Negrophobia and Civil
     War Politics in Ohio, 1863-1865." JOURNAL OF NEGRO
     HISTORY 65:3 (1980): 250-60.

     See F50.

E73. Kantowicz, Edward R. POLISH-AMERICAN POLITICS IN CHICAGO,
     1880-1940. Chicago: University of Chicago Press, 1975.

     Stresses a view of white ethnic urban politics "from
     inside the group itself" in order to write a more interior
     view of ethnic history.

     Argues three main points: 1) that the affinity between
     Chicago's Democratic Party and the city's Polish Americans
     dates at least from the 1880s--not just the 1930s as pre-
     viously believed; 2) 1920 stands as the symbolic watershed
     of acculturation for Chicago's Poles; 3) failure of Polish-
     Americans to elect a mayor in Chicago or to convert their
     numerical strength into a commensurate share of political
     power paradoxically reflects ethnic solidarity, rather than
     factionalism.

E74. Katzman, David. BEFORE THE GHETTO: BLACK DETROIT IN THE
     NINETEENTH CENTURY. Urbana: University of Illinois
     Press, 1973.

Model study of a northern city's Black population before the major migrations of the early 20th century.

E75. Keil, Harmut, and John B. Jentz, eds. GERMAN WORKERS IN INDUSTRIAL CHICAGO, 1850-1910: A COMPARATIVE PERSPECTIVE. DeKalb: Northern Illinois University press, 1983.

See G39.

E76. Keller, Edmond J. "Electoral Politics in Gary: Mayoral Performance, Organization, and the Political Economy of the Black Vote." URBAN AFFAIRS QUARTERLY 15:1 (1979): 43-64.

See F56.

E77. Kern, Richard. FINDLAY COLLEGE: THE FIRST HUNDRED YEARS. Findlay: Findlay College, 1984.

Written for the College's centennial, the volume tells how tensions developed in the alliance that founded the institution and hampered its prosperity: the Church of God (a branch of the German Reformed Church) wanted a denominational college and the townspeople wanted a non-Church affiliated institution.

E78. Kleppner, Paul. CHICAGO DIVIDED: THE MAKING OF A BLACK MAYOR. Dekalb: Northern Illinois University Press, 1985.

See F57.

E79. Kornblum, William. BLUE COLLAR COMMUNITY. Chicago: University of Chicago Press, 1974.

See D92.

E80. Kramer, Frank R. VOICES IN THE VALLEY: MYTH MAKING AND FOLK BELIEF IN THE SHAPING OF THE MIDDLE WEST. Madison: University of Wisconsin Press, 1964.

A neglected but innovative examination by a professor of classics and ancient history at Heidelberg College of the influence of folklore on human thought and motivation in what the author calls "The Great Interior" formed by the Ohio River Valley.

The study explores the power of myth-making and folk belief by examining episodes from the history of ethnic groups: French explorers and missionaries in their contacts with Huron Indians, religion (Peter Cartwright's revival camp meetings), industry (Henry Ford's Highland Park plant), agrarian revolt (the Grange), and the New England Yankees and Pennsylvania Germans who migrated to the upper and lower Midwest.

E81. Krause, Corinne A. "Urbanization Without Breakdown:
Italian, Jewish and Slavik Immigrant Women in Pittsburgh,
1900-1945." JOURNAL OF URBAN HISTORY 4:3 (1978):
291-306.

See G45.

E82. Kusmer, Kenneth L. A GHETTO TAKES SHAPE: BLACK CLEVELAND,
1970-1930. Urbana: University of Illinois Press, 1976.

An excellent comparative analysis that relates developments in Cleveland to events in most other American cities
whose black sections have received scholarly attention.
While Kusmer concentrates his story on 1870-1930, the book
also describes the forces shaping the black community since
the early 1800s.

Utilizing statistical data and sociological models, the
volume is basically an engaging chronological account, one
worthy of imitation by scholars interested in exploring the
topic in other regions.

E83. Levine, David Allan. INTERNATIONAL COMBUSTION: THE RACES
IN DETROIT, 1915-1925. Westport, CT: Greenwood Press,
1976.

Theorizes that the paucity of housing was directly
responsible for racial unrest in the city during this
decade. Neglects white racism, economic discrimination,
and segregation as major factors.

E84. Lewis, Pierce F. "Impact of Negro Migration on the
Electoral Geography of Flint, Michigan, 1932-62: A
Cartographic Analysis." ANNALS OF THE ASSOCIATION OF
AMERICAN GEOGRAPHERS 55 (March 1965): 1-25.

See F63.

E85. Lissak, Rivka. "Myth and Reality: The Pattern of
Relationship Between the Hull House Circle and the 'New
Immigrants' On Chicago's West Side." JOURNAL OF AMERICAN
ETHNIC HISTORY 2 (1983): 21-50.

A critical examination of the role of Hull House in
dealing with the "new immigrants" shows that Jane Addams
and her colleagues failed to understand Russian Jewish
ethnicity as well as the economic and social background of
most Italians. In time, however, the settlement workers
did learn to accept new immigrants, as their later
experience with Greeks demonstrated.

E86. McCree, Wade H., Jr. "The Negro Renaissance in Michigan
Politics." NEGRO HISTORY BULLETIN 26 (October 1962):
7-9, 13.

See F65.

E87. Margen, Martin. "Ethnic Succession In Detroit Politics, 1900-1950." POLITY 11:3 (1979): 343-361.

A study that distinguishes three eras in the ethnic make-up of the city's political elite directly related to shifts in the economic and industrial structure.

E88. Mason, Philip P., ed. DIRECTORY OF JEWISH ARCHIVAL INSTITUTIONS. Detroit: Wayne State University Press, 1975.

Excellent finding aid for research on the Jewish presence and influence in the region.

E89. Meier, August, and Elliot Rudwick. BLACK DETROIT AND THE RISE OF THE UAW. New York: Oxford University Press, 1979.

Describes a major watershed in American race relations in chronicling the rise of an alliance between black Detroiters and the United Auto Workers. Shows unparalleled familiarity with the intricate internal operations of black, labor, and federal organizations. A model study.

E90. Morrison, Theodore. CHAUTAUQUA: A CENTER FOR EDUCATION, RELIGION, AND THE ARTS IN AMERICA. Chicago: University of Chicago Press, 1974.

See H84.

E91. Murray, John J., ed. HERITAGE OF THE MIDDLE WEST. Norman: University of Oklahoma Press, 1958.

See A56.

E92. Myek, Eugene. "Ethnic and Race Segregation, Cleveland, 1910-1970." ETHNICITY 7:4 (1980): 390-403.

Demonstrates how the residential segregation of white ethnics declined from 1910 to 1960 but then reversed over the next decade. For blacks in Cleveland, the pattern was almost exactly the opposite.

E93. Nelli, Humbert S. ITALIANS IN CHICAGO: A STUDY IN ETHNIC MOBILITY, 1880-1930. New York: Oxford University Press, 1970.

Traces the early influx of Italians into the city, especially its West Side, and monitors their economic and social mobility. Uses quantitative data in order to track the movement of certain elements of the ethnic group within the city's neighborhoods. Good on the relations of the Italians and other Chicago ethnics.

E94. Obenhaus, Victor. THE CHURCH AND FAITH IN MID-AMERICA.
      Philadelphia: Westminster, 1963.

          A detailed report based upon 1200 interviews by
      University of Chicago School of Theology students and
      faculty in their attempt to assess the state of religious
      life in the region as of 1960. A sociological as well as
      religious study.

E95. Obidinski, Eugene. "Polish Americans in Buffalo: The
      Transformation of An Ethnic Subcommunity." POLISH
      REVIEW 14:1 (1969): 28-39.

          Explores how a maturing ethnic subcommunity adjusts to a
      dominant society. Traces the evolution of the subculture
      to the 1930s.

E96. Parot, Joseph. "Ethnic versus Black Metropolis: The
      Origins of Polish-Black Housing Tensions in Chicago."
      POLISH AMERICAN STUDIES 29 (Spring-Autumn 1972): 5-33.

          Concentrates on the historical origins of housing
      patterns and tensions in Chicago Polonia, at the time the
      largest white ethnic group in the city, and its
      relationship to the "Black Metropolis" defined by St. Clair
      Drake, Horace Clayton, and others.

E97. Parra, Richardo, Victor Rios, and Armando Gutierrez.
      "Chicano Organizations in the Midwest: Past, Present and
      Future." AZTLAN 7:2 (1976): 235-253.

          Identifies three successive stages of Chicano organi-
      zational development: a) fraternal, cultural, and mutual
      aid societies; b) assimilationist leagues; and most recent-
      ly c) academic organizations such as the Centro de Estudios
      Chicanos at the University of Notre Dame.

E98. Philliber, William W. APPALACHIAN MIGRANTS IN URBAN
      AMERICA: CULTURAL CONFLICT OR ETHNIC GROUP FORMATION?
      New York: Praeger, 1981.

          See G60.

E99. Philliber, William W., and Clyde B. McCoy. THE INVISIBLE
      MINORITY: URBAN APPALACHIANS. Lexington: University
      Press of Kentucky, 1981.

          See G61.

E100. Pitzer, Donald, and Timothy Smith. THE HISTORY OF
       EDUCATION IN THE MIDDLE WEST. Indianapolis: Indiana
       Historical Society, 1978.

          Surveys one broad topic ("Uncommon Schools: Christian
       Colleges and Social Idealism in Midwestern America,

1820-1950") and one specific one ("Education in Utopia: The
New Harmony Experience").

E101. Posadas, Barbara M. "Crossed Boundaries in Interracial
       Chicago Filipino American Families Since 1925."
       AMERASIA 8:2 (1981): 31-52.

       Notes how Chicago immigrants from the Philippines
       differed from their counterparts on the West Coast in that
       they were mostly male and well educated and married white
       females in multi-ethnic Chicago.

E102. Reisler, Mark. "The Mexican Immigrant in the Chicago Area
       During the 1920's." JOURNAL OF THE ILLINOIS STATE
       HISTORICAL SOCIETY 66:2 (1973): 144-58.

       By 1927, Illinois had become the fourth most popular
       destination among Mexican immigrants. The author explains
       the events surrounding this large influx, particularly in
       the border area around East Chicago, Indiana.

E103. Rockaway, Robert A. "Anti-Semitism in an American City:
       Detroit, 1850-1914." AMERICAN JEWISH HISTORICAL
       QUARTERLY 64:1 (1974): 42-54.

       The article pays particular attention to the anti-
       Semitism that occurred before the time of Ford and Father
       Coughlin. "Anti-Semitic sentiment first made its appear-
       ance in Detroit in the nineteenth century and continued to
       plague the city until the present day," the author says.

E104. Rockaway, Robert A. "The Detroit Jewish Ghetto Before
       World War I." MICHIGAN HISTORY 52 (Spring 1968): 28-36.

       Establishes the spatial parameters, economic activities,
       and cultural influences of a minority group often neglected
       in pre-twentieth century Detroit history.

E105. Russell, John A. THE GERMAN INFLUENCE IN THE MAKING OF
       MICHIGAN. Detroit: University of Detroit Press, 1929.

       Although an old work and prone to ethnic boosterism,
       still the best treatment of the subject on the state
       level.

E106. Santos, Richard. "Earnings Among Spanish-Origin Males in
       the Midwest." SOCIAL SCIENCE JOURNAL 19:2 (1982):
       51-59.

       Analyzes the incomes of Spanish-origin males in Illinois,
       Indiana, Michigan, Ohio and Wisconsin, concluding that they
       earn approximately one-fifth less than a comparable group
       of non-Hispanic males.

E107.   Schlereth, Thomas J. THE UNIVERSITY OF NOTRE DAME: A
        PORTRAIT OF ITS HISTORY AND CAMPUS. Notre Dame:
        University of Notre Dame Press, 1976.

        Re-creates the history of the university since its
        founding in 1842 via architectural history, photographic
        analysis, and the use of extensive cartographic data.
        Explores the role of Notre Dame in both regional and
        national terms.

E108.   Schroeder, W. Widick, and Victor Obenhaus. RELIGION IN
        AMERICAN CULTURE: UNITY AND DIVERSITY IN A MID-WESTERN
        COUNTY. New York: Free Press, 1964.

        Sociological study of religious behavior "in an area
        considered to be typical of the Midwestern Corn Belt
        farming region."

E109.   Shiloh, Ailou. BY MYSELF I'M A BOOK! AN ORAL HISTORY OF
        THE IMMIGRANT EXPERIENCE IN PITTSBURGH. Waltham, MA:
        American Jewish Historical Society, 1972.

        Uses data collected from over two hundred interviews with
        Jewish immigrants who came to Pittsburgh between 1890 and
        1924 in order to explore the complexity of immigrant
        adaption in America.

E110.   Simons, William, Samuel Patti, and George Hermann.
        "Bloomfield: An Italian Working-Class Neighborhood."
        ITALIAN AMERICANA 7:1 (1981): 102-116.

        A study in ethnic transformation of a Pittsburgh
        neighborhood initially German and that became, by the
        1940s, largely Italian. Focuses on community leaders,
        physical characteristics, religion and business in the
        area.

E111.   Sponholtz, Lloyd L. "Harry Smith, Negro Suffrage and the
        Ohio Constitutional Convention: Black Frustration in the
        Progressive Era." PHYLON 35:2 (1974): 165-80.

        See F98.

E112.   Suttles, Gerald D. THE SOCIAL ORDER OF THE SLUM: ETHNICITY
        AND TERRITORY IN THE INNER CITY. Chicago: University
        of Chicago Press, 1968.

        See D133.

E113.   Sweet, William Warren. RELIGION IN THE DEVELOPMENT OF
        AMERICAN CULTURE. New York: Scribners, 1952.

        Claims "the Middle West was the first region in
        the new nation to develop its own character, and the

American character produced there furnished the model for
the whole nation west of the Alleghenies."

E114. Taeber, Karl E., and Alma F. Taeber. "The Negro as an
       Immigrant Group: Recent Trends in Racial and Ethnic
       Segregation in Chicago." AMERICAN JOURNAL OF SOCIOLOGY
       69 (January 1964): 374-82.

       A useful update on demographic patterns on the city's
       south and west sides in the middle of the twentieth
       century.

E115. Taylor, Quintard. "The Chicago Political Machine and
       Black-Ethnic Conflict and Accommodation." POLISH
       AMERICAN STUDIES 29 (Spring-Autumn 1972): 40-66.

       See F106.

E116. Thurner, Arthur W. "Polish Americans in Chicago Politics,
       1890-1930." POLISH AMERICAN STUDIES 28 (Spring 1971):
       20-42.

       Chronicles the participation of an ethnic force in
       Chicago's Democratic Party in terms of such issues as voter
       turnout, relation to other ethnic groups, and political
       patronage.

E117. Townsend, Charles. "Peter Cartwright's Circuit Riding
       Days in Ohio." OHIO HISTORY 74 (Spring 1965): 90-98.

       Recreates the routes and routines of one of the Midwest's
       major Protestant evangelists in the early nineteenth
       century.

E118. Tuttle, William. RACE RIOT: CHICAGO IN THE RED SUMMER OF
       1919. New York: Atheneum, 1970.

       The scholarly monograph that places the origins of the
       riot several years before 1919 in the contested
       neighborhoods and racial violence of the city's south side.
       The best summary of this civil disorder.

E119. Vinyard, Jo Ellen. "Inland Urban Immigrants: The Detroit
       Irish, 1850." MICHIGAN HISTORY 57:2 (1973): 121-39.

       Looks at the 3,289 Irish immigrants who made their home
       in early Detroit (1850 population 21,019) with particular
       emphasis on socio-economic status.

E120. Ward, David. CITIES AND IMMIGRANTS: A GEOGRAPHY OF CHANGE
       IN NINETEENTH-CENTURY AMERICA. New York: Oxford
       University Press, 1971.

       A major contribution to a previously little cultivated
       field of American historical scholarship--that which is

usually called historical geography. In addition to
subjecting a wide variety of generalizations or models of
urban growth to careful scrutiny, Ward uses extensive
quantitative data (especially manuscript census returns) to
monitor the inflow of immigrants from the 1820s to the
1920s.

In so doing, he provides us with a model of immigration
to, around, and through cities such as Boston, New York,
Pittsburgh, and Chicago. The book's maps and diagrams are
excellent and demonstrate Ward's breakthrough research on
the historical factors for the establishment of and changing character of ethnic ghettoes in cities east of the
Mississippi.

E121. Washburn, David E., ed. THE PEOPLES OF PENNSYLVANIA: AN
       ANNOTATED BIBLIOGRAPHY OF RESOURCE MATERIALS.
       Pittsburgh: University Center For International Studies,
       University of Pittsburgh, 1981.

       Includes nearly three thousand entries dealing with
       forty-six separate ethnic groups in the commonwealth. Half
       the entries are, in effect, capsule reviews.

E122. Weber, Michael P. "Residential and Occupational Patterns
       of Ethnic Minorities in Nineteenth-Century Pittsburgh."
       PENNSYLVANIA HISTORY 44:4 (1977): 317-334.

       Focuses on four industrial wards during 1880-1920 compar-
       ing native born workers with Irish and German immigrants.

E123. Weisberger, Bernard. THEY GATHERED AT THE RIVER: THE STORY
       OF THE GREAT REVIVALISTS AND THEIR IMPACT UPON RELIGION
       IN AMERICA. Boston: Little, Brown, 1958.

       Emphasizes the interrelations of frontier and revivalist
       belief and practice. Zestfully written and entertaining
       with a sound grasp of the appeal of Protestant
       evangelism in the region.

E124. Wheeler, James O., and Stanley D. Brunn. "An Agricultural
       Ghetto: Negroes in Cass County, Michigan, 1845-1968.
       GEOGRAPHICAL REVIEW 59 (July 1969): 317-29.

       Traces the history from prior to the Civil War until the
       middle of the twentieth century of a community of blacks
       who fled slavery and settled in southwestern Michigan.

E125. Wheeler, James O., and Stanley D. Brunn.   "Negro Migration
       into Rural Southwestern Michigan. GEOGRAPHICAL REVIEW 58
       (April 1968): 214-30.

       An overview of the settlement patterns of slaves and
       freed blacks seeking farming opportunities in Michigan in
       the nineteenth century.

E126. Williams, Peter W. "Religion and the Old Northwest: A
       Bibliography Essay." THE OLD NORTHWEST 5 (Spring 1979):
       37-89.

       An excellent survey that also argues that the concept of
       regionalism still has considerable heuristic potential for
       the study of American religion.

E127. Wilson, Ben C. "Idlewood, Michigan, 1912-1930: Growth of
       One of America's Oldest Black Resorts." JOURNAL OF
       REGIONAL CULTURES 2:1 (Spring/Summer 1982): 56-70.

       See H121.

E128. Wilson, William E. THE ANGEL AND THE SERPENT: THE STORY OF
       NEW HARMONY. Bloomington: Indiana University Press,
       1964.

       A standard history and best overview of the New Harmony
       communitarian experiment.

E129. Wood, Arthur Evans. HAMTRAMCK: A SOCIOLOGICAL STUDY OF A
       POLISH-AMERICAN COMMUNITY. New Haven: Yale University
       Press, 1955.

       See D144.

E130. Wynear, Hubomyr R., et al. ETHNIC GROUPS IN OHIO WITH
       SPECIAL EMPHASIS ON CLEVELAND: AN ANNOTATED
       BIBLIOGRAPHICAL GUIDE. Cleveland: Cleveland State
       University, 1975.

       A substantial reference work, strong on the neighborhood
       level, prepared by the Cleveland Ethnic Heritage Studies
       Development Program.

E131. Zunz, Oliver. THE CHANGING FACE OF INEQUALITY:
       URBANIZATION, INDUSTRIALIZATION, AND IMMIGRANTS IN
       DETROIT, 1880-1920. Chicago: University of Chicago
       Press, 1983.

       See G91.

POLITICS

F1. Abzug, Robert H. "The Copperheads: Historical Approaches
to Civil War Dissent in the Midwest." INDIANA MAGAZINE
OF HISTORY 66:1 (1970): 40-55.

Abzug adopts the definition of Cooperheads as advocates
of peace at any price, and examines the role they played in
opposition to the Union cause.

F2. Allswang, John. A HOUSE FOR ALL PEOPLES: ETHNIC POLITICS
IN CHICAGO, 1890-1936. Lexington: University Press of
Kentucky, 1971.

See E3.

F3. Allswang, John M. "The Chicago Negro Voter and the
Democratic Consensus: A Case Study, 1918-1936." JOURNAL
OF THE ILLINOIS STATE HISTORICAL SOCIETY 60:2 (1967):
145-75.

See E4.

F4. Anderson, David D. "The Odyssey of Petroleum Nasby." OHIO
HISTORY 74:4 (1965): 232-46.

Discusses the life of Nasby, the self-styled speaker of
the midwestern Peace Democrats, who sought to bring the
Civil War to a quick end. Writing in the HANCOCK
JEFFERSONIAN of Findlay, Ohio, Nasby got his pacifist
messages across in an often humorous and homey manner.

F5. Angus, David I. "The Politics of Progressive School
Reform: Grand Rapids, 1900-1910." MICHIGAN ACADEMICIAN
14:3 (1982): 239-58.

Explores the link between school reform and municipal
reform, between reform efforts and charges of corruption,
and between governance reform and curriculum reform.

F6. Barnhart, John D. VALLEY OF DEMOCRACY: FRONTIER IN THE
OHIO VALLEY, 1775-1818. Bloomington: Indiana University
Press, 1953.

Surveys the impact of frontier conditions on politics and
economic development in Ohio's pre-statehood era.

F7. Barrows, Robert G. THEIR INFINITE VARIETY: ESSAYS ON
     INDIANA POLITICIANS. Indianapolis: Indiana Historical
     Bureau, 1980.

     Includes biographical essays describing eleven Hoosier
     politicians who were active from the territorial period to
     the 1950s, and one special study of state legislative lead-
     ers. Highlight of the volume is the long and analytical
     chapter on Louis L. Ludlow, Indianapolis U.S. Congressman
     remembered now only for his effort in the late 1930s to
     secure a constitutional amendment requiring a national
     referendum before Congress could declare war.

F8. Biles, Roger. BIG CITY BOSS IN DEPRESSION AND WAR: MAYOR
     EDWARD J. KELLY OF CHICAGO. DeKalb: Northern Illinois
     University Press, 1984.

     A thoroughly researched and well documented look at
     Kelly, concentrating on his reign as mayor after 1933 and
     in turn providing insight into Chicago's political history
     during the New Deal.

F9. Borough, Reuben W. "The Education of a Midwestern
     Socialist." MICHIGAN HISTORY 50:3 (1966): 235-54.

     The article, a portion of Borough's autobiography, ex-
     plains his early development as a socialist in Michigan,
     before he moved on to much greater fame in Chicago and Los
     Angeles. The excerpt begins at the time when the Borough
     family moved from the tiny village of Samaria to the much
     larger city of Marshall, in 1897.

F10. Bridges, Roger D., and Rodney O. Davis. ILLINOIS: ITS
     HISTORY AND LEGACY. St. Louis: River City Publishers,
     1984.

     See A10.

F11. Brisbin, Richard A., Jr. "Before Bureaucracy: State
     Courts and the Administration of Public Services in the
     Northwest, 1787-1830." THE OLD NORTHWEST 10:2 (Summer
     1984): 141-174.

     This article explores the adjustments in judicial author-
     ity that came after the Revolutionary War with Great
     Britain. The author closely examines the early governments
     of Ohio and Indiana, and finds that as the public increas-
     ingly asserted its power, the legislatures in turn paved
     the way for a bureaucratic structure.

F12. Buffa, Dudley W. UNION POWER AND AMERICAN DEMOCRACY: THE
     UAW AND THE DEMOCRATIC PARTY, 1935-1972. Ann Arbor:
     University of Michigan Press, 1984.

     Traces the interaction of the United Automobile,
     Aerospace, and Agricultural Implement Workers of America

and the Democratic Party with special emphasis on the
state of Michigan.

F13. Buni, Andrew. ROBERT L. VANN OF THE PITTSBURGH COURIER:
      POLITICS AND BLACK JOURNALISM. Pittsburgh: University of
      Pittsburgh Press, 1974.

      A balanced study of one of America's best known black
      journalists and editors and his career in Pittsburgh.

F14. Buroker, Robert L. "From Voluntary Association to Welfare
      State: The Illinois Immigrant's Protective League,
      1908-1926. JOURNAL OF AMERICAN HISTORY 58 (Dec. 1971):
      643-60.

      See E25.

F15. Cassell, Frank A., and Marguerite E. Cassell. "Pride,
      Profits, and Politics: Indiana and the Columbian
      Exposition of 1893." INDIANA MAGAZINE OF HISTORY 80:2
      (June 1984): 93-121.

      See H18.

F16. Carson, Mina J. "Agnes Hamilton of Fort Wayne: The
      Education of a Christian Settlement Worker." INDIANA
      MAGAZINE OF HISTORY 80 (March 1984): 1-34.

      See D33.

F17. Coode, Thomas H., and John F. Bauman. PEOPLE, POVERTY, AND
      POLITICS: PENNSYLVANIANS DURING THE GREAT DEPRESSION.
      Lewisburgh, PA: Bucknell University Press, 1981.

      Chapters one, six, and seven are devoted to the economic,
      social, and political consequences of the Depression and
      the New Deal among southwestern Pennsylvania coal miners.
      Unfortunately treatment of the impact of the Depression in
      northwestern parts of the state or Pittsburgh is not
      treated.

F18. Cowles, Karen. "The Industrialization of Duquesne and the
      Circulation of Elites, 1891-1933." THE WESTERN
      PENNSYLVANIA HISTORICAL MAGAZINE 62 (January 1979):
      1-17.

      See D41.

F19. Danneybaum, Jed. "Immigrants and Temperance: Ethnic
      Cultural Conflict in Cincinnati, 1845-1869." OHIO
      HISTORY 87:2 (1978): 125-139.

      Argues that issues such as anti-Catholicism, nativism,
      and temperance sparked the breakdown of electoral politics
      and the realignment of contemporary cultural mores during
      the 1950s in Cincinnati.

F20.   Davis, Allen F. SPEARHEADS FOR REFORM: THE SOCIAL
       SETTLEMENTS AND THE PROGRESSIVE MOVEMENT, 1890-1914. New
       York: Oxford University Press, 1967.

       See D44.

F21.   Davis, Donald F. "The City Remodelled: The Limits of
       Automotive Industry Leadership in Detroit, 1910-1919."
       SOCIAL HISTORY 13 (1980): 451-486.

       Demonstrates how the city's auto executives responded to
       social disorder by becoming interested in municipal
       reform.

F22.   Diner, Steven J. "Chicago Social Workers and Blacks in the
       Progressive Era." SOCIAL SERVICE REVIEW 44:4 (1970):
       393-410.

       See D49.

F23.   Dunbar, Willis F., and William G. Shade. "The Black Man
       Gains the Vote: The Centennial of 'Impartial Sufferage'
       in Michigan." MICHIGAN HISTORY 56 (1972): 42-57.

       First gives a general history of black enfranchisement,
       then specifically examines the reasons why black suffrage
       was voted down in Michigan in an April, 1868, election.

F24.   Elazar, Daniel J. CITIES OF THE PRAIRIE: THE METROPOLITAN
       FRONTIER AND AMERICAN POLITICS. Lanham, MD: University
       Press of America, 1984.

       Co-published with the Center for the Study of Federalism,
       this book concentrates on the impact of federalism on the
       political institutions of seventeen cities in ten medium-
       sized metropolitan areas in America's midwestern heartland
       during their period of most dramatic change between the end
       of World War II and the Kennedy Administration. The author
       draws upon the varied experience of specific and typical
       communities to illustrate the larger political, social and
       economic trends confronting urban society.

F25.   Elenbalas, Jack D. "The Boss of the Better Class: Henry
       Leland and the Detroit Citizens League, 1912-1924."
       MICHIGAN HISTORY 58:2 (1974): 131-50.

       Supports the Hays and Wieble thesis that the Progressive
       Era was fueled by the upper and upper middle classes, and
       examines the activity of Leland and his upper class out-
       look.

F26.   Engel, J. Ronald. "Social Democracy, the Roots of Ecology,
       and the Presentation of the Indiana Dunes." JOURNAL OF
       FOREST HISTORY 28 (January 1984): 4-13.

Describes the grass-roots organizing strategies and lobbying activities of various coustituencies to set aside the northern Indiana dunelands as an environmental preserve.

F27. Engelmann, Mary. INTEMPERANCE: THE LOST WAR AGAINST LIQUOR. New York: The Free Press, 1979.

Argues that Michigan was the pivotal state in the national crusade against intemperance because it came to be seen by both proponents and opponents of prohibition as a laboratory test once the state enacted its dry law from the spring of 1918 until the Volstead Act went into effect in 1920.

F28. Fanning, Charles. FINLEY PETER DUNNE AND MR. DOOLEY: THE CHICAGO YEARS. Lexington: University Press of Kentucky, 1978.

A straightforward analysis of four basic themes: 1) the daily existence of Chicago's working-class Irish community; 2) the impact on the community of assimilation into American life; 3) the strange phenomenom of late nineteenth-century Irish nationalism as it affected the Chicago Irish; and 4) the view from an Irish ward of American urban politics in the 1890s. Should be read along with Fanning's excellent anthology of Dunne's Chicago pieces: MR. DOOLEY AND THE CHICAGO IRISH (New York: Arno, 1976).

F29. Fenton, John H. MIDWEST POLITICS. New York: Holt, Rinehart and Winston, 1966.

A comparative political study of the Midwest's six states which examines how the systems of traditional two-party politics (Ohio, Indiana, and Illinois) and issue-oriented politics (Michigan, Wisconsin, and Minnesota) affect the performance of state government. Fenton, a political scientist, also sees the three archetypes of traditional two-party politics as the main "job-oriented" states.

F30. Fish, John Hall. BLACK POWER/WHITE CONTROL. Princeton: Princeton University Press, 1973.

See D58.

F31. Flanagan, Maureen A. "The Ethnic Entry into Chicago Politics: The United Societies for Local Self-Government and the Reform Charter of 1907." JOURNAL OF THE ILLINOIS STATE HISTORICAL SOCIETY 75:1 (1982): 2-14.

See E47.

F32. Flinn, Thomas A. "Continuity and Change in Ohio Politics." THE JOURNAL OF POLITICS 24:3 (1962): 521-44.

Discusses the evolution of the party system in Ohio, shows the force of tradition and habit in determining voting preferences, and demonstrates some techniques for measuring continuity and change in voting behavior.

F33. Foster, R. Scott, and Renee A. Perger. PUBLIC-PRIVATE PARTNERSHIP IN AMERICAN CITIES: SEVEN CASE STUDIES. Lexington, MA: D.C. Heath & Co., 1982.

Joel A. Tarr and Shelby Stewman, both of Carnegie-Mellon University, conducted the case study of Pittsburgh's involvement (particularly with the Mellons) in urban revival and expansion, coupling a Democratic mayoral dynasty and the city's Republican corporate elite. A fine piece of public history.

F34. Fox, Dixon Ryan, ed. SOURCES OF CULTURE IN THE MIDDLE WEST: BACKGROUNDS VERSUS FRONTIER. New York: Appleton-Century, 1934.

See A21.

F35. Funchion, Michael F. "Irish Nationalist and Chicago Politics in the 1880s." EIRE-IRELAND 10:2 (1975): 3-18.

Study of the Chicago branch of the Clan na Gael in local politics, 1884-1888.

F36. Ginger, Ray. ALTGELD'S AMERICA: THE LINCOLN IDEAL VERSUS CHANGING REALITIES. New York: Funk and Wagnalls, 1958.

See A24.

F37. Ginger, Ray. THE BENDING CROSS: A BIOGRAPHY OF EUGENE VICTOR DEBS. New Brunswick: Rutgers University Press, 1949.

A long, detailed biography of a national labor figure and president of the American Socialist Party with particular attention to Debs' role in political and labor activities in Indiana and Illinois.

F38. Gosnell, Harold F. MACHINE POLITICS: THE CHICAGO MODEL. Chicago: University of Chicago Press, 1947, 1968.

Best single introduction to the city's political culture, including the rise of bossism, ethnic politics, and protests for political reform.

F39. Gosnell, Harold F. NEGRO POLITICIANS: THE RISE OF NEGRO POLITICS IN CHICAGO. Chicago: University of Chicago Press, 1935, 1967.

Best work on blacks in the city politics prior to the
Cermak administration; for later developments see Horace R.
Clayton and St. Clair Drake, BLACK METROPOLIS (E27).

F40. Gottfried, Alex. BOSS CERMAK OF CHICAGO: A STUDY OF
      POLITICAL LEADERSHIP. Seattle: University of Washington
      Press, 1962.

      Stresses the central role of ethnic groups in Chicago
      politics, the importance of the prohibition issue to
      Cermak, and his high level of political and administrative
      skill. Also an early attempt at biographical
      psychohistory.

F41. Griffin, William W. "The Political Realignment of Black
      Voters in Indianapolis, 1924." INDIANA MAGAZINE OF
      HISTORY 79:2 (1983): 133-166.

      Election statistics and political activities from black
      wards in Indianapolis reveal that by 1924 a shift of
      allegiance from the Republican to the Democratic parties ,
      had begun. This predates by eight to twelve years the
      national shift of black voters. The major reason for the
      earlier shift in Indianapolis was the linking of Ku Klux
      Klan activities and leadership to some of Indiana's
      Republican leaders. Based on local histories, manuscripts,
      and NAACP Annual Reports.

F42. Hart, John Fraser. "The Middle West." REGIONS OF THE
      UNITED STATES. Edited by John Fraser Hart. New York:
      Harper and Row, 1972, pp. 258-282.

      See C72.

F43. Havighurst, Walter. OHIO, A BICENTENNIAL HISTORY. New
      York: W.W. Norton, 1976.

      See A35.

F44. Heinz, John P., and Edward O. Lauman. CHICAGO LAWYERS:
      THE SOCIAL STRUCTURE OF THE BAR. New York: Russell Sage
      Foundation and American Bar Foundation, 1982.

      See D72.

F45. Herrick, Mary. THE CHICAGO SCHOOLS: A SOCIAL AND A
      POLITICAL HISTORY. Beverly Hills: Sage Publications,
      1971.

      See D73.

F46. Holli, Melvin G. REFORM IN DETROIT: HAZEN S. PINGREE AND
      URBAN POLITICS. New York: Oxford University Press,
      1969.

An early book in the Oxford University Press Urban Life in America series that describes the reform coalition put together by Hazen S. Pingree. Contains some comparative analysis with other reform movements in industrial belt cities.

F47. Holt, Michael F. FORGING A MAJORITY. THE FORMATION OF THE REPUBLICAN PARTY IN PITTSBURGH, 1848-1860. New Haven: Yale University Press, 1969.

Using quantitative techniques to determine the appeal, leadership, and constituency of local political parties in the 1850s, Holt contends that local issues were more important than national conflicts in explaining the political behavior of Pittsburghers in the decade prior to the Civil War.

F48. Hook, Alice P. "The YWCA in Cincinnati: A Century of Service, 1868-1968." CINCINNATI HISTORICAL SOCIETY BULLETIN 26 (April 1968): 119-36.

See G33.

F48A. Hubbart, Henry C. THE OLDER MIDDLE WEST, 1840-1880. New York: Appleton-Century, 1936.

Argues that during the crisis of disunion in the 1840s and 1850s, the position of the Old Northwest was a pivotal factor in the struggle for power between slavery and anti-slavery advocates. Suggests that many western leaders of the time were fully conscious of the possibility--many saw it as a moral necessity--of defining a regional position in that struggle.

F49. Hyneman, Charles, C. Richard Hofstetter, and Patrick F. O'Connor. VOTING IN INDIANA: A CENTURY OF PERSISTENCE AND CHANGE. Bloomington: Indiana University Press, 1980.

Primarily an account of how Indiana voters behave on election day. Mainly concerned with state and national elections, it includes data on the period 1880-1920 but focuses principally on the last half century.

F50. Jackson, W. Sherman. "Emancipation, Negrophobia and Civil War Politics in Ohio, 1863-1865." JOURNAL OF NEGRO HISTORY 65:3 (1980): 250-60.

Describes how politicians used threats of negrophobia and urscegenation to enhance the political fortunes of the Copperheads.

F51. Jensen, Richard. ILLINOIS, A BICENTENNIAL HISTORY. New York: W.W. Norton, 1978.

See A42.

F52. Jones, Alan. "Thomas M. Cooley and the Michigan Supreme
      Court: 1865-1885." AMERICAN JOURNAL OF LEGAL HISTORY.

      Examines the historical context of the court under the
      famed guidance of Cooley.

F53. Jones, Gene Delon. "The Origin of the Alliance Between The
      New Deal and The Chicago Machine." JOURNAL OF THE
      ILLINOIS STATE HISTORICAL SOCIETY 67:3 (1974): 253-274.

      Explores the initial antagonism and then the longstanding
      rapport between Chicago's mayor, Edward J. Kelly, and
      Franklin Delano Roosevelt.

F54. Kantowicz, Edward R. POLISH-AMERICAN POLITICS IN CHICAGO,
      1880-1940. Chicago: University of Chicago Press, 1975.

      See E73.

F55. Keeran, Roger. THE COMMUNIST PARTY AND THE AUTO WORKERS
      UNIONS. Bloomington: Indiana University Press, 1980.

      Challenges Cold War historiography which has held the
      American Communist party culpable for numerous labor union
      problems and argues that UAWA Communists and their allies
      not only helped industrial unionism supplant crafts
      unionism in the auto plants, but that they also injected
      their party's social reform objectives into union affairs.

F56. Keller, Edmond J. "Electoral Politics in Gary: Mayoral
      Performance, Organization, and the Political Economy of
      the Black Vote." URBAN AFFAIRS QUARTERLY 15:1 (1979):
      43-64.

      Asserts that Hatcher's continued electoral success is
      based on his superior political organization, and his
      satisfactory policy performance in the eyes of the majority
      of the dominant black electorate.

F57. Kleppner, Paul. CHICAGO DIVIDED: THE MAKING OF A BLACK
      MAYOR. DeKalb: Northern Illinois University Press, 1985.

      The author pays close attention to the shifting ethnic
      and racial loyalties that have always existed, he says,
      just below the surface. Thus, the elections of 1979 and
      1983 were not as surprising as many thought; rather, they
      were the logical occurrences of long-term trends.

F58. Knoke, David. "Political Mobilization by Voluntary
      Associates." JOURNAL OF POLITICAL AND MILITARY
      SOCIOLOGY 10:2 (1982): 171-182.

      Hypotheses about the process by which social associations
      mobilize their members for collective political action are
      tested using 32 Indianapolis organizations.

F59. Kogan, Herman, and Lloyd Wendt. LORDS OF THE LEVEE: THE
      STORY OF BATHHOUSE JOHN AND HINKY DINK. Indianapolis:
      Bobbs-Merrill, 1943.

      Captures the exploits (political and otherwise) of
      Chicago's two most notorious turn-of-the century politicos
      and the machinations of the infamous city council of that
      era. Retitled BOSSES IN LUSTY CHICAGO and reissued by the
      Indiana University Press in 1967.

F60. Kohlmeier, Arthur L. THE OLD NORTHWEST AS KEYSTONE OF THE
      ARCH OF AMERICAN FEDERAL UNION. Bloomington: Indiana
      University Press, 1938.

      Formulated the idea that the five states of the Northwest
      Territory each developed a strong "commonwealth tradition,"
      an essentially mercantilistic view that the interests of
      each state as a single community demanded men's loyalties
      and men's energies. The tradition produced a commitment to
      vigorous governmental enterprise throughout the region.

F61. Kutolowski, Kathleen Smith. "The Janus Face of New York's
      Local Parties: Genesee County, 1821-1827." NEW YORK
      HISTORY 59:2 (1978): 145-172.

      A test of the concept of differential-participant
      politics at the local level.

F62. Leggett, John C. "Class Consciousness and Politics in
      Detroit: A Study in Change." MICHIGAN HISTORY 45
      (December 1964): 289-314.

      See D96.

F63. Lewis, Pierce F. "Impact of Negro Migration on the
      Electoral Geography of Flint, Michigan, 1932-62: A
      Cartographic Analysis." ANNALS OF THE ASSOCIATION OF
      AMERICAN GEOGRAPHERS 55 (March 1965): 1-25.

      A historical geographer's review of the economic, social,
      and political factors prompting black migration to Flint
      and the influence of this demographic shift on the city's
      politics.

F64. McCarthy, Michael P. "Prelude to Armageddon: Charles E.
      Merriam and the Chicago Mayoral Election of 1911."
      JOURNAL OF THE ILLINOIS STATE HISTORICAL SOCIETY 67
      (November 1974): 505-18.

      Reviews the issues and tactics of the University of
      Chicago political scientist who sought to reform the city's
      political machine.

F65. McCree, Wade H., Jr. "The Negro Renaissance in Michigan
      Politics." NEGRO HISTORY BULLETIN 26 (October 1962):
      7-9, 13.

Instead of describing the Negro Renaissance, the author
discusses Negro maturation in Michigan politics, giving
an overview of prominent black politicians.

F66. Maizlish, Stephen E. THE TRIUMPH OF SECTIONALISM: THE
     TRANSFORMATION OF OHIO POLITICS, 1844-1856. Kent: Kent
     State University Press, 1983.

     Denying that pre-Civil War politics were shaped signifi-
     cantly by ethnocultural issues, the author argues in this
     study of Ohio politics that sectionalism was indeed
     responsible for the breakup of the second party system.
     Economic issues, Maizlish claims, brought about the for-
     mation of political parties in Ohio, but as the Democrats'
     economic views (notably on banks) proved impractical in an
     economically maturing state in need of credit sources,
     their party factionalized along hard money/soft money
     lines, causing a once unifying issue to become divisive.
     As party cohesion declined, sectional issues that touched
     on important concerns for Ohioans, such as free labor and
     the fear of southern domination, became important.

F67. Marcus, Maeva. TRUMAN AND THE STEEL SEIZURE CASE: THE
     LIMITS OF PRESIDENTIAL POWER. New York: Columbia
     University Press, 1977.

     Analysis of a regional court case (Youngstown Sheet and
     Tube vs. Sawyer) that had national ramifications during the
     Korean War.

F69. Margen, Martin. "Ethnic Succession in Detroit Politics,
     1900-1950." POLITY 11:3 91979): 340-61.

     The author distinguishes three eras in the ethnic makeup
     of the city's political elite directly related to shifts in
     the economic and industrial structure. Good case study
     with interest in political ecology.

F70. Mayer, Harold M. "Politics and Land Use: The Indiana
     Shoreline of Lake Michigan." ANNALS OF THE ASSOCIATION
     OF AMERICAN GEOGRAPHERS 54 (December 1964): 508-23.

     Reviews the controversies between industrial developers
     and environmentalists over the appropriate public policy
     for the Indiana dune land.

F71. Merrill, Horace Samuel. BOURBON DEMOCRACY OF THE MIDDLE
     WEST, 1865-1896. Baton Rouge: Louisiana State
     University Press, 1953.

An engaging monograph that interprets the post-Civil War Democrats as a cadre of wealthy, self-esteemed politicians. In the three decades studies, Merrill sees mid-America as the principal arena for the continuous advance of industry into agricultural territory carrying with it the influx of Bourbon Democracy which, in turn, gave aid and protection to the region's growing number of industrial entrepreneurs.

F71A. Miller, Zane L. BOSS COX'S CINCINNATI URBAN POLITICS IN THE PROGRESSIVE ERA. New York: Oxford University Press, 1968.

An early study of the interaction of reform and machine or boss politics and the attempt of these two political traditions to deal with the emergence of the modern configuration of the American urban environment.

Centered around the career of Republican city boss, George B. Cox, the study goes beyond the conventional view of urban politics with its emphasis on ethnicity, political organization, status and class. Miller includes the issue of residentiality in his arguement, and his spatial analysis (The Circle, The Zone, The Hilltops) of Cincinnati is integrated with his political examination of what he calls "the Periphery and the Center" in various reform strategies.

F72. Morgan, Iwan. "Fort Wayne and the Great Depression: The New Deal Years, 1933-1940." INDIANA MAGAZINE OF HISTORY 80:4 (December 1984): 348-378.

See G53.

F73. Nord, David P. "The Paradox of Municipal Reform in the Nineteenth Century." WISCONSIN MAGAZINE OF HISTORY 66 (1982-83): 128-142.

The political philosophy of Joseph Medhill, owner and editor of the CHICAGO TRIBUNE, illustrated the dilemma of the upper-class mugwump municipal reformers who led the Citizens' Association of Chicago, the Chicago Civic Federation, and the Municipal Voters League. They opposed paternalistic government, denounced high taxes and resisted public enterprise, but they also wanted government to solve the city's problems and eliminate corruption. This could only be done if the electorate were better informed, a cause the newspapers adopted as a way of building support for municipal reform among lower-class voters. Focuses on the 1870s-90s.

F74. Nord, David P. "The Politics of Agenda Setting in Late 19th Century Cities." JOURNALISM QUARTERLY 58:4 (1981): 565-574.

A comparison of Chicago and St. Louis reformers on strategies for promoting public utility regulation.

F75. Nye, Russell B. MIDWESTERN PROGRESSIVE POLITICS: A HISTORICAL STUDY OF ITS ORIGINS AND DEVELOPMENT, 1870-1950. East Lansing: Michigan State College Press, 1951.

The standard work that has withstood well the revisionist critiques of the 1970s. Excellent book.

F76. O'Connor, Len. CLOUT--MAYOR DALEY AND HIS CITY. Chicago: H. Regnery Co., 1975.

In the absence of a well-researched, scholarly biography of Daley, this account serves as the best interpretive introduction to the city's most famous twentieth-century mayor. O'Connor also has written a detailed account of Daley's last years, REQUIEM: THE DECLINE AND DEMISE OF MAYOR DALEY AND HIS ERA (1977) but it lacks the insights of CLOUT.

F77. Peckham, Charles A. "The Ohio National Guard and Its Police Duties, 1894." OHIO HISTORY 83:1 (1974): 51-67.

Discusses the duties of the Guard during the depression-laden year of 1894, when as many as 3,647 men were called on active duty to preserve public order threatened by unemployed or striking workers, severe fires, and lynching mobs.

F78. Peterson, Jon A. "From Social Settlement to Social Agency: Settlement Work in Columbus, Ohio, 1898-1958." SOCIAL SERVICE REVIEW 39 (June 1965): 191-208.

See D117.

F79. Rakove, Milton L. DON'T MAKE NO WAVES--DON'T BACK NO LOSERS: AN INSIDER'S ANALYSIS OF THE DALEY MACHINE. Bloomington: Indiana University Press, 1975.

Contains an analysis of strategies and behavior patterns of the Richard Daley mayoral reign. Argues that in the next decades, blacks and Chicanos will take control of the machine, considering demographic shifts among white ethnics. In one sense prescient, given the election of Harold Washington as Chicago Mayor.

F80. Rakove, Milton L. WE DON'T WANT NOBODY NOBODY SENT. Bloomington: Indiana University Press, 1979.

An oral history of the Daley organization in Chicago that includes 41 interviews, ranging from one with a precinct captain in the 25th Ward to one with U.S. Senator Adlai Stevenson III. The selectively chosen respondents are

classified into ten categories such as "old guard," "foot
soldiers," "young turks," "women," and "losers."

F81. Ratcliffe, Donald J. "Politics in Jacksonian Ohio:
      Reflections on the Ethnocultural Interpretation." OHIO
      HISTORY 88:1 (1979): 5-36.

      Argues that the party division can be understood only in
      ethnocultural terms.

F82. Ratcliffe, Donald J. "The Experience of Revolution and the
      Beginnings of Party Politics in Ohio, 1776-1816." OHIO
      HISTORY 85:3 (1976): 186-230.

      Chronicles the long and difficult events that led to a
      viable territorial government.

F83. Resch, John Phillips. "Ohio Adult Penal System, 1850-1900:
      A Study in the Failure of Institutional Reform." OHIO
      HISTORY 81:4 (1972): 236-62.

      The article explains early attempts to make prison a
      "moral hospital," where inmates would be "treated" and
      released when "cured." The movement lost vitality,
      however, when reformers adopted a broader vision of social
      perfection, which left the state's penal system floundering
      in the "customary cross currents of public whims, political
      patronage, official self-interest, and institutional
      inertia."

F84. Rosentreter, Roger L. "The County Courthouse: Polestar of
      Michigan's Heritage." MICHIGAN HISTORY 66:4 (1982):
      16-25, 37-48.

      See I77.

F85. Sarasohn, Stephen B., and Vera H. Sarasohn. POLITICAL
      PARTY PATTERNS IN MICHIGAN. Detroit: Wayne State
      University Press, 1957.

      Builds upon and supercedes F.B. Streeter's POLITICAL
      PARTIES IN MICHIGAN, 1837-1860 (1918).

F86. Scheiber, Harry N. OHIO CANAL ERA: A CASE STUDY OF
      GOVERNMENT AND THE ECONOMY, 1820-1861. Athens: Ohio
      University Press, 1968.

      As the title suggests, an inter-disciplinary study of
      internal improvement legislation and economic development
      in a single state prior to the outbreak of the Civil war.

F87. Scheiber, Harry N. "State Policy and the Public Domain:
      The Ohio Canal Lands." JOURNAL OF ECONOMIC HISTORY 25
      (March 1965): 86-113.

      See B48.

F88. Scheiber, Henry N., ed. THE OLD NORTHWEST: STUDIES IN
      REGIONAL HISTORY, 1787-1910. Lincoln: University of
      Nebraska Press, 1969.

      See A69.

F89. Schellenberg, James A. "County Seat Wars: Historical
      Observations." AMERICAN STUDIES 22:2 (1981): 81-95.

      Using the Midwest as his primary data base, the author
      surveys the historical context of county seat wars to
      illustrate two types of conflict. Major factors in
      prompting this conflict were settlement patterns, the
      growth of private enterprise, and spirited local politics.

F90. Schlereth, Thomas J. "City Planning As Progressive
      Reformer: Burnham's Plan and Moody's Manual." JOURNAL
      OF THE AMERICAN PLANNING ASSOCIATION 47 (January 1981):
      70-82.

      Demonstrates how Walter Moody, Chicago public relations
      expert, sold the concept of Daniel Burnham's influential
      1909 Plan of Chicago to the city's populace using books,
      pamphlets, high school courses, pageants, and feature
      films. Moody believed, as a liberal Republican, that if
      you reformed the city, you would reform its citizens.

F91. Schneider, John C. "Detroit and the Problem of Disorder:
      The Riot of 1863." MICHIGAN HISTORY 58:1 (1974): 4-24.

      Argues that Detroit's Civil War riot was not unlike New
      York's four months later. Explains that the former city's
      response to the crisis represents the complexity of urban
      life and outmoded ways of thinking about Detroit as a
      community.

F92. Shade, William Gerald. BANKS OR NO BANKS: THE MONEY ISSUE
      IN WESTERN POLITICS, 1832-1865. Detroit: Wayne State
      University Press, 1972.

      See C141.

F93. Shortridge, Ray M. "Voter Turn Out in the Midwest,
      1840-1872." SOCIAL SCIENCE QUARTERLY 60:4 (1980):
      617-629.

      Utilizing county-level voter turnout data, the author
      divides the potential electorate into core (always voting),
      periphery (sometimes voting) and nonvoting groups, and
      compares the mid-19th-century electorate with that of the
      mid-twentieth century.

F94. Shortridge, Ray M. "Voting For Minor Parties in the
      Antebellum Midwest." INDIANA MAGAZINE OF HISTORY 74:2
      (1978): 117-134.

Examines the Midwest electoral support for three
parties--the Liberty Party, Free Soil Party, and the
American Party--and the role they played in the antebellum
election system, ca. 1840-1860.

F95. Simpson, Vernon, and David Scott. CHICAGO'S POLITICS AND
      SOCIETY, A SELECTED BIBLIOGRAPHY. DeKalb: Northern
      Illinois University Center For Governmental Studies,
      1972.

      Most comprehensive listing of publications to date; has
      had periodic supplements to keep current.

F96. Smith, Roland M. "The Politics of Flood Control,
      1908-1936." PENNSYLVANIA HISTORY 42:1 (1975): 5-24.

      A complex story of conflicting local, state, and national
      interests prior to the great flood of 1936 which provided
      the real impetus for eventual flood control.

F97. Spencer, Thomas T. "Auxiliary and Non-Party Politics:
      The 1936 Democratic Presidential Campaign in Ohio." OHIO
      HISTORY 90:2 (1981): 114-28.

      Sees Ohio as a key state in Roosevelt's 1936 win.

F98. Sponholtz, Lloyd L. "Harry Smith, Negro Suffrage and the
      Ohio Constitutional Convention: Black Frustration in the
      Progressive Era." PHYLON 35:2 (1974): 165-80.

      Sponholtz says that Smith and the convention of 1912
      illustrate black frustrations in the Progressive Era, when
      the civil and economic rights that resulted from the Civil
      War began to erode.

F99. Stave, Bruce M. "The New Deal, The Last Hurrah, and the
      Building of An Urban Political Machine: Pittsburgh
      Committeemen, A Case Study." PENNSYLVANIA HISTORY 33:4
      (1966): 460-483.

      Traces the largely unbroken tradition of Democratic
      control of the city to the coalition forged in the New Deal
      era.

F100. Steffens, Lincoln. THE SHAME OF THE CITIES. New York:
      McClure, 1904.

      A classic muckraker critique of corruption in several
      cities of the industrial belt at the turn of the twentieth
      century.

F101. Stevens, Arthur R. "State Boundaries and Political
      Cultures: An Exploration in the Tri-State Area of
      Michigan, Indiana and Ohio." PUBLIUS 4:1 (1974):
      11-25.

Addresses the question of whether or not separate "state political cultures" can be detected in the attitudes and behavior of persons living in the immediate vicinity of the intersection of three states.

F102. Stickle, Warren E. "Ruralite and Farmer in Indiana: Independent, Sporadic Voter and Country Bumpkin?" AGRICULTURAL HISTORY 48:4 (1974): 543-70.

Examines the stereotypes of rural political participation by comparing the differences and similarities in rural voting behavior in Western Indiana in the 1960s.

F103. Strassberg, Richard, and M. Constance Bulkley. RADICALS AND REACTIONARIES: A PRELIMINARY GUIDE TO PRIMARY SOURCES. Ithaca, NY: Labor-Management Documentation Center, 1974.

Political ramifications of industrial and labor relations.

F104. Suskind, Richard. "Chicago's Bloody Haymarket Riot-- First Anarchist Drama--Evoked Loud Demands, Law-and-Order." SMITHSONIAN 2 (Oct. 1971): 52-59.

See D132.

F105. Tarr, Joel A. A STUDY IN BOSS POLITICS: WILLIAM LORIMER OF CHICAGO. Urbana: University of Illinois Press, 1971.

Argues that as mayor, Lorimer, an immigrant, built a machine in the city to fill the vacuum created by the chaos of rapid industrialization, population growth and other disruptive urban influences in the late 19th century.

F106. Taylor, Quintard. "The Chicago Political Machine and Black-Ethnic Conflict and Accommodation." POLISH AMERICAN STUDIES 29 (Spring-Autumn 1972): 40-66.

Surveys the tensions between ethnic voters, particularly Poles, and blacks in the history of Democratic Party politics in the twentieth century.

F107. Thurner, Arthur W. "Polish Americans in Chicago Politics, 1890-1930." POLISH AMERICAN STUDIES 28 (Spring 1971): 20-42.

See E116.

F108. Tompkins, C. David. "John Peter Altgeld as a Candidate for Mayor of Chicago in 1899." JOURNAL OF ILLINOIS STATE HISTORY SOCIETY 56 (Winter 1963): 654-76.

Describes Altgeld's unsuccessful bid for the mayor's office as partly attributable to the former Illinios

governor's failure in his controversial role in the
Haymarket affair in 1886.

F109. Travis, Anthony R. "Mayor George Ellis: Grand Rapids
       Political Boss and Progressive Reformer." MICHIGAN
       HISTORY 58:2 (1974): 101-30.

       Examines the life of Ellis (mayor from 1906 to 1916) that
       exemplified the puzzling relationship between political
       bossism and urban reform in the early twentieth century.
       As a left-wing progressive, Ellis practiced machine
       politics for the ethnic working class's benefit.

F110. Turano, Peter J. MICHIGAN STATE AND LOCAL GOVERNMENT AND
       POLITICS: A BIBLIOGRAPHY. Ann Arbor: University of
       Michigan, 1955.

       Prepared by the Bureau of Government, Institute of Public
       Administration. Deserves to be updated.

F111. Tutorow, Norman E. "Whigs of the Old Northwest and Texas
       Annexation, 1836-April, 1844." INDIANA MAGAZINE HISTORY
       66 (March 1970): 56-69.

       The article focuses on Whig reactions in Ohio, Indiana,
       Illinois, and Michigan by journalists, and congressmen.
       The issue was a crucial one, both to those concerned about
       slavery and to those who feared a breakup of the Whig
       Party.

F112. Vineyard, Dale, and Roberta S. Sigel. "Newspapers and
       Urban Voters." JOURNALISM QUARTERLY 48:3 (1971):
       486-493.

       Concludes that newspapers, as opposed to radio and tele-
       vision, are preferred by voters for political information
       about local issues and elections.

F113. Walker, Daniel. RIGHTS IN CONFLICT: CHICAGO'S SEVEN BRUTAL
       DAYS. New York: Grosset, 1969.

       A useful and quite detailed report of the tumultuous
       Chicago Democratic political convention of 1968 and its
       urban violence.

F114. Warner, Hoyt L. PROGRESSIVISM IN OHIO, 1897-1917.
       Columbus: Ohio State University Press, 1964.

       An uncritical assessment of the importance of the
       Progressives that seems unaware of the ethnic, religious
       and other factors involved in the reformers' characters or
       their causes.

F115. Whitaker, F.M. "Ohio WCTU and the Prohibition Amendment
       Campaign of 1883." OHIO HISTORY 83:2 (1974): 85-102.

The author discusses the tumultuous campaign that ultimately resulted in frustration and bitterness, and marked the decline of the Ohio WCTU's influence and power.

RURAL/URBAN ISSUES

G1. Abbott, Carl. "'Necessary Adjuncts to its Growth': The
     Railroad Suburbs of Chicago, 1854-1875." JOURNAL OF THE
     ILLINOIS STATE HISTORICAL SOCIETY 73:2 (1980): 117-31.

     Examines the many early suburbs that developed precisely
     because of railroad lines.

G2. Arnold, Eleanor, ed. FEEDING OUR FAMILIES: MEMORIES OF
     HOOSIER HOMEMAKERS. Indianapolis: Indiana Extension
     Homemakers Association, 1983.

     See D8.

G3. Barrows, Robert G. "Hurryin' Hoosiers and the American
     'Pattern': Geographic Mobility in Indianapolis and Urban
     North America." SOCIAL SCIENCE HISTORY 5:2 (1981):
     197-222.

     See D16.

G4. Baskin, John. NEW BURLINGTON; THE LIFE AND DEATH OF AN
     AMERICAN VILLAGE. New York: New American Library, 1977.

     A provocative contemporary oral history of the remaining
     residents of an Ohio farming village that once stood
     between Dayton and Cincinnati and was destroyed in the
     early 1970s when the U.S. Army Corps of Engineers built a
     dam that eventually covered the town site.

     The collected stories of the last few residents--farmers,
     teachers, blacksmiths, doctors, carpenters, widows--provide
     excellent insight into American small town life in the
     twentieth century as well as a cameo study in rural
     sociology.

G5. Becker, Carl W. THE VILLAGE: A HISTORY OF GERMANTOWN,
     OHIO, 1804-1976. Germantown, OH: Historical Society of
     Germantown, 1981.

     A model "local history" study of an obscure small village
     in southwestern Ohio; essentially a narrative history rich
     in description of local personalities.

G6.   Brown, Marilyn A.   "Modelling The Spatial Distribution of
      Suburban Crime."   ECONOMIC GROGRAPHY 58:3 (1982):
      247-261.

      Working with data from Chicago's 126 suburban communities
      gathered from 1969 to 1973, shows where and how suburban
      crime has increased steadily.

G7.   Butera, Ronald J.   "A Settlement House and The Urban
      Challenge: Kingsley House in Pittsburgh, Pennsylvania,
      1893-1920." THE WESTERN PENNSYLVANIA HISTORICAL MAGAZINE
      66 (January 1983): 24-47.

      Analyzes this eastern variant of the settlement movement
      as basically "a middle-class panacea for a working-class
      condition" and describes the tension that such a policy
      produced.

G8.   Chapman, Edmund H.   CLEVELAND: VILLAGE TO METROPOLIS: A
      CASE STUDY OF PROBLEMS OF URBAN DEVELOPMENT IN NINETEENTH
      CENTURY AMERICA.   Cleveland: Western Reserve Historical
      Society, 1965.

      Subtitle says it all; a model analysis of the rural-urban
      topic.

G9.   Clive, Alan.   STATE OF WAR: MICHIGAN IN WORLD WAR II.   Ann
      Arbor: The University of Michigan Press, 1979.

      See D37.

G10. Davis, Allen F.   SPEARHEADS FOR REFORM: THE SOCIAL
      SETTLEMENTS AND THE PROGRESSIVE MOVEMENT, 1890-1914.   New
      York: Oxford University Press, 1967.

      Especially strong on the spread of the Hull House concept
      to cities such as Boston, New York, and throughout Chicago.
      Sympathetic to the nuances of social reformers and their
      various reform strategies and how this led many of them to
      support the Progressive "Bull Moose" party.   Shows how many
      settlement house workers came from rural or small town
      backgrounds.

G11. Davis, C.M.   "The Cities and Towns of the High Plains of
      Michigan."   GEOGRAPHICAL REVIEW 28 (1938): 664-73.

      See C45.

G12. Doenecke, Justus D.   "Myths, Machines, and Markets: The
      Columbian Exposition of 1893."   JOURNAL OF POPULAR
      CULTURE 6:3 (1982): 535-549.

      Sees Chicago's 1893 World's Fair as a conscious attempt
      to humanize the expanding American industrialization by
      enveloping it in pastoral and rural themes.

G13. Dorn, Jacob H. "The Rural Ideal and Agrarian Realities:
      Arthur E. Holt and the Vision of a Decentralized America
      in the Interwar Years. CHURCH HISTORY 52:1 (1983):
      50-65.

      Arthur E. Holt, professor of social ethics at the Chicago
      Theological Seminary, emerged as an authoritative
      interpreter of rural life for liberal Protestantism during
      the 1920s-30s. Holt believed that a just society was
      essentially decentralized and could best be achieved by a
      rural lifestyle.

G14. Dorson, Richard M. LAND OF THE MILLRATS. Cambridge:
      Harvard University Press, 1981.

      A pioneering venture expanding the traditional patterns
      of folklore research beyond the antiquities of rural or
      marginal cultures and into the everyday life of contempor-
      ary industrial work in the Calumet Region of northern
      Indiana's steel industry. Excellent.

G15. Duis, Perry. "Whose City? Public and Private Places in
      Nineteenth-Century Chicago." CHICAGO HISTORY 12 (1983):
      Part I (2-27); Part II (2-23).

      Describes the effects of industrialization on cities,
      using 19th-century Chicago as an example; both public and
      private life was changed as a result of urbanization.
      Part II examines the impact of rapid urban growth on
      social organization, transportation, architecture and
      crime.

G16. Dunbar, Willis. KALAMAZOO AND HOW IT GREW. Kalamazoo:
      Western Michigan University, 1959.

      Good local study by a faculty member at Western Michigan
      University. Kalamazoo is studied in the wider context of
      urban development in other Michigan cities.

G17. Duncan, Otis Dudley, et al. METROPOLIS AND REGION.
      Baltimore: The Johns Hopkins Press, 1960.

      See C52.

G18. Dunlop, M.H. "Curiosities Too Numerous to Mention: Early
      Regionalism and Cincinnati's Western Museum." AMERICAN
      QUARTERLY 36:4 (Fall 1984): 524-548.

      See H32.

G19. Elazar, Daniel J. CITIES OF THE PRAIRIE: THE METROPOLITAN
      FRONTIER AND AMERICAN POLITICS. New York: Basic Books,
      Inc., 1970.

      Focused primarily on eight medium-sized Illinois
      metropolitan communities (e.g., Joliet, Quad Cities,

Peoria), this study attempts to assess, within a regional
context, the impact of four decisive forces that the author
believes shaped American civilization: the frontier, immigration, sectionalism, and federalism. Based on extensive
fieldwork, including both personal interviewing and the
distribution of questionnaires.

G20. Eversole, Theodore W. "The Cincinnati Union Bethel: The
Coming of Age of the Settlement Idea in Cincinnati."
CINCINNATI HISTORICAL SOCIETY BULLETIN 32 (Spring-Summer
1974): 47-59.

See D55.

G21. Exoo, Calvin. "Ethnic Culture and Political Language in
Two American Cities." JOURNAL OF ETHNIC STUDIES 11:2
(1983): 79-105.

See E41.

G22. Flanagan, Maureen A. "The Ethnic Entry into Chicago
Politics: The United Societies for Local Self-Government
and the Reform Charter of 1907." JOURNAL OF THE ILLINOIS
STATE HISTORICAL SOCIETY 75:1 (1982): 2-14.

See E47.

G23. Fuller, Wayne E. THE OLD COUNTRY SCHOOL: THE STORY OF
RURAL EDUCATION IN THE MIDDLE WEST. Lincoln: University
of Nebraska Press, 1982.

A detailed analysis of one of America's major cultural
symbols; should be read in conjunction with Andrew
Gulliford's AMERICA'S COUNTRY SCHOOLS (Washington:
Preservation Press, 1984).

G24. Gates, Paul W. THE ILLINOIS CENTRAL AND ITS COLONIZATION
WORK. Cambridge: Harvard University Press, 1934.

See C60.

G25. Gehring, Wes D. "Kim Hubbard's Abe Martin: A Figure of
Transition in American Humor." INDIANA MAGAZINE OF
HISTORY 78:1 (1982): 26-37.

See H44.

G26. Graham, James Q., Jr. "Family and Fertility in Rural Ohio:
Wood County, Ohio, IN 1860." JOURNAL OF FAMILY HISTORY
8:3 (1983): 262-278.

Applies techniques pioneered in urban studies to a rural
county in Ohio. Examines basic demographics from sex to
ethnicity. Confirms patterns described by the urban
literature. Based on census manuscripts.

G27. Groh, George W. THE BLACK MIGRATION: THE JOURNEY TO URBAN
      AMERICA. New York: Weybright and Tallen, 1972.

      Strong on several industrial belt cities where whole
      black populations increased substantially during the early
      20th century.

G27A. Hart, John Fraser. THE LOOK OF THE LAND. Englewood
      Cliffs, NJ: Prentice-Hall, 1975.

      Despite its general title, this classic in American cul-
      tural and historical geography is thoroughly grounded in
      the Midwest region that Hart has researched while teaching
      at Indiana University and the University of Minnesota. The
      first third of the book examines basic geological concepts
      as well as land division formulae. The remainder of this
      excellent primer is devoted to farm size, tenure, manage-
      ment, buildings, houses, and regions.

G28. Heller, Charles F., Jr., and Stanley F. Moore. "Continuity
      in Rural Land Ownership: Western Kalamazoo County,
      Michigan, 1830-1861." MICHIGAN HISTORY 56:3 (1972):
      233-46.

      Focuses on the question of whether or not "continuous
      owners" and their holdings were significantly different
      from other original purchasers who shortly left the area,
      and finds that higher assessments characterize those
      continuously owned compared to those non-continuously
      owned.

G29. Hesslink, George K. BLACK NEIGHBORS: NEGROES IN A NORTHERN
      RURAL COMMUNITY. Indianapolis: Bobbs-Merrill, 1974.

      A case-study of black migration from the south during the
      antebellum era and their life in Cass County, Michigan, in
      the twentieth century.

G30. Hirsch, Arnold R. MAKING THE SECOND GHETTO: RACE AND
      HOUSING IN CHICAGO, 1940-1960. Cambridge: Cambridge
      University Press, 1983.

      The author shows how whites worked to create large con-
      centrations of poor blacks living within carefully deter-
      mined geographic boundaries during the post-World War II
      years. Those who were responsible for this black removal
      to the south and west of the city, Hirsch says, were
      corrupt political machine bosses, powerful business elites,
      and white bastions like the University of Chicago.

G31. Hoffman, John. "The 'Upward Movement' in Illinois: Henry
      B. Fuller's Record of Cultural Progress, 1867-1917."
      JOURNAL OF THE ILLINOIS STATE HISTORICAL SOCIETY 16
      (Winter 1983): 257-72.

      See H60.

G32. Homel, Michael W. DOWN FROM EQUALITY: BLACK CHICAGOANS
      AND THE CHICAGO PUBLIC SCHOOLS, 1920-1941. Urbana:
      University of Illinois Press, 1984.

      See E70.

G33. Hook, Alice P. "The YWCA in Cincinnati: A Century of
      Service, 1868-1968." CINCINNATI HISTORICAL SOCIETY
      BULLETIN 26 (April 1968): 119-36.

      A centennial history of an important urban institution
      and its role in the history of women.

G34. Jebsen, Harry. "Preserving Suburban Identity In An
      Expanding Metropolis: The Case of Blue Island, Illinois."
      THE OLD NORTHWEST 7:2 (1981): 127-145.

      During the era 1872-1929, Blue Island serves as an
      example of how a suburb, although pressured by the central
      city, retained its self-determination through a combination
      of unilateral action and cooperation with the metropolis.

G35. Jensen, Richard. ILLINOIS, A BICENTENNIAL HISTORY. New
      York: W.W. Norton, 1978.

      See A42.

G36. Jones, Robert Leslie. HISTORY OF AGRICULTURE IN OHIO TO
      1880. Kent: Kent State University Press, 1983.

      This thoroughly detailed volume focuses on the state's
      main lines of commercial development through 1880, when
      changes then began to raise new issues and presented
      problems different from those of the pioneering stage.

G37. Jordy, William H. "The Commercial Style and the 'Chicago
      School.'" PERSPECTIVES IN AMERICAN HISTORY 1 (1967):
      390-400.

      See I48.

G38. Katz, Michael B., and Mark J. Stern. "Migration and the
      Social Order in Erie County, New York, 1855." JOURNAL OF
      INTER-DISCIPLINARY HISTORY 8:4 (1978): 659-701.

      SEE D86.

G39. Keil, Harmut, and John B. Jentz, eds. GERMAN WORKERS IN
      INDUSTRIAL CHICAGO, 1850-1910: A COMPARATIVE PERSPECTIVE.
      DeKalb: Northern Illinois University Press, 1983.

      This collection of fourteen essays argues that German-
      American workers were similar in many ways to other
      European-Americans working in the city during this period;
      the study also holds that life for Chicago's immigrant

workers was prototypical for industrial America as a
whole.

G40. Kern, Richard. FINDLAY COLLEGE: THE FIRST HUNDRED YEARS.
      Findlay: Findlay College, 1984.

      See E77.

G41. Kirschner, Don S. CITY AND COUNTRY: RURAL RESPONSES TO
      URBANIZATION IN THE 1920S. Westport: Greenwood, 1970.

      Examines attitudes about urbanization held by rural
      Midwesterners in the decade following the first federal
      census that declared the U.S. had over fifty percent
      urban population.

G42. Kleinberg, Susan J. "Technology and Women's Work: The
      Lives of Working Class Women in Pittsburgh, 1870-1900."
      DYNAMOS AND VIRGINS REVISITED. Edited by Martha
      Trescott. Metuchen, NJ: Scarecrow Press, 1979, pp.
      185-204.   .

      Changes in domestic technology (for example, washing
      machines) and municipal services (for example, sewers,
      public water supplies) did not improve the life of
      lower class women as quickly as it did for their wealthier
      counterparts.

G43. Knight, Marian. "Historic Mount Adams." CINCINNATI
      HISTORICAL SOCIETY BULLETIN 28 (Spring 1970): 27-38.

      Local history of an important nineteenth-century hilltop
      suburb of Cincinnati.

G44. Korson, George G., ed. COAL DUST ON THE FIDDLE: SONGS AND
      STORIES OF THE BITUMINOUS INDUSTRY. Philadelphia:
      University of Pennsylvania Press, 1943.

      Good material on the folklore of the coal culture in
      Pennsylvania, Ohio, Indiana and Illinois.

G45. Krause, Corinne A. "Urbanization Without Breakdown:
      Italian, Jewish and Slavic Immigrant Women in Pittsburgh,
      1900-1945." JOURNAL OF URBAN HISTORY 4:3 (1978):
      291-306.

      Concludes that most immigrant women adjusted to the
      cultural shock of immigration without serious or lasting
      problems due to neighborhood ethnicity and other bridges to
      the old world.

G46. Lee, James H. "The Ohio Agricultural Commission, 1913-
      1915." OHIO HISTORY 79 (Summer-Autumn 1970): 219-30.

      Describes Governor James M. Cox's efforts to organize Ohio
      agriculture with the creation of the Ohio Agriculture

Commission on April 15, 1913. While intentions were good, the Commission proved to be deeply controversial among rural folk.

G47. Leet, Don R. "Interrelations of Population Density, Urbanization, Literacy, and Fertility." EXPLORATIONS IN ECONOMIC HISTORY 14:4 (1977): 388-401.

A county-by-county analysis of fertility rates in Ohio in 1850 revealing a close association among population density, land availability, and land values.

G48. Lovin, Hugh T. "The Ohio 'Farmer-Labor' Movement In The 1930s." OHIO HISTORY 87:4 (1978): 419-437.

Reviews Thomas Amlie and Herbert Hard's attempt to build a viable farmer-labor coalition as a third party to the left of the New Deal.

G49. McMillen, Wheeler. OHIO FARM. Columbus: Ohio State University Press, 1974.

A personal narrative of the activities of field, barn, house and neighborhood of a small family farm in western Ohio during 1900-1915. Author considers this reminiscence in accord "with the experience of those who farmed there and elsewhere in the Midwest."

G50. Margulis, Harry L. "Housing Mobility in Cleveland and Its Suburbs 1975-1980." GEOGRAPHICAL REVIEW 72:1 (1982): 36-49.

Examines how rental assistance programs in the city and its suburbs did not promote racial and economic integration, or interjurisdictional mobility as had been hoped.

G51. Miller, Zane L., SUBURB: NEIGHBORHOOD AND COMMUNITY IN FOREST PARK, OHIO, 1936-1976. Knoxville: University of Tennessee Press, 1981.

A case study of the planning and growth of a greenbelt town of the Resettlement Administration of the 1930s; emphasizes changing community definitions of itself. A detailed urban suburb as well as an intellectual history of the changing values of suburban dwellers.

G52. Modell, John. "Family and Fertility on the Indiana Frontier, 1820." AMERICAN QUARTERLY 23 (December 1971): 615-34.

See D108.

G53. Morgan, Iwan. "Fort Wayne and the Great Depression: The New Deal Years, 1933-1940." INDIANA MAGAZINE OF HISTORY 80:4 (December 1984): 348-378.

The author raises Fort Wayne up as the archetypal example
of Franklin Delano Roosevelt's New Deal accomplishments
(unemployment relief, city improvements, and increased
trade union power) and limitations (continued urban decay
and fiscal problems), also addressing the role that local
interest groups played.

G54. Nawrocki, Dennis Alan. "Art Outside the Mainstream--
      Detroit Style." JOURNAL OF REGIONAL CULTURES 2:1
      (Spring/Summer 1985): 78-98.

      See H87.

G55. Paredes, America, and Ellen J. Stekent, eds. THE URBAN
      EXPERIENCE AND FOLK TRADITION. Austin: University of
      Texas Press, 1971.

      Contains papers from a symposium held at Wayne State in
      Detroit in 1968. Industrial belt cities are given good
      coverage.

G56. Parkerson, Donald H. "How Mobile Were Nineteenth-Century
      Americans?" HISTORICAL METHODS 15:3 (1982): 99-109.

      See D115.

G57. Peters, Bernard C. "Early Town-Site Speculation in
      Kalamazoo County." MICHIGAN HISTORY 56 (Fall 1972):
      201-15.

      Explores the activities and results of three men who
      founded the county's first three towns: Titus Bronson
      (Bronson, renamed Kalamazoo in 1836), Horace H. Comstock
      (Comstock), and Lucius Lyon (Schoolcraft). The author
      holds that his generalizations hold for most of the
      agricultural interior of southern Michigan.

G58. Peterson, Fred W. "Vernacular Building and Victorian
      Architecture: Midwestern American Farm Homes." JOURNAL
      OF INTERDISCIPLINARY HISTORY 12:3 (1981): 409-27.

      See I69.

G59. Pflug, Warner W., ed. A GUIDE TO THE ARCHIVES OF LABOR
      HISTORY AND URBAN AFFAIRS. Detroit: Wayne State
      University Press, 1974.

      Finding aid for a major research center.

G60. Philliber, William W. APPALACHIAN MIGRANTS IN URBAN
      AMERICA: CULTURAL CONFLICT OR ETHNIC GROUP FORMATION?
      New York: Praeger, 1981.

      Traces the origins, motivations, and differences of
      Appalachian migrants to Cincinnati and concludes that

in this major city of the industrial belt, the Appalachians
have tended toward ethnic grouping and identity.

G61. Philliber, William W., and Clyde B. McCoy. THE INVISIBLE
      MINORITY: URBAN APPALACHIANS. Lexington: University
      Press of Kentucky, 1981.

      A collection of papers originally presented at a 1974
      meeting in Columbus, Ohio, designed to assess what has
      happened to the 3.3 million people who have left Appalachia
      since 1950 for the cities of the South, East, and Midwest.
      In addition to migration patterns, deals with Appalachians
      as an urban ethnic group and their attainments in city
      life.

G62. Pickar, Madge, and R. Carlyle Buley. THE MIDWEST PIONEER:
      HIS ILLS, CURES AND DOCTORS. New York: Henry Schuman,
      1976.

      An early social history of the frontier era with particu-
      lar emphasis on the medical history of the common man in
      relation to his everyday life. A popular study wherein the
      authors sketch a lively portrait of an era--a portrait in
      which the central figures are the Pioneer Doctor, who
      boldly faced the wilderness, and the Pioneer, who bravely
      faced the doctor. Includes a 20-page bibliography strong
      on folklore scholarship.

G63. Pierce, Bessie Louise, ed. AS OTHERS SEE CHICAGO,
      IMPRESSIONS OF VISITORS, 1673-1933. Chicago: University
      of Chicago Press, 1933.

      An excellent anthology of the impressions of a wide range
      of visitors and travelers who have come to Chicago begin-
      ning with Jacques Marquette in 1674 and concluding with
      Morris Markey in 1932. Contains an excellent introduction
      by the premier historian of nineteenth-century Chicago and
      a detailed bibliography of travelers' accounts. Deserves
      to be updated for the last fifty years and republished.

G64. Power, Richard. PLANTING CORN BELT CULTURE: THE IMPRESS OF
      THE UPLAND SOUTHERNER AND YANKEE IN THE OLD NORTHWEST.
      Indianapolis: Indiana Historical Society, 1957.

      Builds upon and greatly expands, especially in economic
      analysis, Lois Kimball's THE EXPANSION OF NEW ENGLAND.
      Deliberately neglects influences in the region emanating
      from the Middle Atlantic states through depots such as
      Pittsburgh.

G65. Quandt, Jean B. FROM SMALL TOWN TO GREAT COMMUNITY: THE
      SOCIAL THOUGHT OF PROGRESSIVE INTELLECTUALS. New
      Brunswick: Rutgers University Press, 1970.

      See D120.

G66. Roberts, Warren E. "The Tools Used in Building Log Houses
      in Indiana." PIONEER AMERICA 9 (July 1977): 30-61.

      See I75.

G67. Rohrbough, Malcolm J. THE TRANS-APPALACHIAN FRONTIER
      PEOPLE, SOCIETIES, AND INSTITUTIONS 1775-1850. New York:
      Oxford University Press, 1978

      An economic-social history that now ranks as the standard
      work. Excellent chapters on "Michigan: The Great Lakes
      Frontier" and on Illinois as one of the states of "The Last
      Frontier of The Old Northwest." A superb set of maps drawn
      to delineate the shifting boundaries of various frontiers.

G68. Rosentreter, Roger L. "The County Courthouse: Polestar of
      Michigan's Heritage.' MICHIGAN HISTORY 66:4 (1982):
      16-25, 37-48.

      See I77.

G69. Ross, D. Reid, and C.W. Weister. "The Relationship Between
      Urban Growth and Transportation Development in the
      Cincinnati-Northern Kentucky Area." CINCINNATI
      HISTORICAL SOCIETY BULLETIN 21 (April 1963): 112-32.

      Compares the different transportation patterns and city
      morphologies of Covington, Kentucky, and Cincinnati, Ohio.

G70. Scheiber, Harry N. "Urban Rivalry and Internal
      Improvements in the Old Northwest, 1820-1860." OHIO
      HISTORY 71 (October 1962): 227-39.

      Discusses the improvements that fledgling villages
      keenly fought for. Boosters looked for opportunities
      that might land them a county seat, a federal land
      office, or a government installation like an arsenal
      or a prison.

G71. Scheiber, Henry N., ed. THE OLD NORTHWEST: STUDIES IN
      REGIONAL HISTORY, 1787-1910. Lincoln: University of
      Nebraska Press, 1969.

      See A69.

G72. Schlereth, Thomas J. "Mail-Order Catalogs As Resources in
      American Cultural Studies." PROSPECTS: AN ANNUAL JOURNAL
      OF AMERICAN CULTURAL STUDIES 7 (1981): 141-161.

      Suggests that catalogs, particularly those produced by
      the Midwest industrial giants like Sears, Roebuck and
      Montgomery Ward, are vital sources for the analysis of
      rural/urban interaction, popular literature, language,
      consumer patterns, advertising techniques, and behavior
      modeling.

G73. Schneider, John C. DETROIT AND THE PROBLEM OF ORDER,
      1830-1880: A GEOGRAPHY OF CRIME, RIOT, AND POLICING.
      Lincoln: University of Nebraska Press, 1980.

      Argues that Detroit's shift from a highly compact city of
      mixed land use in the 1830s and 1840s to a more spatially
      differentiated environment in the 1850s and 1860s both
      prompted a breakdown in law and order and helped shape the
      nature of the response to that disorder. Adds a new
      dimension to the study of police reform in the nineteenth-
      century city.

G74. Schneider, John C. "Urbanization and the Maintenance of
      Order: Detroit, 1824-1847." MICHIGAN HISTORY 60:3
      (1976): 260-81.

      Examines the difficulty Detroit had in maintaining order
      without jeopardizing democratic individualism.

G75. Scholo, David E. HIRED HANDS AND PLOWBOYS: FARM LABOR IN
      THE MIDWEST, 1816-1860. Urbana: University of Illinois
      Press, 1976.

      See C140.

G76. Sehr, Timothy J. "Three Gilded Age Suburbs of Indianapolis:
      Irvington, Brightwood and Woodruff Place." INDIANA
      MAGAZINE OF HISTORY 77:4 (1981): 305-332.

      See I83.

G77. Shepherd, Rebecca A. "Restless Americans: The Geographic
      Mobility of Farm Laborers in the Old Midwest, 1850-1870."
      OHIO HISTORY 89:1 (1980): 25-45.

      Looks closely at the lives of six groups of farm laborers
      in an effort to determine what factors influenced their
      decisions to move or to stay where they were.

G78. Smith, Carl S. CHICAGO AND THE LITERARY IMAGINATION,
      1880-1920. Chicago: The University of Chicago Press,
      1984.

      See H110.

G79. Steinnes, Donald N. "Suburbanization and the 'Malling of
      America': A Time-Series Approach." URBAN AFFAIRS
      QUARTERLY 17:4 (1982): 401-418.

      See I85.

G80. Still, Bayard. "Patterns of Mid-Nineteenth Century
      Urbanization in the Middle West." MISSISSIPPI VALLEY
      HISTORICAL REVIEW (September 1941): 187-206

An early attempt to explain how industrial belt cities grew and what spatial configurations they shared in common.

G81.   Wade, Louise. GRAHAM TAYLOR: PIONEER FOR SOCIAL JUSTICE. Chicago: University of Chicago Press, 1964.

A detailed study of Jane Addams' male counterpart in Chicago's social reform circles of the turn of the century; Taylor established his settlement house in the University of Chicago neighborhood and maintained close contact with its social science faculty on the issue of modern urbanism.

G82.   Wade, Richard C. THE URBAN FRONTIER: THE RISE OF WESTERN CITIES, 1790-1830. Cambridge: Cambridge University Press, 1959.

An innovative comparative study of several cities in the industrial belt and how they developed in response to economic pressures from their hinterlands. Also examined is their intense "urban rivalry," that is, competition among them for advantages that would promote their growth and enhance their attractiveness to immigrants and investors. A classic of the new urban history.

G83.   Weisenburger, Francis P. "The Urbanization of the Middle West: Town and Village in the Pioneer Period." INDIANA MAGAZINE OF HISTORY 61 (1945): 14-30.

A pioneering statement of how quickly urban communities developed in the Old Northwest in response to the commercial needs of the surrounding country. Should be compared with Richard Wade's THE URBAN FRONTIER (G82).

G84.   Wheeler, James O., and Stanley D. Brunn. "An Agricultural Ghetto: Negroes in Cass County, Michigan, 1845-1968. GEOGRAPHICAL REVIEW 59 (July 1969): 317-29.

See E124.

G85.   Wheeler, Thomas C., ed. A VANISHING AMERICA: THE LIFE AND TIMES OF THE SMALL TOWN. New York: Holt, Rinehart and Winston, 1964.

Twelve personal essays, each by an author dealing with a place he knows and cherishes. Wallace Stegner's introduction is a gem.

G86.   Whitaker, James W., ed. FARMING IN THE MIDWEST, 1840-1900. Washington: The Agricultural History Society, 1974.

See C164.

G87.   White, John H., Jr. "The Cincinnati Inclined Plane Railway Company: The Mount Auburn Incline and the Lookout

House." CINCINNATI HISTORICAL BULLETIN 27 (January
1969): 7-29.

A case study of the development and operation of an
important transportation feature that played a role in the
growth of one of Cincinnati's hill-top suburbs.

G88. Winters, Donald L. "Agricultural Tenancy in the Nineteenth-
Century Middle West: The Historiographical Debate."
INDIANA MAGAZINE OF HISTORY 78:2 (1982): 128-153.

An excellent review of the published literature on this
topic since the 1930s.

G89. Woodford, Frank B., and Arthur W. ALL OUR YESTERDAYS: A
BRIEF HISTORY OF DETROIT. Detroit: Wayne State
University Press, 1969.

A highly personal, interpretive survey with particular
emphasis on twentieth century developments.

G90. Yon, Paul D. A GUIDE TO OHIO COUNTRY AND MUNICIPAL
RECORDS FOR URBAN RESEARCH. Columbus: Ohio Historical
Society, 1972.

Strong on governmental materials at the local and
metropolitan levels.

G91. Zunz, Oliver. THE CHANGING FACE OF INEQUALITY:
URBANIZATION, INDUSTRIALIZATION, AND IMMIGRANTS IN
DETROIT, 1880-1920. Chicago: University of Chicago
Press, 1983.

A massive statistical study of the changing social
structure of Detroit that argues that spatially based
ethnic communities provided a moderating influence rather
than a disruptive one in a rapidly changing and industrializing city.

CULTURAL EXPRESSION

H1. Anderson, David. "Louis Bromfield's Myth of the Ohio
    Frontier." THE OLD NORTHWEST 6:1 (1980): 63-74.

    Discusses the novels, THE GREEN BAY TREE (1924) and THE
    FARM (1933), against Bromfield's first twenty years spent
    in Mansfield, Ohio.

H2. Anderson, David. "Sherwood Anderson's Ohio." THE OLD
    NORTHWEST 5:2 (1979): 181-189.

    Reviews the small-town Ohio influence on a major
    Midwestern writer.

H3. Angle, Paul. "The Armory Show in Chicago, 1913." CHICAGO
    HISTORY 6:12 (1963): 353-60.

    Examines the newspaper accounts of the Show when it came
    to the Art Institute; the scandalized reaction was not
    unlike New York's.

H4. Armstrong, Richard. "Report From Detroit: Was Cass
    Corridor A Style?" ART IN AMERICA (August 1983): 29-32.

    Discusses an exhibit of paintings and sculptures done by
    artists who lived on Detroit's Cass Avenue, a street
    eventually known as Cass Corridor, and who left the city
    after they felt they had not received recognition of their
    artistic talents.

H5. Arndt, Karl, and Richard D. Wetzel. "Harmonist Music:
    Pittsburgh Musicians in Early Economy." WESTERN
    PENNSYLVANIA HISTORY MAGAZINE 54:2 (1971): 125-157;
    3 (1971): 284-211; 4 (1971): 391-413.

    Emphasizes the import of Johann Christopher Muller's
    MEMORANDUM BOOK OF THE MUSIC BAND OF ECONOMY: 1828-1831.

H6. Atherton, Lewis. MAIN STREET ON THE MIDDLE BORDER.
    Bloomington: Indiana University Press, 1954.

    See D11.

H7. Atkeson, Mary M. A STUDY OF THE LOCAL LITERATURE OF THE
    UPPER OHIO VALLEY, WITH SPECIAL REFERENCE TO THE EARLY
    PIONEER AND INDIAN TALES, 1820-1840. Columbus: Ohio
    State University Press, 1921.

Pioneer research on an often overlooked era and genre; one of the most complete compendiums of basic information on the topic in this specific geographical section of the region.

H8.   Badger, Reid. THE GREAT AMERICAN FAIR: THE WORLD'S COLUMBIAN EXPOSITION AND AMERICAN CULTURE. Chicago: Nelson-Hall Publishers, 1979.

Contends that the Exposition of 1893, a major cultural event in the Midwest, concealed fundamental problems and questions about life in America in the 1890s. Contradictions, the author maintains, abounded at the fair despite efforts by Daniel Burnham and others to achieve artistic and architectural unity. Should be read in juxtaposition to Burg's CHICAGO'S WHITE CITY (H-14).

H9.   Bakerman, Jane S. "When God Looks Down, It's the Bottom-- Tony Morrison's Images of the Midwest." JOURNAL OF REGIONAL CULTURES 2:1 (Spring/Summer 1982): 24-32.

Bakerman explores Morrison's midwestern novels and concludes that while the author constructs archetypal figures and myths in her realism, she also destroys the myth that the North (including the Midwest) is a better place for blacks to live than the South. Morrison shows that the racism in the North and Midwest make the region no different from the South.

H10. Boelio, Bob. "A Literary Tour of Michigan." CHRONICLE 16:1 (1980): 18-22.

Brief accounts of the lives and works of authors who once lived in Michigan including Ring Lardner, Carl Sandburg, and Ernest Hemingway.

H11. Bray, Robert. "Robert Herrick, A Chicago Trio." THE OLD NORTHWEST 1:1 (1975): 63-84.

Emphasizes THE COMMON LOT (1904) and THE MEMOIRS OF AN AMERICAN CITIZEN (1905). Examples of Midwestern progressive fiction and Chicago's social history.

H12. Bronner, Simon J. CHAIN CARVERS: OLD MEN CRAFTING MEANING. Lexington: University Press of Kentucky, 1984.

Examines the history of carving chains out of wood and analyzes the symbolism of the designs and their use by carvers and their audiences in southern Indiana. Study focuses on four life histories.

H13. Bruegmann, Robert. "Holabird & Roche and Holabird & Root: The First Two Generations." CHICAGO HISTORY 9 (Fall 1980): 130-65.

See I13.

H14. Burg, David F. CHICAGO'S WHITE CITY OF 1893. Lexington:
      University Press of Kentucky, 1976.

      Claims that the 1893 World's Fair received its impetus
      and its reason for being from the same forces that were
      then shaping Chicago. Where others have seen a tension, a
      paradox in the relation between grimy Chicago and the white
      city created by the fair, Burg sees a natural extension of
      its culture, its political and social ideals.

H15. Burger, Mary W. "I, Too, Sing America: The Black
      Autobiographer's Response To Life in the Midwest and
      Mid-Plains." KANSAS QUARTERLY 7:3 (1975): 43-57.

      Contends that unique self-perceptions and racial identi-
      ties of black autobiographers such as William Wells Brown,
      Henry Bruse, Langston Hughes, and Gordon Parks resulted
      from their origins in the Midwest, 1840-1970.

H16. Byrne, Kathleen, and Richard C. Snyder. CHRYSALIS: WILLA
      CATHER IN PITTSBURGH, 1896-1906. Pittsburgh: Historical
      Society of Western Pennsylvania, 1950.

      A cult-like collection of most of what is discernable of
      Cather's Pittsburgh apprenticeship--from Cather's own
      writings, from oral sources and correspondence, from other
      scholarly works, and from photography.

H17. Carter, Denny T. "Cincinnati and Its 19th-Century
      Artists." AMERICAN ART AND ANTIQUES 2:5 (1979): 102-109.

      Traces how Cincinnati patrons attempted to create an art
      center in the west and how a number of artists, including
      James H. Beade and Joseph De Camp, began their careers
      there.

H18. Cassell, Frank A., and Marguerite E. Cassell. "Pride,
      Profits, and Politics: Indiana and the Columbian
      Exposition of 1893." INDIANA MAGAZINE OF HISTORY 80:2
      (June 1984): 93-121.

      The authors detail the boosterism and controversy that
      were part of the development of the Indiana exhibit. The
      article outlines the wide range of exhibits, from farm
      plows to needle work, and discusses the implications the
      fair had on Hoosiers.

H19. Chambers, Bruce W. THE WORLD OF DAVID GILMOUR BLYTHE
      (1815-1865). Washington, D.C.: Smithsonian Institution
      Press, 1980.

      Investigates the most important artist working in western
      Pennsylvania in the nineteenth century as one whose paint-
      ings "provide us with a rare glimpse into the compelling
      moral preoccupations of a rapidly urbanizing and indus-
      trializing society."

H20. Clark, Edna Marie. OHIO ART AND ARTISTS. Detroit: Gale
      Research Company, 1976.

Reprint of a standard reference work.

H21.   Clauson Schlereth, Wendy L. THE CHAP BOOK: A JOURNAL OF
       AMERICAN INTELLECTUAL LIFE IN THE 1890S. Ann Arbor: UMI
       Research Press, 1982.

       The definitive study of the nation's first "little maga-
       zine" that appeared in Chicago in the 1890s.

H21A. William L. Clements Library. HISTORY OF THE WILLIAM L.
       CLEMENTS LIBRARY, 1923-1973. Ann Arbor: University of
       Michigan, 1973.

       A modern history of a great Midwestern research
       facility.

H22.   Davis, Ronald L. A HISTORY OF OPERA IN THE AMERICAN WEST.
       Englewood Cliffs, NJ: Prentice-Hall, 1965.

       A revealing study of the widespread impact of opera in
       many Midwestern cities where it is not commonly known to
       have existed.

H23.   DeChambrun, Clara Longworth. CINCINNATI: STORY OF THE
       QUEEN CITY. New York: Scribner's, 1939.

       See A19.

H24.   Demarest, David P., ed. FROM THESE HILLS, FROM THESE
       VALLEYS: SELECTED FICTION ABOUT WESTERN PENNSYLVANIA.
       Pittsburgh: University of Pittsburgh Press, 1976.

       An anthology stressing creative writing about the
       region's historical dimensions, industrialism, the social
       aspects of workers and their ethnicity as well as labor
       toil.

H25.   Dewhurst, C. Kurt, and Marsha MacDowell. "Expanding
       Frontiers: The Michigan Folk Art Project." PERSPECTIVES
       ON AMERICAN FOLK ART. Edited by Ian M. G. Quimby and
       Scott T. Swank. New York: W.W. Norton, 1980, pp.
       54-78.

       Excellent summary of the background, theory, method, and
       outcome of a statewide survey of folk art in the state.

H26.   Dewhurst, C. Kurt, and Marsha MacDowell. RAINBOWS IN THE
       SKY: THE FOLK ART OF MICHIGAN IN THE TWENTIETH CENTURY.
       East Lansing: Michigan State University, 1978.

       Offers a typology for understanding art that is tradi-
       tional and art traditions influenced by popular culture.
       The brief biographies of artists included are based on
       folkloristic fieldwork.

H27.   Dewhurst, C. Kurt, and Marsha MacDowell. "The Folk Arts of
       Illinios." CHICAGO HISTORY 10 (Winter 1981-1982):

198-204.

Cautions against responding only to the formal properties of a folk art form, as meaning can be best realized by understanding that the life of the folk artist shapes the folk object in a region.

H28.   Doenecke, Justus D. "Myths, Machines, and Markets: The Columbian Exposition of 1893." JOURNAL OF POPULAR CULTURE 6:3 (1982): 535-549.

See G12.

H29.   Duffey, Bernard. THE CHICAGO RENAISSANCE IN AMERICAN LETTERS. East Lansing: Michigan State Press, 1954.

Claims the emergence of literary creativity in Chicago, 1890-1920, can be best studied by dividing the city's authors into a genteel tradition and a realistic tradition. Still the standard interpretation for this era of the city's literary past.

H30.   Duis, Perry. THE CHICAGO: CREATING NEW TRADITIONS. Chicago: Chicago Historical Society, 1976.

A succintly written, heavily illustrated museum catalog prepared to accompany a major Chicago Historical Society exhibition of the city's populism in architecture, city planning, urban reform, cultural literature, and merchandising. An up-to-date bibliography, particularly good on Chicago's marketing prowess, is included.

H31.   Duncan, Hugh D. CULTURE AND DEMOCRACY: THE STRUGGLE FOR FORM IN SOCIETY AND ARCHITECTURE IN CHICAGO AND THE MIDDLE WEST DURING THE LIFE AND TIMES OF LOUIS H. SULLIVAN. Totowa, NJ: Bedminster Press, 1965.

The title summarizes this sociologist's attempt to interrelate the city's politics, economic growth, literary achievement, architectural innovation, and social theory. The volume is, however, more concerned with the sources and impact of the democratic philosophy espoused by the city's creative elite than their actual literary and artistic achievements.

H32.   Dunlop, M.H. "Curiosities Too Numerous to Mention: Early Regionalism and Cincinnati's Western Museum." AMERICAN QUARTERLY 36:4 (Fall 1984): 524-548.

This study traces the early beginnings and eventual decline of the Museum that saw its purpose to be one of providing regional knowledge; the many forces that caused this failure are, the author says, "of both local and national import," and provide a good background to early Cincinnati.

H33.   Eble, Kenneth E. "Howells and Twain: Being and Staying Friends." THE OLD NORTHWEST 10:1 (Spring 1984): 91-106.

The article explores the first meeting of the two writers when Howells was the editor of the Atlantic Monthly, and the ensuing growth of friendship that followed. Eble sheds interesting light on the inconspicuous Howells and the extroverted Twain.

H34. Engel, Bernard. "Some Nineteenth-Century Midwestern Poets." THE OLD NORTHWEST 3:4 (1977): 360-378.

Discusses Henry Rowe Schoolcraft, Frederick William Thomas, Henry Whiting, John Milton Harney, and Samuel Beach.

H35. Fanelli, Dom Devine. "Stone Men: Indiana Limestone Craftsmen as Folk Artists." Ph.D. dissertation. Indiana University, 1983.

Examines limestone quarrymen and mill fabricators who create limestone art at home. Limestone artists are viewed as the secular counterpart to local mortuary art.

H36. Firelands Association For The Visual Arts. QUILTS AND CAROUSELS: FOLK ART IN THE FIRELANDS. Oberlin, OH: Firelands Association For The Visual Arts, 1983.

Essays which treat popular and folk artifacts from the region around Oberlin, Ohio.

H37. Flanagan, John T. "A Decade of Middlewestern Autobiography." CENTENNIAL REVIEW 26:2 (1982): 115-133.

Discusses eleven autobiographies written in the 1930s by authors with origins in the Midwest. Ten have strong links to Chicago and all offer a wide range of observation on their experiences during times of economic and social problems.

H38. Flanagan, John T., ed. AMERICA IS WEST: AN ANTHOLOGY OF MIDDLE-WESTERN LIFE AND LITERATURE. Minneapolis: University of Minnesota Press, 1945.

Although first selected forty years ago, this important anthology places special emphasis upon various Midwestern ethnic concentrations and locales throughout the region. It contains pertinent excerpts from the works of Garland, Rolvaag, Lewis, Sandburg, and Anderson.

H39. Flanagan, John T. "Middlewestern Regional Literature." RESEARCH OPPORTUNITIES IN AMERICAN CULTURAL HISTORY. Edited by John F. McDermott. Lexington: University Press of Kentucky, 1961.

A concise assessment of the needs and opportunities for future research on the topic. Integrates intellectual history and literary history in a call for more scholarly

biographies and critical editions of the region's major and
minor literary figures.

H40. Flanagan, John T. "Poetic Voices In The Early Middle
      West." CENTENNIAL REVIEW 24:3 (1980): 269-283.

      Review of 19th-century poetry of the region. Finds most
      noted work, which appeared near the end of the century,
      done in dialect verse, with James Whitcomb Riley among the
      leading practitioners of the form.

H41. Frederick, John T., ed. OUT OF THE MIDWEST: A COLLECTION
      OF PRESENT-DAY WRITING. New York: Whittlesey House,
      1944.

      An anthology similar to Flanagan's AMERICA IS WEST but
      with more emphasis on writers dealing with the Midwest west
      of the Mississippi. Reflects Frederick's own influential
      literary and aesthetic interests as longtime editor of THE
      MIDLAND.

H42. Fuller, Wayne E. THE OLD COUNTRY SCHOOL: THE STORY OF
      RURAL EDUCATION IN THE MIDDLE WEST. Lincoln: University
      of Nebraska Press, 1982.

      See G23.

H43. Gazell, James Albert. "The High Noon of Chicago's
      Bohemias." JOURNAL OF THE ILLINOIS STATE HISTORICAL
      SOCIETY 65:1 (1972): 54-68.

      The temporary dwellings built for the Columbian
      Exposition were taken over by South Side bohemia between
      1910 and 1930; among those who lived and wrote in them were
      Anderson, Dreiser, Lindsay, Masters, and Sandburg.

H44. Gehring, Wes D. "Kin Hubbard's Abe Martin: A Figure of
      Transition in American Humor." INDIANA MAGAZINE OF
      HISTORY 78:1 (1982): 26-37.

      Attempts to place a key humorist and his most famous
      central Indiana character in the context of nineteenth-
      century American culture.

H45. Gibson, Arthur H. ARTISTS OF EARLY MICHIGAN: A
      BIOGRAPHICAL DICTIONARY OF ARTISTS NATIVE TO OR ACTIVE IN
      MICHIGAN, 1801-1900. Ann Arbor: University of Michigan
      Press, 1975.

      A standard reference work.

H46. Ginger, Ray. ALTGELD'S AMERICA, THE LINCOLN IDEAL VERSUS
      CHANGING REALITIES. New York: Funk and Wagnalls, 1958.

      See A24.

H47. Governor, Alan B. OHIO FOLK⁄TRADITIONS: A NEW GENERATION.
      Columbus: Ohio Arts Council and Ohio Program in the
      Humanities, 1981.

      Brief biographies of central Ohio folk artists cover
      skills of chain saw sculpture, quilting, stonecarving,
      tattooing, and rag rug making.

H48. Grey, Lennox B. "Chicago And The Great American Novel: A
      Critical Approach To The American Epic." Ph.D. disser-
      tation. University of Chicago, 1935.

      Useful primarily for its bibliography.

H49. Groselose, Barbara. "Itinerant Painting in Ohio: Origins
      and Implications." OHIO HISTORY 90:2 (1981): 120-140.

      A model state study that probes both the role of
      itinerant painting in the development of the region's art
      and also the implications upon the individual artist's
      career. Thomas Cole and James Beard are given special
      attention.

H50. Gross, Barry. "The Midwest on the Broadway Stage."
      JOURNAL OF REGIONAL CULTURES 2:1 (Spring/Summer 1982):
      33-43.

      Gross shows that when the Midwest is on stage (and not a
      point of departure in a drama), the region is fictitiously
      portrayed as "peaceful and provincial, a Spoon River with-
      out trauma, a Winesburg without terror, a Gopher Prairie
      without cruelty." The author says that New York is
      idolized by the Midwesterner for its freedom, something
      that the Midwest is not perceived to possess.

H51. Hallwas, John E. "The Midwestern Poetry of Eliza Snow."
      WESTERN ILLINOIS REGIONAL STUDIES 5:2 (1982): 136-145.

      Studies a local poet of regional interest during the
      nineteenth century.

H52. Hansen, Harry. MIDWEST PORTRAITS: A BOOK OF MEMORIES AND
      FRIENDSHIPS. New York: Harcourt, 1923.

      Combines personal memoirs and biographical sketches of
      several Midwest writers and scenes known to the author.

H53. ter Harmsel, Larry. "Dutch Language Remnants in Holland,
      Michigan." JOURNAL OF REGIONAL CULTURES 2:1
      (Spring/Summer 1982): 71-77.

      The author finds that Dutch lexical remnants persist in
      areas such as street names, surnames, religious phrases,
      and slang, and also discovers influence on syntax, usage,
      and pronunciation of English.

H54. Hatcher, Harlan. THE BUCKEYE COUNTRY, A PAGEANT OF OHIO.
      New York: G.P. Putnam's Sons, 1940.

      A well-written paean to Ohio's cultural achievements in
      architecture, education, literature, and art by a native
      son who traces his roots back to the state's earliest white
      pioneers. Hatcher pays some attention to economic and
      political events primarily through his discussion of
      transportation patterns, particularly the Ohio River, the
      National Road, and Lake Erie. In several ways, the book is
      a one-man WPA state guide.

H55. Havighurst, Walter, ed. LAND OF LONG HORIZONS. New York:
      Coward-McCann, 1960.

      Can be considered as one updated version of Flanagan's
      AMERICA IS WEST. Havighurst's anthology is stronger on
      general cultural criticism and contains interpretive essays
      by Frank Lloyd Wright, Theodore Dreiser, and Robert and
      Helen Lynd.

H56. Havighurst, Walter, ed. THE GREAT LAKES READER. New York:
      Macmillan, 1966.

      Using the 350 years of history surrounding the waterways
      of America's inland seas as his interpretive metaphor,
      Havighurst collected a wide range of first-hand accounts
      and narratives of people who witnessed episodes in the
      shaping of the area from the voyagers to the iron ore
      freight captains.

      Havighurst, one of the deans of Midwestern regional
      studies, provides an introductory commentary to the
      selections which, in addition to first-person tales, also
      include the work of twentieth-century historians,
      novelists, and biographers.

H57. Hendrickson, Walter B. "Science and Culture in the
      American Middle West." ISIS 64:223 (1973): 326-40.

      Explores the movement that led to the founding of
      numerous natural history societies or academies.

H58. Hibbs, Jack Eugene. "A History of the Toledo Public
      Library, 1873-1964." NORTHWEST OHIO QUARTERLY 46:3
      (1974): 72-116.

      A well-researched and factual article, the author looks
      at the long history of the library, particularly the events
      that led to its inception.

H59. Hilfer, Anthony Channell. THE REVOLT FROM THE VILLAGE,
      1915-1930. Chapel Hill: University of North Caroline
      Press, 1969.

With Carl Van Doren's 1921 essay, "The Revolt from the Village," in THE NATION as his lodestone, Hilfer analyzes several regional writers--Edgar Lee Masters, Sherwood Anderson, Sinclair Lewis, Zona Gale, and Booth Tarkington as to their literary and cultural perspectives on the Midwestern small town.

H60. Hoffman, John. "The 'Upward Movement' in Illinois: Henry B. Fuller's Record of Cultural Progress, 1867-1917." JOURNAL OF THE ILLINOIS STATE HISTORICAL SOCIETY 16 (Winter 1983): 257-72.

An assessment of an important Chicago novelist's perspective on the city's self-consciousness as an aspiring cultural center in literature and the arts.

H61. Hogeland, Ronald W. "Coeducation of the Sexes at Oberlin College: A Study of Social Ideas in Mid-Nineteenth Century America." JOURNAL OF SOCIAL HISTORY 6 (Winter 1972-73): 160-76.

Detailed study of the first Midwestern liberal arts college to establish coeducation and its impact on social attitudes.

H62. Holt, Glen E. "Private Plans for Public Spaces: The Origins of Chicago's Park System, 1850-1875." CHICAGO HISTORY 8 (Fall 1979): 173-84.

Evaluates early attempts by the city's private citizenry to establish public green spaces prior to the work of the Chicago Park Commission.

H63. Homel, Michael W. DOWN FROM EQUALITY: BLACK CHICAGOANS AND THE CHICAGO PUBLIC SCHOOLS, 1920-41. Urbana: University of Illinois Press, 1984.

See E70.

H64. Horowitz, Helen Lefkowitz. CULTURE AND THE CITY: CULTURAL PHILANTHROPY IN CHICAGO FROM THE 1880S TO 1917. Lexington: University Press of Kentucky, 1976.

See D78.

H65. Howe, Barbara. "Uniting The Useful and Beautiful: The Arts in Cincinnati. THE OLD NORTHWEST 4:4 (1978): 319-336.

Historical analysis of the Cincinnati Art Museum and Art Academy.

H66. Howells, William Dean. STORIES OF OHIO. New York: American Book Company, 1897.

An outline view of the history of the state for young
readers that reveals much about its author's view of the
region.

H67. Hutton, Graham. MIDWEST AT NOON. Chicago: University of
      Chicago Press, 1946.

      See D81.

H68. Jackle, John A. IMAGES OF THE OHIO VALLEY. New York:
      Oxford University Press, 1977.

      See B22.

H69. Jensen, Merrill. REGIONALISM IN AMERICA. Madison:
      University of Wisconsin Press, 1951.

      See A41.

H70. Jordy, William H. "The Commercial Style and the 'Chicago
      School.'" PERSPECTIVES IN AMERICAN HISTORY 1 (1967):
      390-400.

      See I48.

H71. Karlowicz, Titus M. "Notes on the Columbian Exposition's
      Manufactures and Liberal Arts Building." JOURNAL OF THE
      SOCIETY OF ARCHITECTURAL HISTORIANS 33 (October 1974):
      214-18.

      See I49.

H72. Kern, Richard. FINDLAY COLLEGE: THE FIRST HUNDRED YEARS.
      Findlay: Findlay College, 1984.

      See E77.

H73. Kiel, Charles. URBAN BLUES. Chicago: University of
      Chicago Press, 1966.

      Stresses the importance of Chicago and other belt cities
      in the development of the musical forms that came north
      with the black migrations.

H74. Kramer, Dale. CHICAGO RENAISSANCE: THE LITERARY LIFE IN
      THE MIDWEST, 1900-1980. New York: Appleton-Century,
      1966.

      Stresses Duffey's (H29) realistic tradition of authors;
      (Drieser, Anderson, Sandburg) as the key figures in the
      Chicago literary revival; also takes the story farther into
      the twentieth century than most writers on the topic. A
      popular treatment.

H75. Lawrence College Faculty. THE CULTURE OF THE MIDDLE WEST.
      Appleton, WI: Lawrence College, 1944.

A charming faculty lecture series done at a small,
Midwest college during the early years (1941-42) of World
War II; includes papers on geography, literature, and
politics and sociology.

H76. Lee, Edward B. A PENCIL IN PENN. SKETCHES OF PITTSBURGH
      AND SURROUNDING AREAS. Pittsburgh: Meridian Gravure Co.,
      1970.

      A collection of western Pennsylvania landscapes by
      Pittsburgh architect, Edward Brown Lee (1876-1956) edited
      and introduced by his son.

H77. Loar, Peggy. INDIANA STONEWARE. Indianapolis:
      Indianapolis Museum of Art, 1974.

      Argues that Indiana pottery is inferior in variety and
      quality to that of eastern states but that no other folk
      art is better represented in Indiana.

H78. McCarthy, Kathleen. NOBLESSE OBLIGE: CHARITY AND CULTURAL
      PHILANTHROPHY IN CHICAGO, 1849-1929. Chicago:
      University of Chicago Press, 1982.

      See D102.

H79. Mackenzie, Donald R. "Collections and Exhibits. Early Ohio
      Painters: Cincinnati, 1830-50." OHIO HISTORY 73 (Spring
      1964): 111-18.

      Study of regional art and its public display in a city
      that hoped to become a major art center in early Midwestern
      history.

H80. Mander, Daniel. HUGH HENRY BRACKENRIDGE. New York: Twayne
      Publishers, 1968.

      Useful digest of a Western Pennsylvania author and his
      literary, artistic and political activities.

H81. Maxwell, Margaret. SHAPING A LIBRARY: WILLIAM L. CLEMENTS
      AS A COLLECTOR. Amsterdam: N. Israel, 1973.

      A revision of the author's thesis that describes how the
      great research library of William Lawrence Clements
      (1861-1934) came into existence. Compares Clements to
      other major collectors in the Midwest.

H82. Meador, Roy. "The Pittsburgh Years of Robinson Jeffers."
      WESTERN PENNSYLVANIA HISTORY MAGAZINE 63:1 (1980):
      17-29.

      Argues that the poet was strongly influenced by his
      Pittsburgh childhood, although he was to write primarily
      about the Big Sur area around Carmel, California.

H83. Meyer, Roy W. THE MIDDLE WESTERN FARM NOVEL IN THE
      TWENTIETH CENTURY. Iowa City: University of Iowa Press,
      1975.

      A very solid genre study: includes an annotated list of
      novels and a bibliography.

H84. Morrison, Theodore. CHAUTAUQUA: A CENTER FOR EDUCATION,
      RELIGION, AND THE ARTS IN AMERICA. Chicago: University
      of Chicago Press, 1974.

      Best book on subject to date; particularly good on the
      links between the New York State institution and the
      development of the University of Chicago in the 1890s under
      William Rainey Harper.

H85. Muelder, Herman R. THE FIRST HUNDRED YEARS OF KNOX
      COLLEGE. Urbana: University of Illinois Press, 1984.

      The book focuses on the Galesburg, Illinois, college from
      four different perspectives: the students, the alumni, the
      faculty, and the representation in society; the latter
      emphasizes Knox's history of social reform zeal in areas
      such as abolitionism and progressive change.

H86. Murray, John J., ed. HERITAGE OF THE MIDDLE WEST. Norman:
      University of Oklahoma Press, 1958.

      See A56.

H87. Nawrocki, Dennis Alan. "Art Outside the Mainstream--
      Detroit Style," JOURNAL OF REGIONAL CULTURES 2:1
      (Spring/Summer 1985): 78-98.

      The article sees Detroit's "urban expressionism" as a
      conscious rejection of mainstream New York modern art; it
      is a style influenced both by Abstract Expressionism and
      the decaying inner-city neighborhoods, where the majority
      of the artists discussed lived and worked.

H88. Nemanic, Gerald, ed. A BIBLIOGRAPHICAL GUIDE TO
      MIDWESTERN LITERATURE. Iowa City: University of Iowa
      Press, 1981.

      The current master guide; not only comprehensive on
      literature and language but also strong on history, folk-
      lore, architecture, and Chicago; in short, a Midwest bibli-
      ography in relation to Midwest literature. Outstanding
      book; should be in every reference library.

H89. Nicholson, Meredith. THE HOOSIERS. New York: Macmillan,
      1900.

      An autobiographical account and evaluation of writers
      from the "Hoosier" school including James Whitcomb Riley,

Booth Tarkington, Lew Wallace and others by a contemporary who knew many of them personally.

H90. Pargellis, Stanley, ed. A MIDWEST BIBLIOGRAPHY. Chicago: The Newberry Library, 1947.

See A60.

H91. Parmalee, Paul W., and Forrest D. Loomis. DECOYS AND DECOY CARVERS OF ILLINOIS. DeKalb: Northern Illinois University Press, 1969.

Emphasizes the carvers who provide decoys during the period 1870-1940 for the three major hunting areas in Illinois: Mississippi River region, Lake Michigan and Chicago, and the Illinois River.

H92. Paul, Sherman. LOUIS SULLIVAN: AN ARCHITECT IN AMERICAN THOUGHT. Englewood Cliffs, NJ: Prentice-Hall, 1962.

Interprets Sullivan as a major literary and philosophical figure in turn of the century intellectual history. Includes an important analysis of his relationship to transcendentalism and pragmatism.

H93. Payne, Alma J. "The Ohio World of William Dean Howells-- Ever Distant, Ever Near." THE OLD NORTHWEST 10:1 (Spring 1984): 127-137.

Payne shows how Howells displayed a phenomenon shared by other Midwest writers from Edgar Watson Howe to Joyce Carol Oates: "A rhythm of repulsion and attraction, of the use of the geographical area as a literary quarry from which the artist obtains materials vital to his or her work, while retreating personally from the immediate physical scene."

H94. Peat, Wilbur. PIONEER PAINTERS OF INDIANA. Indianapolis: Art Association of Indianapolis, 1954.

Summaries of over 150 painters active in the state from the late 18th century to the late nineteenth. Emphasis is on identifiable painters.

H95. Peck, Herbert. "The Amateur Antecedents of Rockwood Pottery." CINCINNATI HISTORICAL SOCIETY BULLETIN 26 (October 1968): 317-37.

Provides a decorative arts historical background for one of Cincinnati's most famous ceramic firms.

H96. Prior, Moody E. "Lost (and Found) Cities." AMERICAN SCHOLAR 46:4 (1976-77): 506-513.

Uses Chicago as a model of the American city. Traces architectural and ethnic diversity since its beginning; sees a new renaissance in the city's achievements.

H97. Prosser, Daniel J. "Chicago and the Bungalow Boom of the 1920s." CHICAGO HISTORY 10 (Summer 1981): 86-95.

See I71.

H98. Michael C. Rockefeller Arts Center. AMERICAN FOLK ART IN CHAUTAUQUA. Fredonia, NY: State University Gallery, 1976.

Surveys folk art in a New York county in the industrial belt. Organized by medium (metal, glass, textile, wood) and contains a brief general bibliography on American traditional arts.

H99. Rusk, Ralph Leslie. THE LITERATURE OF THE MIDDLE WESTERN FRONTIER, 2 vols. New York: Columbia University Press, 1925.

An encyclopedic overview of writing in all fields--literary, historical, journalistic--in the region prior to the arbitrary terminal point of 1840. Contains references to early and now largely unknown individuals who wrote something during the pioneer or territorial status of the area.

H100. Russo, Dorothy R., and Thelma Lois Sullivan. SEVEN AUTHORS OF CRAWFORDSVILLE, INDIANA. Indianapolis: Indiana Historical Society, 1952.

Biographical studies of Lew and Susan Wallace, Maurice and Will Thompson, Mary Hannah, Caroline Virginia Krout, and Meredith Nicholson and their regional achievement in American letters.

H101. Schlereth, Thomas J. "America, 1871-1919: A View Of Chicago." AMERICAN STUDIES 17 (Fall: 1976): 87-100.

Argues that if one knows Chicago's cultural history--its economics, politics, ethnic and racial patterns, literature, and architecture--during the period from the city's great fire in 1871 to the south side race riot of 1919, he knows all the key urban history configurations taking place in other major American cities during that time period.

H102. Schlereth, Thomas J. "A 'Robin Egg Renaissance': Chicago Culture, 1893-1933." CHICAGO HISTORY 8 (Fall: 1979): 144-145.

Using Sherwood Anderson's metaphor for the cultural renaissance that Chicago experienced, 1890-1920, a review is made of the interconnections among regional

literature, music (classical, jazz, and opera), films, and
radio programing.

H103.   Schlereth, Thomas J. "Big Money and High Culture: The
        Commercial Club of Chicago and Charles L. Hutchinson."
        GREAT LAKES REVIEW: A JOURNAL OF MIDWEST CULTURE 3:1
        (Summer 1976): 15-27.

        See C137.

H104.   Schlereth, Thomas J. "Regional Studies In America: The
        Chicago Model." AMERICAN STUDIES INTERNATIONAL 13
        (Autumn 1974): 20-35.

        See A70.

H105. Schlereth, Thomas J. "Regional Studies On the Chicago Model
       Since 1975." SOURCES FOR AMERICAN STUDIES. Edited by
       Robert Walker and J.B. Kellog. Westport, CT: Greenwood
       Press, 1980, pp. 518-532.

       See A71.

H106.   Schulze, Franz. FANTASTIC IMAGES: CHICAGO ART SINCE 1945.
        Chicago: Follett, 1972.

        Covers the movements and major figures in the city;
        provides data on Chicago's aspiration to become the
        industrial belt's leading art center since WW II.

H107.   Scriabine, Christine. "Upton Sinclair and the Writing of
        THE JUNGLE." CHICAGO HISTORY 10:1 (1981): 26-37.

        Focuses on how Sinclair amassed material for his muck-
        raking exposé of the Chicago meatpacking industry.

H108.   Seeney, J. Gray. "Great Lakes Marine Painting of the
        Nineteenth Century: A Michigan Perspective." MICHIGAN
        HISTORY 67:3 (1983): 24-33.

        Presents paintings by Seth Eastman, George Catlin, Thomas
        Moran, Seth A. Whipple, Thomas Birch, Vincent D. Nickerson,
        Gilbert Munger, Eastman Johnson, and Robert Hopkin.

H109.   Shaw, Henry K. "The Founding of Butler University,
        1847-1855." INDIANA MAGAZINE OF HISTORY 58 (September
        1962): 233-64.

        Treats the educational rationale and early curricular
        format of the founding years of an important private
        Indiana university.

H110.   Smith, Carl S. CHICAGO AND THE LITERARY IMAGINATION,
        1880-1920. Chicago: The University of Chicago Press,
        1984.

        Described by Smith as "a literary study with ties to
        social and intellectual history," this book concentrates on

Chicago's representation in novels and discusses the railroad, the skyscraper, and the stockyards with commentary
from historical and literary angles.

H111. Speiss, Phillip D., II. "Exhibitions and Expositions in
       Nineteenth Century Cincinnati." CINCINNATI HISTORICAL
       SOCIETY BULLETIN 28 (Fall 1970): 171-92.

       Surveys the industrial fairs and cultural exhibitions
       that took place in the Queen city; particular attention is
       paid to the role of the Cincinnati Music and Exhibition
       Hall.

H112. Stryck, Lucien, ed. HEARTLAND: POETS OF THE MIDWEST.
       DeKalb: Northern Illinois University Press, 1967.

       Best anthology of contemporary Midwestern poetry; has a
       supplement, HEARTLAND II, by the same editor and publisher
       that came out in 1975.

H113. Sylvesser, Lorna Lutes. "Conner Prairie Pioneer Settlement
       and Museum." INDIANA MAGAZINE OF HISTORY 65 (March
       1969): 1-24.

       The article explains how brothers John and William Conner
       ventured into an Indian Territory with their Delaware
       Indian wives and proceeded to civilize the central Indiana
       wilderness. Profusely illustrated with contemporary views
       of the museum sites.

H114. Tingley, Donald F. "The Robin's Egg Renaissance: Chicago
       and the Arts, 1910-1920." JOURNAL OF THE ILLINOIS STATE
       HISTORICAL SOCIETY 63 (Spring 1970): 35-54.

       Reviews the blossoming of cultural activity in poetry,
       theater, fiction that Sherwood Anderson identified as novel
       to Chicago in this decade.

H115. Venable, William H. BEGINNINGS OF LITERARY CULTURE IN THE
       OHIO VALLEY. Cincinnati: P. Smith, 1949 (1891).

       A pioneering study of Cincinnati as a center of regional-
       ism as early as the 1830s. Insightful sketches of figures
       such as Timothy Flint, James Hall, Daniel Drake and others.
       Notes on early western magazines are especially useful to
       the student of American journalism.

H116. Waggoner, Madeline S. THE LONG HAUL WEST: THE GREAT CANAL
       ERA, 1817-1850. New York: Putnam, 1958.

       See C157.

H117. Walsh, Justin E. "Radically and Thoroughly Democratic:
       Wilbur F. Storey and the Detroit Free Press, 1853 to
       1861." MICHIGAN HISTORY 47 (September 1963): 193-225.

A brief portrait of a Midwestern editor and his
newspaper's role in regional and national politics.

H118. Omitted.

H119. Williams, Kenny J., and Bernard Duffey, eds. CHICAGO'S
       PUBLIC WITS: A CHAPTER IN THE AMERICAN COMIC SPIRIT.
       Baton Rouge: Louisiana State University Press, 1983.

       This book examines the humorists that Chicago daily
       newspapers have fostered since the 1840s; lacks proper
       bibliography.

H120. Williams, Kenny J. PRAIRIE VOICES: A LITERARY HISTORY OF
       CHICAGO FROM THE FRONTIER TO 1893. Nashville: Townsend
       Press, 1980.

       Unlike most studies of literary Chicago, this monograph
       focuses on the period prior to 1890 rather than the thirty
       years afterward usually known as the Chicago Renaissance.
       Valuable mostly for its bibliographical detail, the book
       also contains two useful appendices. Appendix A lists
       approximately a thousand newspapers and magazines in exis-
       tence in Chicago between 1893 and 1933, arranged in cate-
       gories according to their dominant appeal--Agriculture,
       Commercial World, Foreign Language, Religion and the like;
       Appendix B summarizes the Chicago novel from 1883 to 1893
       and includes a list of published novels.

H121. Wilson, Ben C. "Idlewood, Michigan, 1912-1930: Growth of
       One of America's Oldest Black Resorts." JOURNAL OF
       REGIONAL CULTURES 2:1 (Spring/Summer 1982): 56-70.

       This brief but well-illustrated article outlines the rise
       in popularity in the black middle class resort in Lade
       County, Michigan, that became known throughout the
       country.

BUILT ENVIRONMENT

I1. Abbott, Carl. "The Plank Road Enthusiasm in the Antebellum
     Middle West." INDIANA MAGAZINE OF HISTORY 67:2 (1971):
     95-116.

     Abbott says the reason why westerners seized upon the
     idea of plank roads was because of the miserable condition
     of common roads and the exorbitant cost of moving goods,
     although financial problems plagued toll companies and
     resulted in the failure of the plank road. Well researched
     and illustrated.

I2. Abbott, Edith. THE TENEMENTS OF CHICAGO, 1908-1935.
     Chicago: University of Chicago Press, 1936, 1956.

     An important study by one of the members of the Chicago
     School. It is an analysis and summary of 25 years of
     research by the School of Social Service Administration.
     The development of tenements and tenement legislation is
     surveyed in the 19th century tenement housing in Chicago
     with the bulk of the book devoted to a detailed study of
     tenements in the first third of the twentieth century. The
     discussion has wide significance, e.g., for ethnic, legal,
     architectural history, etc., as well as for social
     conditions. Abbott argues that housing is bad and it will
     not improve until there is a stronger housing code with
     more officers to enforce it.

I3. Alberts, Robert C. THE SHAPING OF THE POINT: PITTSBURGH'S
     RENAISSANCE PARK. Pittsburgh: University of Pittsburgh
     Press, 1980.

     Discusses the significance of the Point (formed by the
     convergence of the Allegheny and the Monongahela Rivers to
     form the Ohio) in local and national history and then to
     the landscape architecture at Point Park.

I4. Andrews, Wayne. ARCHITECTURE IN CHICAGO AND MID-AMERICA: A
     PHOTOGRAPHIC HISTORY. New York: Atheneum, 1968.

     A picture book with no real architectural history or
     criticism.

I5. Andrews, Wayne. ARCHITECTURE IN MIGHIGAN: A REPRESENTATIVE
     PHOTOGRAPHIC SURVEY. Detroit: Wayne State University,
     1967.

Focuses primarily on historic houses; no major attempt to analyze the buildings illustrated.

I6.   Badger, Reid. THE GREAT AMERICAN FAIR: THE WORLD'S
      COLUMBIAN EXPOSITION AND AMERICAN CULTURE. Chicago:
      Nelson-Hall Publishers, 1979.

      See H8.

I7.   Barnes, Joseph W. "Rochester's City Halls." ROCHESTER
      HISTORY 40:2 (1978): 1-24.

      Traces how the Rochester city government has been housed
      in stores, clerk's offices, and official court houses and
      city halls.

I8.   Bastian, Robert W. "Indiana Folk Architecture: A Lower
      Midwestern Index." PIONEER AMERICA 9:2 (1977): 113-136.

      Tests the Kniffen-Lewis-Glassie model of architectural
      diffusion and finds it holds for most structural types in
      the region surveyed, except for I-houses, two-bay
      dwellings, and single-level, and three-bay barns.

I9.   Bowly, Devereux. THE POORHOUSE: SUBSIDIZED HOUSING IN
      CHICAGO, 1895-1976. Carbondale: Southern Illinois
      University Press, 1978.

      Bowly concludes "the history of Chicago's subsidized
      housing is in many respects a story of decline." It has
      failed to make the residents more self-sufficient or
      contented. The fundamental reason for the failure of
      public housing was that it isolated the poor in enclaves.

I10. Bridges, Roger D., and Rodney O. Davis. ILLINOIS: ITS
      HISTORY AND LEGACY. St. Louis: River City Publishers,
      1984.

      See A10.

I11. Brooks, H. Allen. "Chicago Architecture; Its Debt to the
      Arts and Crafts." JOURNAL OF THE SOCIETY OF
      ARCHITECTURAL HISTORIANS 30 (December 1971): 312-16.

      An overview of the Prairie Style, with particular
      emphasis on Frank Lloyd Wright, and its interaction with
      and influence upon the Arts and Craft movement 1890-1910.

I12. Brooks, H. Allen. THE PRAIRIE SCHOOL: FRANK LLOYD WRIGHT
      AND HIS MIDWEST CONTEMPORARIES. Toronto: University of
      Toronto Press, 1972.

      A well-researched, illustrated synthesis of the entire
      School. A standard work, but one that assumes some prior
      knowledge. Brooks argues that the link between the Chicago
      School and the Prairie School was the work of Louis
      Sullivan.

I13. Bruegmann, Robert. "Holabird & Roche and Holabird & Root:
      The First Two Generations." CHICAGO HISTORY 9 (Fall
      1980): 130-65.

      An architectural history of one of Chicago's most famous
      and productive partnerships.

I14. Campen, Richard N. THE ARCHITECTURE OF THE WESTERN
      RESERVE, 1800-1900. Cleveland: Case Western Reserve
      University Press, 1971.

      A superb analysis and catalog of the distinctive
      architecture in "Ohio's New England." A model sub-region
      study.

I15. Caress, Richard. "The Terminals of Chicago." NATIONAL
      RAILWAY BULLETIN 45:1 (1980): 27-41.

      A descriptive overview of the city's main passenger
      stations and their changing role in Chicago's rail history.

I16. Coffey, Brian. "Nineteenth-Century Barns of Geauge County,
      Ohio." PIONEER AMERICA. 10:2 (1978): 53-63.

      Review of barns in northeastern Ohio for their relation-
      ship to the ethnicity of their builders and the farming
      practices of their users.

I17. Condit, Carl. AMERICAN BUILDING ART: THE NINETEENTH
      CENTURY. New York: Oxford University Press, 1960.

      Although national in scope, many examples used in this
      exploration of building materials and techniques are from
      the Midwest. Strong on wood and iron framing, wood and
      iron bridge trusses, and the development of the suspension
      bridge.

I18. Condit, Carl. CHICAGO: BUILDING, PLANNING, AND URBAN
      TECHNOLOGY. 2 vols. Chicago: University of Chicago
      Press, 1973, 1974.

      An evaluation of Chicago's urban planning, transpor-
      tation, networks; has bibliographies, arranged by chapter,
      include newspaper articles as well as traditional sources.

I19. Condit, Carl. THE CHICAGO SCHOOL OF ARCHITECTURE; A
      HISTORY OF COMMERCIAL AND PUBLIC BUILDING IN THE CHICAGO
      AREA, 1875-1925. Chicago: University of Chicago Press,
      1964.

      The book that first identified, documented, and inter-
      preted the existence of a "Chicago School of Architecture."
      Based upon the author's early (1948) pioneering study, THE
      RISE OF THE SKYSCRAPER, the study interprets Chicago

commercial building as an extremely influential form of
indigenous American architecture.

Condit places particular emphasis on the contributions of
engineers and architects in the history of building technology. The commercial work of the city's main architects--
Daniel Burnham, John Root, Solon Beman--and its principal
firms--Adler and Sullivan, Holabird and Roche--receives
detailed analysis.

Although a basic text in the history of office and
commercial building in the U.S., Chicago's enormous
architectural influence elsewhere during its period
(1875-1925) is not examined.

I20. Condit, Carl. THE RAILROAD AND THE CITY: A TECHNOLOGICAL
      AND URBANISTIC HISTORY OF CINCINNATI. Columbus: Ohio
      State University Press, 1977.

      More than a history of the "impact" of the railroad on a
      major industrial belt city and its region; attempts a
      "systems analysis to a series of interlocking, inter-
      dependent and yet, paradoxically competing technological
      systems." Special attention is given to Cincinnati's Union
      Terminal as a brilliant solution to an enormous technical
      problem.

I21. Conover, Jewel H. NINETEENTH-CENTURY HOUSES IN WESTERN NEW
      YORK. Albany: State University of New York, 1966.

      A brief history of the region is followed by a discussion
      of the stylistic developments in regional architecture.
      Most of the book is devoted to photographs of this style
      sequence.

I22. Danz, Ernst. ARCHITECTURE OF SKIDMORE, OWINGS, AND
      MERRILL, 1950-1962. New York: Praeger, 1963.

      Study of early years of Chicago's (and the Midwest's)
      largest firm, tracing its design influence, through the
      region. Text and technical notes are in both English and
      German.

I23. DeWit, Wim. "Apartment Houses and Bungalows: Building the
      Flat City." CHICAGO HISTORY 12 (Winter 1983-84): 19-29.

      An overview of the bungalow and the apartment as building
      types in Chicago and the nature of their diffusion across
      the urban grid.

I24. Drexler, Arthur. LUDWIG MIES VAN DER ROHE. New York:
      George Braziller, 1960.

      A concise biography and analysis of one of the masters of
      contemporary architecture. Strong emphasis on Mies'

Chicago projects and his almost total concern for structure alone.

I25. Drexler, Arthur, and Alex Menges. ARCHITECTURE OF SKIDMORE, OWINGS, AND MERRILL, 1963-1973. New York: Architectural Book Publishers, 1974.

Updates the Ernst Danz 1963 treatment of the SOM firm. Detailed and illustrated are many of the major companies, libraries and skyscrapers designed throughout the 1960s.

I26. Drury, John. HISTORIC MIDWEST HOUSES. Minneapolis: University of Minnesota Press, 1947.

Treats houses, some architecturally significant, others important only because of a famous inhabitant. Very little information on building materials or style.

I27. Duncan, Hugh D. CULTURE AND DEMOCRACY: THE STRUGGLE FOR FORM IN SOCIETY AND ARCHITECTURE IN CHICAGO AND THE MIDDLE WEST DURING THE LIFE AND TIMES OF LOUIS H. SULLIVAN. Totowa, NJ: Bedminster Press, 1965.

See H31.

I28. Eckert, Kathryn. "Midwestern Resort Architecture: Earl H. Mead in Harbor Springs." MICHIGAN HISTORY 63:1 (1979): 10-20.

Impact of a popular summer resort architect's work in northwestern lower Michigan. Excellent local study of a usually neglected architecture genre.

I29. Edward, Susan. "Cobblestone Houses: A Part of The Land." HISTORIC PRESERVATION 30:3 (1978): 81-86.

Surveys the design, materials, and construction of more than 600 cobblestone structures built during 1825-1860 and presents the period as one of western New York's distinctive vernacular architectural styles.

I30. Fairbanks, Robert B. "Housing The City: The Better Housing League and Cincinnati, 1916-1939." OHIO HISTORY 89:2 (1980): 157-180.

A case study of one of the country's most effective local housing associations.

I31. Ferry, W. Hawkins. THE BUILDINGS OF DETROIT. Detroit: Wayne State University Press, 1968.

A photographic history of both public and domestic architecture that also includes architectural criticism of several of the city's structures. The text and 466 illustrations are basically a chronological survey from 1700 to the present.

132. Field, Cynthia. "The City Planning of D.H. Burnham."
      Ph.D. dissertation. Columbia University, 1974.

      A long, careful analysis of Burnham's work in planning.
      Field studies the 1893 Fair, Burnham's involvement with
      Washington's McMillan Commission Plan, the Group Plan for
      Cleveland, the Plans for West Point and for Manila, to show
      the development of his key ideas. These came together in
      the Plan of Chicago. In all of these plans Burnham worked
      from 19th century values which provided no new ideas for
      the solution of 20th century problems.

133. Frary, Ihna T. EARLY HOMES OF OHIO. Richmond, VA:
      Garrett, 1936.

      An early discussion of the transplanting of architectural
      forms and ideas from the East to Ohio.

134. Glass, James A. "The Architects Town and Davis and the
      Second Indiana Statehouse." INDIANA MAGAZINE OF HISTORY
      80:4 (December 1984): 329-347.

      A representative piece on early Indiana architectural
      history, the article examines the design and construction
      of the state's first Greek Revival design that, the
      author says, implanted the mode of architecture in
      Indianapolis.

135. Hardin, Thomas L. "The National Road in Illinois."
      JOURNAL OF THE STATE HISTORICAL SOCIETY 60 (Spring 1967):
      5-22.

      A survey of the first federally funded highway (now U.S.
      40) in the state prior to the Civil War.

136. Hatcher, Harlan. THE BUCKEYE COUNTRY, A PAGEANT OF OHIO.
      New York: G.P. Putnam's Sons, 1940.

      See H54.

137. Hilliard, Celia. "'Rent Reasonable to Right Parties': Gold
      Coast Apartment Buildings 1906-1929." CHICAGO HISTORY 8
      (Summer 1979): 66-77.

      A social and architectural history of a Chicago building
      type and its role in the real estate development of the
      near North side.

138. Hines, Thomas. BURNHAM OF CHICAGO: ARCHITECT AND PLANNER.
      New York: Oxford University Press, 1974.

      Definitive biographical treatment of Chicago's most
      prolific commercial builder and master city planner.
      Burnham's firm, the Skidmore, Owings, and Merrill of its
      day, was America's largest and his ideas (especially

the Beaux Arts design of the 1893 World's Columbian
Exposition) influenced the downtown of numerous Midwestern
cities.

139. Hoffman, Donald. THE ARCHITECTURE OF JOHN WELLBORN ROOT.
     Baltimore: The Johns Hopkins University Press, 1973.

     A brief biographical and historical chapter is followed
     by intensive documentation of Root's work on major projects
     and buildings as well as by an account of his general role
     in the formation of the Chicago of Commercial School of
     Architecture.

140. Holleman, Thomas J., and James P. Gallagher Smith. HINCHMAN
     & GRYLL: 125 YEARS OF ARCHITECTURAL ENGINEERING, 1853-
     1978. Detroit: Wayne State University Press, 1978.

     History of major Detroit firm.

141. Holt, Glen E. "Private Plans for Public Spaces: The
     Origins of Chicago's Park System, 1850-1875." CHICAGO
     HISTORY 8 (Fall 1979): 173-84.

     See H62.

142. Hoyt, Homer. ONE HUNDRED YEARS OF LAND VALUES IN CHICAGO:
     THE RELATIONSHIP OF CHICAGO TO THE RISE IN ITS LAND
     VALUES, 1830-1933. Chicago: University of Chicago
     Press, 1933.

     See D79.

143. Hugill, Peter J. "Houses in Cazenovia: The Effects of Time
     and Class." LANDSCAPE 24:2 (1980): 10-15.

     Traces city growth and housing construction in a western
     New York community that was founded in the 1790s; focuses
     on the quality of housing, additions, and modifications on
     older houses, and changing house styles.

144. Jensen, Merrill. REGIONALISM IN AMERICA. Madison:
     University of Wisconsin Press, 1951.

     See A41.

145. Johannesen, Eric. "Charles W. Heard, Victorian Architect."
     OHIO HISTORY 77:4 (1968): 130-42.

     Examines the life and major works (mainly in Cleveland)
     of the midwestern electic architect who began his career in
     the carpenter-builder tradition. Includes illustrations of
     designs.

146. Johannesen, Eric. "Simeon Porter: Ohio Architect." OHIO
     HISTORY 74:3 (1965): 169-90.

Looks at the mid-ninteenth century designs of Porter on
the western reserve; nicely illustrated text shows designs
ranging from Greek Revival to Eclecticism.

147. Johnson, Leland R. THE HEADWATERS DISTRICT: A HISTORY OF
      THE PITTSBURGH DISTRICT, U.S. ARMY CORPS OF ENGINEERS.
      Pittsburgh: U.S. Army corps of Engineers, 1978.

      Part of the nationwide project of the Corps to publish
      regional histories of its activities. Focuses on watershed
      improvements.

148. Jordy, William H. "The Commercial Style and the 'Chicago
      School.'" PERSPECTIVES IN AMERICAN HISTORY 1 (1967):
      390-400.

      A historiographical essay assessing the appropriate
      architectural history terminology ("Commercial Style" or
      "Chicago School") for the work of Chicago builders in the
      era, 1880-1920.

149. Karlowicz, Titus M. "Notes on the Columbian Exposition's
      Manufactures and Liberal Arts Building. JOURNAL OF THE
      SOCIETY OF ARCHITECTURAL HISTORIANS 33 (October 1974):
      214-18.

      An architectural and engineering analysis of the world's
      largest building in 1893.

150. Karpel, Bernard. "What Men Have Written About Frank Lloyd
      Wright: A Bibliography Arranged by Decades From 1900-
      1955." HOUSE BEAUTIFUL 97 (November 1955): 22-32.

      Should be used in conjunction with the James Muggenberg
      follow-up bibliography (I61).

151. Kidney, Walter C., and Louise King Ferguson. JAMES D. VAN
      TRUMP: LIFE AND ARCHITECTURE IN PITTSBURGH. Pittsburgh:
      Pittsburgh History & Landmarks Foundation, 1983.

      An anthology of 67 essays by one of the city's most
      prolific architectural historians. Includes solid fine
      arts criticism coupled with nostalgic urban history that
      takes little notice of the city's great mills (except on
      aesthetic terms), transportation networks or forms of land
      speculation.

152. Knight, Marian. "Historic Mount Adams." CINCINNATI
      HISTORICAL SOCIETY BULLETIN 28 (Spring 1970): 27-38.

      See G43.

153. Leckie, Shirley. "Brand Whitlock and the City Beautiful
      Movement in Toledo, Ohio." OHIO HISTORY 91 (1982): 5-36.

Traces Whitlock's unsuccessful attempt to build a city hall and civic center complex.

154. Lee, Edward B. A PENCIL IN PENN. SKETCHES OF PITTSBURGH AND SURROUNDING AREAS. Pittsburgh: Meridian Gravure Co., 1970.

See H76.

155. McKee, Harley J. "Glimpses of Architecture in Michigan." MICHIGAN HISTORY 50 (March 1966): 1-27.

An overview of the state's architectural gems with special attention to those surveyed by the Historic American Building Survey.

156. Madden, Betty J. ARTS, CRAFTS, AND ARCHITECTURE IN EARLY ILLINOIS. Urbana: University of Illinois Press in cooperation with the Illinois State Museum, 1974.

Describes a range of artifacts in order to illustrate general settlement patterns and other forms of cultural diffusion. Bibliography and inventory of early artists included.

157. Margulis, Harry L. "Housing Mobility in Cleveland and its Suburbs 1975-1980." GEOGRAPHICAL REVIEW 72:1 (1982): 36-49.

See G50.

158. Meyer, Katherine M., ed. DETROIT ARCHITECTURE: AMERICAN INSTITUTE OF ARCHITECTS GUIDE. Detroit: Wayne State University Press, 1971.

Typical AIA format with emphasis on structures designed by architects; strongest on the city's contemporary structures.

159. Miller, Ross. "Chicago Architecture After Mies." CRITICAL INQUIRY 6:2 (1979): 271-289.

Traces the influence of Ludwig Mies van der Rohe (1886-1969) on the architecture of Chicago from 1938, and considers the challenges to the his ideas since the 1960s by a younger generation of Chicago architects.

160. Morrison, Hugh. LOUIS SULLIVAN: PROPHET OF MODERN ARCHITECTURE. New York: W.W. Norton, 1935.

Remains one of the most authoritative and important study of Sullivan's career. Evaluates Sullivan's contributions to Midwest architectural history and discusses important buildings upon which he makes his declaration.

161. Muggenberg, James R. "Frank Lloyd Wright in Print, 1959-
      1970." AMERICAN ASSOCIATION OF ARCHITECTURAL
      BIBLIOGRAPHERS PAPERS 9 (1972): 85-132.

      An exhaustive update on the architect about whom more has
      been written than any other American in the profession.
      For earlier sources see Bernard Karpal's bibliographical
      listing (I50).

162. Mullin, John R. "Henry Ford and Field and Factory: An
      Analysis of The Ford Sponsored Village Industries
      Experiment In Michigan, 1918-1941." JOURNAL OF THE
      AMERICAN PLANNING ASSOCIATION 48:4 (1982): 419-431.

      Suggests that the Ford experiment was important despite
      a significant body of literature calling for the decentral-
      ization of American industry during this period because
      there were few efforts that were comprehensively implemen-
      ted, few that included rural areas, and even fewer that
      were totally financed by the private sector.

163. Newcomb, Rexford G. ARCHITECTURE OF THE OLD NORTHWEST
      TERRITORY. Chicago: University of Chicago Press, 1950.

      Although three decades old, still the best overall intro-
      duction to nineteenth-century building in the region.

164. Noble, Allen G. "Barns As Elements in the Settlement
      Landscape of Ohio." PIONEER AMERICA 9:1 (1977): 62-79.

      Uses a perception survey of county agricultural agents in
      the state to classify a large number of barns over a wide
      area. Results yield 10 barn types accounting for 95
      percent of Ohio's barns.

165. Ohman, Marian M. "Diffusion of Foursquare Courthouses To
      The Midwest, 1786-1886." GEOGRAPHICAL REVIEW 72:2
      (1982): 171-189.

      Traces the foursquare building type from its probable
      origins in New Haven, Connecticut, in 1683 through its
      diffusion in the Midwest region and beyond in the
      nineteenth century.

166. O'Kelley, Dorame. "Late Nineteenth Century Courthouse
      Architecture in Northwestern Ohio." OHIO HISTORY 88:3
      (1979): 311-326.

      Sample study of 30 buildings in the height of the county
      public building craze; excellent on the elaborate rituals
      and ceremonies involved in the laying of cornerstones or
      the completion of the structure.

167. Patton, Glenn. "James Keys Wilson (1828-1894): Architect of the Gothic Revival in Cincinnati." JOURNAL OF THE SOCIETY OF ARCHITECTURAL HISTORIANS 26 (Dec. 1967): 850-93.

A concise assessment of a significant regional architect.

168. Peat, Wilbur D. INDIANA HOUSES OF THE NINETEENTH CENTURY. Indianapolis: Indiana Historical Society, 1962.

A survey of the elite style domestic architecture in the south and central portions of the state; deserves to have a twentieth-century counterpart.

169. Peterson, Fred W. "Vernacular Building and Victorian Architecture: Midwestern American Farm Homes." JOURNAL OF INTERDISCIPLINARY HISTORY 12:3 (1981): 409-27.

Examines the interaction of academic styles and vernacular tastes in 19th century rural buildings.

170. Poesch, Jessie J. THE CHICAGO SCHOOL IN PRINT: AN ANNOTATED BIBLIOGRAPHY. Charlottesville, VA: American Association of Architectural Bibliographers, 1959.

A good guide to the published writings of Chicago architects.

171. Prosser, Daniel J. "Chicago and the Bungalow Boom of the 1920s." CHICAGO HISTORY 10 (Summer 1981): 86-95.

Survey of one of the city's most popular building types with particular attention to the so-called "Chicago bungalow."

172. Quinlan, Majorie L. "Spanish Revival Homes in Buffalo." NIAGARA FRONTIER 28:1 (1981): 1-23.

Places the Buffalo style in the 1920s within the nation-wide "Spanish Craze" in general beginning with the 1901 Buffalo Pan-American Exposition.

173. Randall, Frank Alfred. HISTORY OF THE DEVELOPMENT OF BUILDING CONSTRUCTION IN CHICAGO. Urbana: University of Illinois Press, 1949.

The most important reference work on Chicago building between North Avenue and 12th Street and from the River to the Lake up to 1946. The book contains an introductory essay, a detailed list of milestones in building construction to 1931 arranged by year of construction, an annotated presentation of part of Rand McNally's 1898 VIEWS OF CHICAGO, and indexes to architects and engineers, buildings, and locations. A very detailed bibliography is supplied in each building description.

174. Reps, John W. CITIES OF THE AMERICAN WEST: A HISTORY OF
     FRONTIER URBAN PLANNING. Princeton: Princeton University
     Press, 1979.

     The opening chapters of this mammoth survey provide us
     with a cogent and updated summary of recent scholarship
     (his own and others) as well as useful reproductions of the
     plans of industrial belt towns such as Marretta, Cleveland,
     Detroit, Cincinnati, Indianapolis, Columbus, and Chicago.
     A valuable reference work for all types of cartographic,
     architectural, and town planning information by the senior
     scholar in the field.

175. Roberts, Warren E. "The Tools Used in Building Log Houses
     in Indiana." PIONEER AMERICA 9 (July 1977): 30-61.

     Analyses the technology employed in materials preparation
     and construction technique in timber framing.

176. Roos, Frank John, Jr. "Ohio: Architectural Cross-Road,"
     SOCIETY OF ARCHITECTURAL HISTORIANS JOURNAL 12 (May,
     1953): 3-8.

     Argues the state is a crucial architectural nexus where
     Northeast and Southeast styles meet. Briefly discusses
     developments from 1772 to the Civil War and the conflict of
     styles that results.

177. Rosentreter, Roger L. "The County Courthouse: Polestar of
     Michigan's Heritage." MICHIGAN HISTORY 66:4 (1982):
     16-25, 37-48.

     Describes how important courthouses were, particularly in
     their design, to boosters who were concerned with county
     and civic pride.

178. Ross, D. Reid, and C.W. Weister. "The Relationship Between
     Urban Growth and Transportation Development in the
     Cincinnati-Northern Kentucky Area." CINCINNATI
     HISTORICAL SOCIETY BULLETIN 21 (April 1963): 112-32.

     See G69.

179. Schlereth, Thomas J. "City Planning As Progressive
     Reformer: Burnham's Plan and Moody's Manual." JOURNAL
     OF THE AMERICAN PLANNING ASSOCIATION 47 (January 1981):
     70-82.

     See F90.

180. Schlereth, Thomas J. "Regional Studies In America: The
     Chicago Model." AMERICAN STUDIES INTERNATIONAL 13
     (Autumn 1974): 20-35.

     See A70.

I81. Schlereth, Thomas J. "Regional Studies On The Chicago Model
      Since 1975." SOURCES FOR AMERICAN STUDIES. Edited by
      Robert Walker and J.B. Kellog. Westport, CT: Greenwood
      Press, 1980, pp. 518-532.

      See A71.

I82. Schofield, Mary Peale. LANDMARK ARCHITECTURE OF CLEVELAND.
      Pittsburgh: Ober Park Associates, 1976.

      Aspires to "present to urban historians some basic
      materials for more detailed, in-depth studies of the his-
      tory of Cleveland" using buildings as primary resource
      material; an especially good summary of the city's
      Progressive "Group Plan" for civic buildings.

I83. Sehr, Timothy J. "Three Gilded Age Suburbs of
      Indianapolis: Irvington, Brightwood, and Woodruff Place."
      INDIANA MAGAZINE OF HISTORY 77:4 (1981): 305-332.

      Raises several questions about a number of the tradition-
      al reasons for post-Civil War development, particularly
      with the rise of street-car suburbs.

I84. Sprague, Paul E. "The Origin of Balloon Framing." JOURNAL
      OF THE SOCIETY OF ARCHITECTURAL HISTORIANS 40 (December
      1981): 311-19.

      A revisionist assessment of the development of building
      construction techniques originating in Chicago in the late
      1830s.

I85. Steinnes, Donald N. "Suburbanization and the 'Malling of
      America': A Time-Series Approach." URBAN AFFAIRS
      QUARTERLY 17:4 (1982): 401-418.

      Using residential and business location data in 46 stand-
      ard metropolitan statistical areas in the North Central
      States during 1948-72, the author confirms earlier studies
      that document the suburbanization of jobs and people in
      modern America. Examines the role of the shopping mall
      in this process.

I86. Szuberla, Guy. "Irving Kane Pond: A Michigan Architect in
      Chicago." THE OLD NORTHWEST 5:2 (1979): 109-140.

      A survey of Pond's early commissions (1886-1910) suggesting
      his homage to traditional architectural forms, his insistence
      on functional design and, in his settlement architecture such
      as Jane Addams' Hull House, his humanitarian concerns.

I87. Tager, Jack. "Partners in Design: Chicago Architects,
      Entrepreneurs, And The Evolution of Urban Commercial
      Architecture." SOUTH ATLANTIC QUARTERLY 76:2 (1977):
      204-218.

Traces role of business clients in the city's evolution
as an architectural center in the late 19th century.

188. Toker, Franklin B., and Helen Wilson. THE ROOTS OF
ARCHITECTURE IN PITTSBURGH AND ALLEGHENY COUNTY: A GUIDE
TO RESEARCH SOURCES. Pittsburgh: Historical Society of
Western Pennsylvania, 1980.

Best bibliography for topic.

189. White, John H., Jr. "The Cincinnati Inclined Plane Railway
Company: The Mount Auburn Incline and the Lookout House."
CINCINNATI HISTORICAL BULLETIN 27 (January 1969): 7-29.

See G87.

190. Wilson, Ben C. "Idlewood, Michigan, 1912-1930: Growth of
One of America's Oldest Black Resorts." JOURNAL OF
REGIONAL CULTURES 2:1 (Spring/Summer 1982): 56-70.

See H121.

INSTITUTIONAL RESOURCES

Part I--Serial Publications

J1. APPALACHIAN JOURNAL: A REGIONAL STUDIES REVIEW

    Focus: Politics, literature, and culture of Appalachia and environs.

    Affiliation: Appalachian State University

    Address: Appalachian State University
                 Boone, NC 28608

J2. THE BULLETIN OF THE HISTORICAL SOCIETY OF MONTGOMERY COUNTY (PENNSYLVANIA)

    Focus: Events, personalities, trends in Montgomery County or adjacent areas of southeast Pennsylvania, from colonial to present times.

    Affiliation: Historical Society of Montgomery County

    Address: P.O. Box 92
                 Collegeville, PA 19426

J3. BUSINESS HISTORY REVIEW

    Focus: Business enterprise throughout the world with particular emphasis on U.S. economic development since industrialization.

    Affiliation: Harvard Business School

    Address: Harvard University
                 215 Baker Library
                 Soldiers Field
                 Boston, MA 02163

J4. CHICAGO HISTORY

Focus: Chicago and environs

Affiliation: Chicago Historical Society

Address: Chicago Historical Society
             Clark Street at North Avenue
             Chicago, IL 60614

J5. CINCINNATI HISTORICAL SOCIETY BULLETIN

Focus: Cultural, economic, political and social aspects
             of Cincinnati, the Miami Valley, the Old
             Northwest Territory.

Affiliation: Cincinnati Historical Society

Address: Cincinnati Historical Society
             Eden Park
             Cincinnati, OH 45202

J6. DEARBORN HISTORY

Focus: Primary interests include Michigan (especially
             Dearborn) daily life, historic buildings,
             collections, 1820-present.

Affiliation: Dearborn Historical Commission

Address: Dearborn Historical Commission
             915 Brady Street
             Dearborn, MI 48124

J7. DETROIT IN PERSPECTIVE: A JOURNAL OF REGIONAL HISTORY

Focus: Detroit, Southeastern Michigan, Southern Ontario

Affiliation: Department of History, Wayne State University
             and Detroit Historical Society.

Address: Department of History
             Wayne State University
             Detroit, MI 84202

J8. ECHOES

    Focus: Ohio archives, museums, historic sites and
                 historic perservation.

    Affiliation: Ohio Historical Society

    Address: Ohio Historical Society
                 I-71 and 17th Avenue
                 Columbus, OH   43211

J9. ENVIRONMENTAL REVIEW

    Focus: Interdisciplinary studies in an environmental
                 context.

    Affiliation: Duquesne University

    Address: Department of History
                 Duquesne University
                 Pittsburgh, PA   15219

J10. HAYES HISTORICAL JOURNAL

    Focus: The period of Rutherford B. Hayes, his family
                 and interests.

    Affiliation: The Rutherford B. Hayes Library and Museum

    Address: Speigel Grove
                 1337 Hayes Avenue
                 Fremont, OH   43420

J11. HISTORICAL SOCIETY OF MICHIGAN

    Focus: Michigan

    Affiliation: Historical Society of Michigan

    Address: Historical Society of Michigan
                 2117 Washtenaw Avenue
                 Ann Arbor, MI   48104

J12.   INDIANA HISTORY BULLETIN

    Focus: Indiana and Midwest

    Affiliation: Indiana Historical Bureau

    Address: 408 State Library and Historical Building
                  140 North Senate Avenue
                  Indianapolis, IN 46204

J13.   INDIANA MAGAZINE OF HISTORY

    Focus: Indiana and Old Northwest

    Affiliation: Indiana Historical Society and History
                  Department, Indiana University

    Address: Department of History
                  742 Ballantine Hall
                  Indiana University
                  Bloomington, IN 47401

J14.   INDIANA SOCIAL STUDIES QUARTERLY

    Focus: Social sciences

    Affiliation: Ball State University and Indiana Council for
                  the Social Studies

    Address: History Department
                  Ball State University
                  Muncie, IN 47306

J15.   INLAND SEAS: QUARTERLY JOURNAL OF THE GREAT LAKES
      HISTORICAL SOCIETY

    Focus: The discussion and illustration of the
                  history, geography, geology, transportation,
                  and industry of the Great Lakes region.

    Affiliation: Great Lakes Historical Society

    Address: Great Lakes Historical Society
                  2237 Westminster Road
                  Cleveland Heights, OH 44118

J16. JOURNAL OF AMERICAN CULTURE

Focus: Americal culture

Affiliation: Bowling Green State University

Address: Popular Culture Center
              Bowling Green State University
              Bowling Green, OH 43403

J17. JOURNAL OF AMERICAN HISTORY

Focus: All periods and methods in American history

Affiliation: Organization of American Historians

Address: 702 Ballantine Hall
         Indiana University
         Bloomington, IN 47405

J18. JOURNAL OF ERIE STUDIES

Focus: Northwest Pennsylvania

Affiliation: Mercyhurst College

Address: 501 East 38th Street
              Erie, PA 16501

J19. JOURNAL OF INTERDISCIPLINARY HISTORY

Focus: Social sciences

Affiliation: Massachusetts Institute of Technology

Address: Massachusetts Institute of Technology
              Cambridge, MA 02139

J20. JOURNAL OF POPULAR CULTURE

Focus: Popular culture

Affiliation: Bowling Green State University

Address: Popular Culture Center
              Bowling Green State University
              Bowling Green, OH 43403

J21. JOURNAL OF REGIONAL CULTURES

    Focus: All aspects of Ámerican regional culture, their impact on the larger culture and its impact on them.

    Affiliation: Bowling Green University

    Address: Bowling Green University
                  Popular Press
                  Bowling Green, OH   43403

J22. JOURNAL OF SOCIAL HISTORY

    Focus: Social history

    Affiliation: Carnegie-Mellon University

    Address: Department of History
                  Carnegie-Mellon University
                  Pittsburgh, PA   15213

J23. JOURNAL OF THE ILLINOIS STATE HISTORICAL SOCIETY

    Focus: Original research on Illinois subjects

    Affiliation: Illinois State Historical Society

    Address: Illinois State Historical Society
                  Springfield, IL   62706

J24. LIMNOS/SEAWAY REVIEW

    Focus: The magazine of the Great Lakes Foundation. A quarterly containing scientific and educational articles concerning the Great Lakes Basin.

    Affiliation: Great Lakes Foundation

    Address: 221 Water Street
                  Boyne City, MI   49712

J25. MICHIGAN BUSINESS REVIEW

    Focus: American business

    Affiliation: Ann Arbor,
                  School of Business Administration, University
                  of Michigan

    Address: School of Business Administration
                  University of Michigan
                  Ann Arbor, MI   48104

J26. MID-AMERICA

    Focus: United States, especially the nineteenth and
                  twentieth centuries.

    Affiliation: Loyola University

    Address: Loyola University
                  6525 Sheridan Road
                  Chicago, IL   60626

J27. THE NEW-YORK HISTORICAL SOCIETY

    Focus: New York State and American history in general,
                  but not foreign policy.

    Affiliation: The New-York Historical Society

    Address: The New-York Historical Society
                  170 Central Park West
                  New York, NY   10024

J28. NEW YORK HISTORY

    Focus: All aspects of New York

    Affiliation: New York State Historical Association

    Address: New York State Historical Association
                  Cooperstown, NY   13326

J29. NIAGARA FRONTIER

Focus: Western New York

Affiliation: Buffalo and Erie County Historical Society

Address: Buffalo and Erie County Historical Society
                25 Nottingham Court
                Buffalo, NY 14216

J30. NORTHWEST OHIO QUARTERLY

Focus: Maumee Valley region, which consists of
                northwest Ohio, southwest Michigan, and
                northeastern Indiana.

Affiliation: Maumee Valley Historical Society; Bowling Green
                State University.

Address: Wolcott Howe Museum
                1031 River Road
                Maumee, OH 43537

J31. OHIO HISTORY

Focus: Ohio

Affiliation: Ohio Historical Society

Address: Ohio Historical Society
                I-71 and 17th Avenue
                Columbus, OH 43211

J32. THE OLD NORTHWEST: A JOURNAL OF REGIONAL LIFE AND LETTERS

Focus: Interdisciplinary studies of the Old Northwest
                Territory and the states which developed from
                it: Ohio, Indiana, Michigan, Wisconsin,
                Illinois.

Affiliation: Miami University

Address: Bachelor Hall
                Miami University
                Oxford, OH 45056

J33. PENNSYLVANIA FOLKLIFE

    Focus: Folklife and folk culture of any and all ethnic
                  groups in Pennsylvania, particularly of a
                  comparative nature; crafts, personalities, folk
                  heritage from settlement to the present.

    Affiliation: Ursinus College and Pennsylvania Folklife
                  Society

    Address: P.O. Box 92
                  Collegeville, PA   19426

J34. PENNSYLVANIA HERITAGE

    Focus: Pennsylvania

    Affiliation: Quarterly of the Pennsylvania Historical and
                  Museum Commission.

    Address: Pennsylvania Museum and
                  Historical Commission
                  Box 1026
                  Harrisburg, PA   17120

J35. PENNSYLVANIA HISTORY

    Focus: Pennsylvania

    Affiliation: Pennsylvania Historical Association

    Address: Wilkes College
                  Wilkes-Barre, PA   18766

J36. THE PENNSYLVANIA MAGAZINE OF HISTORY AND BIOGRAPHY

    Focus: Pennsylvania

    Affiliation: The Historical Society of Pennsylvania

    Address: 1300 Locust Street
                  Philadelphia, PA   19107

J37. RAILROAD HISTORY

Focus: Impact of railroads on the United States

Affiliation: Railroad and Locomotive Historical Society

Address: Division of Transportation
                Smithsonian Institution
                Washington, DC   20560

J38. ROCHESTER HISTORY

Focus: Rochester and Western New York

Affiliation: Rochester Public Library

Address: Rochester Public Library
                115 South Avenue
                Rochester, NY   14604

J39. SOCIAL SCIENCE

Focus: Economics, political science, sociology

Affiliation: Pi Gamma Mu

Address: Department of Sociology
                Toledo University
                Toledo, OH   43606

J40. SOCIAL SCIENCE HISTORY

Focus: The study of social theory within an
                empirical, historical context.

Affiliation: Bowling Green University.

Address: Department of History
                111 Williams Hall
                Bowling Green University
                Bowling Green, OH   43402

J41. SWEDISH PIONEER HISTORICAL QUARTERLY

    Focus: Swedish emigration and the Swedish presence in North America.

    Affiliation: Swedish Pioneer Historical Society, Chicago.

    Address: Department of History
                  Southern Illinois University
                  Carbondale, IL   62901

J42. WESTERN PENNSYLVANIA HISTORICAL MAGAZINE

    Focus: Western Pennsylvania

    Affiliation: Historical Society of Western Pennsylvania

    Address: 4338 Bigelow Boulevard
                  Pittsburgh, PA   15213

Part II--Research Institutions

J43. JANE ADDAMS HULL HOUSE

    Collections: Photographs; documents; artifacts;
                             memorabilia; furniture; manuscripts; papers
                             letters, and clippings relating to the
                             history of Hull House, Jane Addams, and the
                             surrounding neighborhood.

    Research Fields: History of settlement house movement in
                             Chicago; the life of Jane Addams; local
                             history.

    Address: 800 S. Halsted Street, Chicago IL 60680.
                             Mailing Address: Box 4348, Chicago, IL
                             60680

J44. THE ADLER PLANETARIUM

    Collections: Antique scientific instruments in
                             astronomy, time-keeping, navigation and
                             engineering.

    Research Fields: Astronomy, astrophysics, history of
                             science.

    Address: 1300 S. Lake Shore Drive
                             Chicago, IL 60605

J45. ALLEN COUNTY-FORT WAYNE HISTORICAL SOCIETY MUSEUM

    Collections: Manuscripts and archives pertaining to
                             Fort Wayne, Allen County and Northeastern
                             Indiana; 19th and 20th century clothing;
                             paintings; toys; china; glass; maps; tools;
                             sheet music; dolls; Indian artifacts;
                             industrial products and equipment.

    Research Fields: 19th and 20th century local history;
                             politics; industry; architecture.

    Address: 302 E. Berry Street
                             Fort Wayne, IN 46802

J46. AMERICAN BAPTIST HISTORICAL SOCIETY

Collections: Consists of papers of the American Baptist
                    Foreign Mission Society, the American
                    Baptist Home Mission Society, the Board of
                    Education and Publication, the American
                    Bible Union, and other individuals and
                    organizations connected with the American
                    Baptist church.

Research Fields: Baptist faith and life

Address: 1106 South Goodman Street
                    Rochester, NY 14620

J47. AMERICAN BAR FOUNDATION

Collections: Taped interviews relating to the history
                    of the organized bar in the United States,
                    with special emphasis on the history of the
                    American Bar Foundation, American Bar
                    Association, and the American Bar
                    Endowment. Covers not only institutional
                    history but also important issues that the
                    legal profession has faced since about 1936
                    to the present time.

Research Fields: Americal legal history

Address: 1155 East 60th Street
                    Chicago, IL 60637

J48. AMERICAN JEWISH ARCHIVES

Collections: Materials relating to Jewish history in
                    the Western Hemisphere. The primary focus
                    is on the United States; includes such
                    topics as anti-Semitism, civil rights,
                    immigration, and social welfare activities.
                    Has personal papers, organization records,
                    Yiddish plays in manuscript, memoirs,
                    diaries, genealogical data, photographs,
                    and oral history recordings.

Research Fields: Manuscripts, institution and organization
                    records, photographs, and oral history
                    tapes and transcripts, relating to Jewish
                    history.

Address: 3101 Clifton Avenue
                    Cincinnati, OH 45220

J49. THE ANTHROPOLOGY MUSEUM

Collections: Ethnographic materials from Plains,
                     Southwest and Northwest coasts and eastern
                     North American, Mexico, South America,
                     Pacific Islands, Southeast Asia, Africa and
                     Greece; North American archaeology material;
                     human and non-human primate skeletal
                     material; pathological human skeletal
                     material.

Research Fields: Archaeology; ethnography; physical
                     anthropology.

Address: Northern Illinois University
                     DeKalb, IL 60115

J50. ARCHDIOCESE OF CINCINNATI

Collections: A collection of manuscripts and memo-
                     rabilia concerning the Catholic Church in
                     the Midwest, especially in Ohio. The bulk
                     of the collection consists of corre-
                     spondence of the bishops and archbishops of
                     Cincinnati. Also included are diaries,
                     ledgers, statistical reports, registers of
                     defunct parishes, and records of Mount St.
                     Mary's Seminary.

Research Fields: Records and manuscripts of parishes and
                     institutions of the Archdiocese of
                     Cincinnati. Also accepts memorabilia and
                     manuscripts relating to Cincinnati and Ohio
                     history.

Address: Mount St. Mary's Seminary
                     5440 Moeller Avenue
                     Cincinnati, OH 45212

J51. ARCHIVES AND COMPANY MUSEUM OF ELI LILLY AND COMPANY

Collections: Materials relating to the company, the
                     pharmaceutical industry and early medicine;
                     pictures relating to operation from 1876 to
                     present; archives; herbarium; replica of
                     original Lilly Laboratory.

Research Fields: Eli Lilly and Company and pharmaceutical
                     history

Address: Lilly Center
                     893 S. Delaware
                     Indianapolis, IN 46285

J52. THE ART CENTER

    Collections: Nineteenth and twentieth century American &
                           European paintings & works on paper;
                           historic & contemporary Indian art.

    Research Fields: Historic and contemporary Indian art

    Address: 120 S. St. Joseph Street
                   South Bend, IN 46601

J53. THE ART INSTITUTE OF CHICAGO

    Collections: All periods of European and American painting; sculpture; prints; drawings; decorative arts; textiles; Oriental art (Chinese, Japanese, Indian, Middle Eastern); European medieval art; classical art; photography; Primitive art (African, Oceanic, pre-Hispanic); architectural drawings and fragments and armor.

The Ryerson Library has minutes of the Society for the Advancement of Truth in Art, and artists' business letters from the Art Institute of Chicago, including several letters of Georgia O'Keeffe, Mary Cassatt, and John Singer Sargent. The Architecture Archive in the Burnham Library has Daniel H. Burnham material including diaries, office letters, and personal letters; Louis Henri Sullivan material including his manuscript for 'System of Ornament' (with 20 drawings), and correspondence with Charles H. Whitaker and John Van Allen; Frank Lloyd Wright correspondence concerning a bank in Dwight, IL; a business letter book, a scrapbook, and two small sketchbooks of Howard Van Doren Shaw; Edward H. Bennett papers; and materials concerning the World's Columbian Exposition of 1893, including photographs, Burnham's final report as Director of Work, and a letter book of McKim, Mead, and White.

There is also a major collection of architectural drawings and blueprints from the offices of Burnham and Root; D.H. Burnham and Company; Adler and Sullivan; Louis H. Sullivan; Tallmadge and Watson; and other Chicago architects. Also held are 39 microfilm reels containing architectural drawings of early buildings in the Chicago area and documents concerning them, and 18,640 mounted

photographs of architecture. Illuminated
medieval and Renaissance manuscripts are
housed in the Institute's Department of
Prints and Drawings.

Research Fields: Manuscripts, letters, architectural
drawings, and photographs pertaining to
the visual fine arts and to architecture.

Address: Michigan Avenue at Adams Street
Chicago, IL 60603

J54. AUBURN-CORD-DUESENBERG MUSEUM

Collections: Antique and classic cars; radios;
photographs; clothing exhibit; literature
and memorabilia on those cars manufactured
in or associated with the city of Auburn,
Indiana.

Research Fields: Automobile manufacturing operations based
in Auburn, Ind., from 1900 to 1937.

Address: 1600 S. Wayne Street
Auburn, IN 46706.

J55. BALZEKAS MUSEUM OF LITHUANIAN CULTURE

Collections: Lithuanian memorabilia; numismatics;
philately; Lithuanian hagiology; rare
books and maps; textiles; armor and
antique weapons; United States presidents;
genealogy; Lithuanian art; folklore;
ethnology; costumes; amber exhibit.

Research Fields: Lithuanian history; Lithuanians in
America; photographs.

Address: 4012 Archer Avenue
Chicago, IL 60632

J56. BELLE ISLE NATURE CENTER

Collections: Natural science artifacts

Research Fields: Urban ecology

Address: Belle Isle Park
                      Detroit, MI   48207

J57. BISHOP HILL HERITAGE ASSOCIATION

    Collections: Artifacts of Bishop Hill Colony.
                      Historic buildings include: 1857
                      blacksmith shop; 1853 Bishop Hill colony
                      stone; 1854 steeple; 1855 hospital; 1882
                      barn.

    Research Fields: History of Swedish emmigration; history
                      of Bishop Hill colony.

    Address: P.O. Box 1853
                      Bishop Hill, IL   61419

J58. BOWLING GREEN STATE UNIVERSITY

    Collections: Materials on the history of nineteenth
                      century northwestern Ohio counties;
                      records of county and municipal govern-
                      ments, churches, businesses, railroads,
                      and voluntary and charitable associations.
                      The Center also maintains an extensive
                      Great Lakes collection of photographs,
                      diaries, ships' logs, correspondence,
                      shipbuilding records, and port development
                      materials.

    Research Fields: Manuscripts, archives, visual documents,
                      audible documents, non-current machine-
                      readable records, and microforms relating
                      to the nineteenth century northwestern
                      Ohio counties within the collecting scope
                      of this institution.

    Address: 5th Floor, University Library
                      Bowling Green, OH   43403

J59. BUFFALO AND ERIE COUNTY HISTORICAL SOCIETY

    Collections: Papers relating chiefly to Buffalo and
                      the Niagara frontier with special emphasis
                      on military and Great Lakes history.

    Research Fields: Buffalo and the Niagara frontier.

    Address: 25 Nottingham Court
                      Buffalo, NY   14216

J60. BUFFALO AND ERIE COUNTY PUBLIC LIBRARY

Collections: The collection contains some 2,000
                      letters and literary manuscripts,
                      representing many of the most eminent
                      authors of 19th century America and Great
                      Britain. Among the more significant
                      manuscripts are Mark Twain's "Huckleberry
                      Finn," Ralph Waldo Emerson's
                      "Representative Men," and Elbert Hubbard's
                      "A Message to Garcia." The modern local
                      authors collection includes manuscripts by
                      Taylor Caldwell, Julius W. Pratt, Sloan
                      Wilson, and many others. There are also
                      local history materials, including church
                      and organization records and a large
                      quantity of genealogical materials.

Research Fields: American and local authors and artists.

Address: Lafayette Square
                      Buffalo, NY 14203

J61. BURPEE ART MUSEUM/ROCKFORD ART ASSOCIATION

Collections: 19th and 20th century American and
                      European paintings, sculpture, graphics,
                      and decorative arts; American impression-
                      ists and Taos Society of Artists collec-
                      tions; Arnold Gilbert collection of photo-
                      graphs.

Research Fields: 19th and 20th century American painting

Address: 737 Main Street
                      Rockford, IL 61103

J62. BURPEE MUSEUM OF NATURAL HISTORY

Collections: Natural history; zoology; geology;
                      science; paleontology; mineralogy;
                      archaeology; anthropology; American
                      Indian; herpetology; herbarium; handcarved
                      black and cherry woodwork.

Research Fields: Related to the collections.

Address: 813 N. Main Street
                      Rockford, IL 61103

J63. THE CAMBRIDGE GLASS MUSEUM

Collections: Over 4,000 pieces of Cambridge glass made from 1902 to 1954; 100 pieces of Cambridge art pottery made from 1901 to 1923.

Research Fields: Glass and pottery

Address: 812 Jefferson Avenue
                      Cambridge, OH 43725

J64. THE CANTON ART INSTITUTE

Collections: American, Italian and Spanish paintings; 18th and 19th century English and American portraiture; 20th century national and regional art graphics; sculpture decorative arts; costumes; art objects.

Research Fields: Related to collections

Address: 1001 Market Avenue, N.
                      Canton, OH 44702

J65. CARNEGIE LIBRARY OF PITTSBURGH

Collections: Materials relating chiefly to Pittsburgh and western Pennsylvania, with special focus on the period 1791-1906, when Pittsburgh was a military supply base, and including papers relating to the Whiskey Rebellion.

Research Fields: Pennsylvania history

Address: 4400 Forbes Avenue
                      Pittsburgh, PA 15213

J66. CASE WESTERN RESERVE UNIVERSITY

Collections: Materials relating to science and technology, especially the papers of individuals and organizations, 1850 to the present. Many materials focus on developments in the Cleveland area.

Research Fields: The University's academic programs, with particular emphasis on the history of science and technology.

Address: 11161 East Blvd.
                   Cleveland, OH 44106

J67. CENTER FOR RESEARCH LIBRARIES

      Collections: Humanities and social sciences

      Research Fields: Research materials as required by member
                         libraries

      Address: 5721 Cottage Grove Avenue
                         Chicago, IL 60637

J68. CENTER OF SCIENCE AND INDUSTRY OF THE FRANKLIN COUNTY
      HISTORICAL SOCIETY

      Collections: Industry; marine; medicine; mineralogy;
                         science; history technology.

      Research Fields: Industry; marine, medicine, planetarium;
                         science, history.

      Address: 280 E. Broad Street
                         Columbus, OH 43215

J69. CENTRAL MICHIGAN UNIVERSITY

      Collections: Collections relating to the history and
                         culture of Michigan, the Northwest
                         Territory, and the Great Lakes area.
                         Included are records and papers of
                         organization, businesses, military and
                         political figures, pioneer settlers,
                         literary artists, religious figures, and
                         families and individuals; unpublished
                         memoirs and histories; and collections of
                         ephemera and audio-visual materials.

      Research Fields: Michigan, the Northwest Territory, and
                         the Great Lakes area.

      Address: Clarke Historical Library
                         Mt. Pleasant, MI 48859

J70. CHICAGO ARCHITECTURE FOUNDATION

      Collections: Glesner House: original Isaac Scott
                         furniture and drawings, original H.H.
                         Richardson furniture, decorative objects

and photographs owned by the Glessner family.

Research Fields: Chicago architecture; urban planning and design; Prairie Avenue Historic District; Richardson; Glessner family; Clarke family; decorative arts 1830-1900; Greek Revival architecture in the Midwest.

Address: 1800 S. Prairie Avenue
                      Chicago, IL 60616

J71. CHICAGO BOTANIC GARDEN

Collections: Midwest and other botanical species

Research Fields: Botany; horticulture

Address: P.O. Box 400
                      Glencoe, IL 60022

J72. CHICAGO HISTORICAL SOCIETY

Collections: Chicago and Illinois history; Civil War; Lincoln; Americal folk art, costumes, prints, broadsides and maps; photographs; pre-1865 city views; printed books; decorative arts; graphics; manuscripts; paintings and sculpture.

Research Fields: Chicago and Illinois history; urban history; history of American costume, Lincoln, Civil War.

Address: Clark Street at North Avenue
                      Chicago, IL 60614

J73. THE CHICAGO PUBLIC LIBRARY

Collections: Autograph specimens of prominent 19th and 20th century literary and art figures; Materials relating to Ralph G. Newman, Nathan Leopold, Otto Eisenschiml, the World's Columbian Exposition, the Goodman Theatre of the Art Institute of Chicago; the Civil War; Carl Sandburg; and manuscript maps of Chicago. The Chicago Public Library Archives includes blueprints, financial records,

correspondence, photographs, scrapbooks,
and publications. There are also reports
of the Subversive Activities Control
Board, and graphic material, including
cartoons of John T. McCutcheon.

Research Fields: Material on the World's Columbian
Exposition of 1893; material from the
Goodman Theatre files and family of
Kenneth Sawyer Goodman; and historical
documents relating to the history of
libraries in Chicago. Civil War diaries,
correspondence, rosters; typescripts and
annotated galley proofs of works by
Chicago authors; and Carl Sandburg
correspondence.

Address: 425 North Michigan Avenue
Chicago, IL 60611

J74. CHICAGO PUBLIC LIBRARY CULTURAL CENTER

Collections: Grand Army of the Republic Memorial Hall
and Collections, Old War military equip-
ment; documents; photographs; musical
instruments; permanent art collection;
contemporary works; World War I & II
posters.

Research Fields: Civil War including regimental histories
and official records of the war;
Chicagoans in Special Collections
Division; other fields to appropriate
library divisions.

Address: Washington Street
Chicago, IL 60602

J75. CHICAGO THEOLOGICAL SEMINARY

Collections: Records of individual Midwest congregational churches. Included are reports
of synods of Evangelical and Reformed
churches, especially in the Midwest;
reports of the American Board of
Commissioners for Foreign Missions; and
yearbooks of the Congregational ministers,
and the records of the Chicago Community
Renewal Society.

Research Fields: Midwest Congregationalism; personal
                    papers of theological faculty members;
                    Congregational church merger papers.

Address: 5757 South University Avenue
                    Chicago, IL 60637

J76. CHICAGO ZOOLOGICAL PARK (BROOKFIELD ZOO)

Collections: Dolphinarium; aviary; herpetology; art
                    and photo exhibits; films; slides; photos;
                    animal medicine; natural history; nature
                    center; animal preservation project;
                    science; pathology.

Research Fields: Animal behavior; functional morphology
                    of animals; pathology; evolution.

Address: 8400 W. 31st Street
                    Brookfield, IL 60513

J77. CHILDREN'S MUSEUM (Detroit)

Collections: Ethnology; history; science; folk arts;
                    costumes; textiles; dolls; toys; musical
                    instruments related to school
                    curriculum.

Research Fields: Ethnic studies

Address: 67 East Kirby
                    Detroit, MI 48202

J78. THE CHILDREN'S MUSEUM (Indianapolis)

Collections: Archaeology; ethnology; geology; history;
                    natural history; palentology; transpor-
                    tation with exhibits on railroading;
                    natural acience; physical science; pre-
                    history; emergence of man; ancient Egypt,
                    Africa, Eskimos, Native Americans,
                    Americana; cabinetmaking; wheeled
                    vehicles; operating Dentzel carousel;
                    operating toy train layout; antique toy
                    trains; model trains; toys; dolls.

Research Fields: History of childhood

Address: 3000 N. Meridian Street
                    Indianapolis, IN 46208

J79. CINCINNATI ART MUSEUM

    Collections: Records of the Cincinnati Art Museum and
                          photographs pertaining to art.

    Research Fields: Manuscripts, photographs, biographical
                          information, clippings, and exhibition
                          information on artists who have lived or
                          worked in Cincinnati.

    Address: Eden Park
                          Cincinnati, OH 45202

J80. CINCINNATI HISTORICAL SOCIETY

    Collections: History; manuscripts, as well as a
                          collection of personal and family papers,
                          institutional records, photographs and
                          motion pictures dealing with all aspects
                          of American history, with primary emphasis
                          on Cincinnati and the surrounding area.

    Research Fields: Local history; Southwest Ohio; Old
                          Northwest Territory

    Address: Eden Park
                          Cincinnati, OH 45202

J81. CINCINNATI MUSEUM OF NATURAL HISTORY

    Collections: Anthropology; archaeology; conchology;
                          entomology; ethnology; geology;
                          mineralogy; paleontology; archaeology;
                          ornithology; herpetology.

    Research Fields: Archaelogy; arachnology; orinthology;
                          ethnology

    Address: 1720 Gilbert Avenue
                          Cincinnati, OH 45202

J82. WILLIAM L. CLEMENTS LIBRARY, UNIVERSITY OF MICHIGAN

    Collections: 350 collections, chiefly of British and
                          American materials relating to the
                          colonial and Revolutionary War periods,
                          the War of 1812, and other aspects of
                          American history, including the anti-
                          slavery movement and the Civil War. There

are also collections pertaining to Latin American history, including some dating as early as 1542.

Research Fields: Americana 1500-1865; American sheet music in manuscript, prior to 1900.

Address: South University Avenue
                   Ann Arbor, MI 48109

J83. CLEVELAND HEALTH EDUCATION MUSEUM

Collections: Robert L. Dickenson collection on human reproduction; anatomy and physiology.

Research Fields: Physiology; environmental health.

Address: 8911 Euclid Avenue
                   Cleveland, OH 44106

J84. CLEVELAND MUSEUM OF ART

Collections: Art from all cultures and periods; paintings; sculpture; graphics; arts; music; numismatics; textiles; photography.

Research Fields: Paintings; sculpture; graphics; decorative arts; music; numismatic; textiles; photography.

Address: 11150 East Blvd.
                   Cleveland, OH 44106

J85. CLEVELAND MUSEUM OF NATURAL HISTORY

Collections: 70-foot Haplocanthosaurus; 37-foot Allosauras; Johnston mastodon; Dunkleosteus, armored fish of the Devonian period; prehistoric Ohio & other North American Indian cultures; formation of 4 1/2 billion year history of the earth, plants, mammals, birds and insects of Ohio; paleontology; entomology; geology; mineralogy; zoology herbarium; ethnology; archaeology; anthropology; medical arboretology; astronomy; botany; decorative arts; herpetology; aviary; fossil man.

Research Fields: Ornithology; botany; paleontology;
                       archeology; entomology; physical
                       anthropology; herpetology; ecology.

Address: University Circle
                       Cleveland, OH 44106

J86. CLEVELAND PUBLIC LIBRARY

Collections: Records of the Cleveland Public Library;
                       folklore materials collected by Newbell N.
                       Puckett; over 15,000 photographs of
                       Cleveland in the 19th and 20th centuries;
                       and over 135,000 items, primarily
                       photographs, relating to the theater and
                       motion pictures.

Research Fields: Cleveland history

Address: 325 Superior Avenue
                       Cleveland, OH 44114

J87. CONNER PRAIRIE PIONEER SETTLEMENT

Collections: Historic buildings; 1836, Central Indiana
                       rural settlement with houses, store,
                       blacksmith ship, pottery, carpenter shop,
                       school house, barns and other out-
                       buildings; farmstead with two cabins, barn
                       and supporting structures; loomhouse;
                       second school relating to the Midwest,
                       central Indiana, Hamilton County, and the
                       Conner family in the 19th century.
                       History, social life, folklore and folk-
                       life, commerce, music, and agriculture are
                       among topics of interest.

Research Fields: Pioneer life and architecture 1820-1850.
                       Also a collection of manuscripts relating
                       to central Indiana and two of its early
                       settlers, John and William Conner, includ-
                       ing Conner family papers and genealogical
                       data, as well as ledgers, correspondence,
                       photographs and other materials.

Address: 13400 Allisonville Road
                       Noblesville, IN 46060

J88. CORNELL UNIVERSITY

Collections: Literary papers and manuscripts, letters
                      and diaries of writers, and other related
                      materials, chiefly of the 19th and 20th
                      centuries.

Research Fields: Modern literature

Address: Department of Rare Books
                      Ithaca, NY 14855

J89. CORNELL UNIVERSITY LIBRARIES

Collections: Over 8,000,000 manuscript items and
                      32,000 collective bargaining agreements,
                      plus other materials relating to indus-
                      trial and labor relations. Included are
                      the records of 6 national labor unions, 5
                      New York State labor organizations,
                      several labor education and labor legis-
                      lation groups, and individuals with
                      significant careers in industrial and
                      labor relations. Principal subject areas
                      represented include New York State
                      industrial relations, labor education,
                      arbitration, labor legislation, rail
                      transportation, public employment, the
                      garment industry, and the history of the
                      National Labor Relations Board.

Research Fields: Union records; management records related
                      to industrial relations; personal papers
                      of individuals related to the labor
                      movement or active in labor and industrial
                      relations, management theory, and
                      personnel theory; and oral history
                      materials. Particularly interested in New
                      York State based groups.

Address: 144 Ives Hall
                      Ithaca, NY 14850

J90. CORNELL UNIVERSITY LIBRARIES

Collections: More than 6,000 collections relating to
                      Cornell University and to United States
                      history, both domestic and foreign,
                      especially in the 19th and 20th centuries.
                      There is also extensive documentation
                      relating to upstate New York. Holdings

include individuals' papers and organization records, as well as audio tape recordings, photographs and architectural drawings.

Research Fields: Cornell University, upstate New York, and U.S. agriculture, political activities, architecture and planning, medical services, land utilization, and family photography.

Address: 101 Olin Library
                    Ithaca, NY 14853

J91. CRANBROOK INSTITUTE OF SCIENCE

Collections: Mineralogy; anthropology; zoology; botany; geology.

Research Fields: Limnology; botany; ornithology; anthropology; education; herpetology.

Address: 500 Lone Pine Road
                    Bloomfield Hills, MI 48013

J92. ROBERT CROWN CENTER FOR HEALTH EDUCATION

Collections: Human biology and physiology; human growth and development; audio-visual animated exhibits on the brain, nervous system, reproduction, circulatory and other systems.

Research Fields: Human biology and physiology.

Address: 21 Salt Creek Lane
                    Hinsdale, IL 60521

J93. DEARBORN HISTORICAL MUSEUM

Collections: A collection of manuscripts, archives, history files, maps, photographs, and oral history tapes and transcripts related to all aspects of Dearborn history. Included is information on buildings and residences, business and industry, churches, and organizatons, education, events, families and genealogies, government, streets, roads, bridges, and

transportation. There is a special
emphasis on the Arsenal-Commandant's
Quarters and the McFadden-Ross House. The
collection also includes extensive
materials on Henry Dearborn, the city's
namesake.

Research Fields: Dearborn history

Address: 915 Brady Street
                   Dearborn, MI   48124

J94. EUGENE V. DEBS HOME

Collections: Furnished as it was when Debs occupied
                   it; mementos of his campaigns for
                   Presidency; other memorabilia.

Research Fields: Labor history

Address: 451 N. Eighth Street
                   Terre Haute, IN   47807

J95. DEERE & COMPANY

Collections: Financial records, correspondence,
                   minutes, reports, house organs, news
                   releases, product information, policy
                   statements, and pictorial material
                   relating to the worldwide operations of
                   Deere & Company and any of its
                   acquisitions. Personal papers of John
                   Deere and his descendants and items
                   relating to the development of the
                   agricultural implement industry in the
                   United States and the history of the
                   Quad-City area are also held.

Research Fields: Deere & Company; development of agri-
                   cultural implement industry in U.S.

Address: John Deere Road
                   Moline, IL   61265

J96. DETROIT HISTORICAL MUSEUM

Collections: Detroit   or Michigan related social,
                   cultural, urban, industrial, military and
                   Great Lakes maritime history; streets of

old Detroit; period rooms from 1840 to 1905; costumes; decorative arts; furniture, regional, pioneer and colonial arts and crafts; tools; transportation & automotive items; ethnic exhibits.

Research Fields: Urban, social, industrial, architectural, military and marine history.

Address: 5401 Woodward Avenue
                      Detroit, MI 48202

J97. THE DETROIT INSTITUTE OF ARTS

Collections: European, modern and ancient art; decorative arts; graphic arts; American art; Oriental art; theatre arts; textiles; Near-Eastern art; French-Canadian art; period rooms; African, Oceania & New World culture and art.

Research Fields: All objects of art in permanent collection.

Address: 5200 Woodward Avenue
                      Detroit, MI 48202

J98. DETROIT PUBLIC LIBRARY

Collections: The Burton Historical Collection at the Library includes over 6,500 linear feet of letters, papers, ledgers, and other documents relating to the history of Detroit, Michigan, and the Old Northwest, including papers of pioneers, officeholders, businesspersons, traders, and organizations, as well as non-current records of the city and county. Other collections include papers and photographs regarding black music and musicians, literature, fine arts, and automotive history.

Research Fields: The history of the Old Northwest, Michigan, and Detroit; automotive history; black music and musicians, and fine arts.

Address: 5201 Woodward Avenue
                      Detroit, MI 48202

J99. DISCOVERY HALL MUSEUM

Collections: Studebaker Historic Vehicle Collection of
                      carriages, wagons and automobiles;
                      products manufactured in South Bend and
                      Mishawaka, IN, from 1830 to the present.

Research Fields: South Bend area industrial and commercial
                      history.

Address: 120 S. St. Joseph Street
                      South Bend, IN 46601

J100. DOSSIN GREAT LAKES MUSEUM

Collections: Ship models; paintings; antique and
                      modern nautical photographs; information
                      files of Great Lakes ships.

Research Fields: Great Lakes history and culture.

Address: Belle Isle
                      Detroit, MI 48022

J101. DUSABLE MUSEUM OF AFRICAN AMERICAN HISTORY

Collections: African, Afro-American art; memorabilia;
                      historical artifacts.

Research Fields: African & African-American History;
                      Chicago & Illinois history.

Address: 740 E. 56th Place
                      Chicago, IL 60637

J102. ELMHURST HISTORICAL MUSEUM

Collections: Local history artifacts; manuscripts;
                      literature on local history; photographs;
                      slides; history of town and citizens.

Research Fields: Northern Illinois history.

Address: 120 E. Park
                      Elmhurst, IL 60126

J103. EPISCOPAL DIOCESE OF CHICAGO

Collections: Records of the parishes, chapels, missions, schools, charitable institutions, organizations and guilds of the Episcopal Church in Illinois, especially in the Diocese of Chicago. Included are diocesan Journals of Convention, annual reports, and statistics. There is also correspondence of the former bishops of the diocese; biographical items concerning bishops, priests, deacons, deaconesses, members of religious orders and laity; and items concerned with the formation of the Reformed Episcopal Church.

Research Fields: American church history, especially relating to the Episcopal Church nationally or regionally; Illinois church history; Chicago church history; civil groups, church-state relations, inter-church relations, abortion, penal reform, women's liberation, gay liberation, drug problems, alcoholism, and pornography.

Address: 65 East Huron Street
                      Chicago, IL   60611

J104. EVANSTON ENVIRONMENTAL ASSOCIATION

Collections: Natural history of region; history of Grosse Pointe Lighthouse; maritime history; native wildflowers; energy conservation; wind generators. Historic Building: 1874, Grosse Pointe Lighthouse Station.

Research Fields: Maritime history; natural landscaping, interpretive services, solar greenhouse, environmental studies, alternate energy systems.

Address: 2024 McCormick Blvd.
                      Evanston, IL   60201

J105. EVANSTON HISTORICAL SOCIETY

    Collections: General Charles G. Dawes memorabilia; historical Evanston artifacts; archival material; extensive costume collection, photograph and newspaper archives.

    Research Fields: Genealogical; Evanston history and architecture.

    Address: 225 Greenwood Street
                           Evanston, IL 60201

J106. EVANSVILLE MUSEUM OF ARTS AND SCIENCE

    Collections: Painting; sculpture; prints and drawings; decorative arts; transportation; arms and armor; steam locomotive and cars; R.R. station; science displays including anthropology, natural history and geology.

    Research Fields: Related to collections.

    Address: 411 S.E. Riverside Drive
                           Evansville, IN 47713

J107. FIELD MUSEUM OF NATURAL HISTORY

    Collections: Anatomy; anthropology; archaeology; archives; botany; costumes; entomology; ethnology; geology; herbarium; herpetology; Indian; mineralogy; natural history; paleontology; science; textiles; zoology.

    Research Fields: Archaeology; botany; geology; zoology; anthropology.

    Address: Roosevelt Road at Lake Shore Dr.
                           Chicago, IL 60605

J108. THE FIRESTONE TIRE & RUBBER COMPANY

    Collections: Personal papers and records of Harvey S. Firestone and his family, and his business papers from the founding of the company to his death in 1938; business correspondence, speeches, photographs, and other materials of Harvey S. Firestone, Jr. (1920-73); and non-current company records of archival value.

Research Fields: Company advertising; Public Relations Department information on personnel changes, new plants, new products, and price increases, and proofs of magazine advertisements.

Address: 2930 West Market Street
Akron, OH

Mailing Address:
1200 Firestone Parkway
Akron, OH 44317

J109. HENRY FORD MUSEUM AND GREENFIELD VILLAGE

Collections: Personal papers and business files of Henry Ford; records from offices of the Ford Motor Company, as well as subsidiary companies and companies owned by Henry Ford. Company records include information on production, public operations, international operations, organization, and administration. There are also personal papers of individuals associated with Henry Ford or the company, as well as nearly 400,000 photographs and 400 oral histories.

Research Fields: Henry Ford and family; Ford Motor Company; Ford non-automotive enterprises; related non-Ford automotive history of driving conditions and vehicles in use.

Address: 20990 Oakwood Avenue
Dearborn, MI 48121

J110. FORT WAYNE MUSEUM OF ART

Collections: 19th and 20th century American & European prints and paintings; pioneer painters of Indiana; Japanese woodcuts; West African sculpture; Medieval and ancient sculpture; Weatherhead and Tannenbaum contemporary art; Fairbanks print collection; 19th and 20th century Theime and Hamilton collections of prints and paintings;

Ashcan & Regionalist schools; contemporary art; Japanese prints; African arts; American Indian basketry; antiquities.

Research Fields: Parallel to collections

Address: 311 E. Main Street
                    Fort Wayne, IN 46802

J111. FORT WAYNE PUBLIC LIBRARY

Collections: The Cocks Collection relating to the history of the motion picture industry, containing 10,000 stills, autographed pictures of movie stars, promotional material, sample film contracts, booking records, and profit and loss records.

Research Fields: American motion picture history; Indiana

Address: 900 Webster Street
                    Fort Wayne, IN 46802

J112. GARRETT-EVANGELICAL THEOLOGICAL SEMINARY

Collections: Correspondence, lecture notes and other papers of the faculty of the Garrett Biblical Institute; sermons, correspondence and journals of early Methodist preachers in the Midwest; papers of Methodist bishops; and research materials on Mormons and polygamous marriage.

Research Fields: Methodist Episcopal Church, the Methodist Church, and the United Methodist Church.

Address: 2121 Sheridan Road
                    Evanston, IL 60201

J113. GOODYEAR TIRE & RUBBER COMPANY

Collections: A collection of materials relating to the formation, history and growth of the Goodyear Tire & Rubber Company. There are also some materials on Charles Goodyear, one of the discoverers of the process of vulcanization.

Research Fields: Materials relating to the Goodyear
                    Company.

Address: 1144 East Market Street
                    Akron, OH 44316

J114. GRAND RAPIDS PUBLIC MUSEUM

Collections: Furniture; decorative arts c. 1830-1930;
                    birds of Western Michigan; Hopewell
                    archaeological material; history; eth-
                    nology; geology; archaeology; costumes;
                    Indian artifacts; paleontology; natural
                    history; Michigan mammals in habitat
                    settings. Historic buildings: 1836,
                    Calkins Law Office; 1869, Stilwill
                    Horseshoe Shop, 1853, Star Schoolhouse;
                    1879, historic site; Norton Indian Mounds
                    (Hopewell).

Research Fields: Paleontology and Michigan History

Address: 54 Jefferson
                    Grand Rapids, MI 49503

J115. GREAT LAKES HISTORICAL SOCIETY MUSEUM

Collections: Great Lakes ship models; paintings;
                    photographs; marine artifacts and relics;
                    marine engines; yachting and racing
                    artifacts.

Research Fields: Shipping and passenger vessels on the
                    Great Lakes; ship wrecks on the Great
                    Lakes.

Address: 480 Main Street
                    Vermillion, OH 44089

J116. THE JEROME J. GREENE HERBARIA

Collections: 250,000 speciments; Greene collection of
                    Western and Middle Atlantic state plants;
                    Nieuwland collections of Midwestern
                    plants.

Research Fields: Plant taxonomy; plant geography; ecology.

Address: University of Notre Dame
                    Notre Dame, IN 46556

J117. GREENTOWN GLASS MUSEUM, INC.

Collections: Glassware manufactured by the Indiana
                      Tumbler & Goblet Co. of Greentown from
                      1894 to 1903; Chocolate glass from other
                      factories poured by Jacob Rosenthal,
                      developer of chocolate glass at Greentown;
                      tools and materials used in the making of
                      glassware.

Research Fields: History of the town at the time of the
                      glassworks; history of the glassworks and
                      the people working there; glassware poured
                      at the Indiana Tumbler and Goblet Co.

Address: 112 N. Meridian
                      Greentown, IN 46936

J118. RUTHERFORD B. HAYES LIBRARY

Collections: Rutherford B. Hayes family and
                      northeastern Ohio materials.

Research Fields: Rutherford B. Hayes and to other 19th
                      century individuals in political, civil,
                      or military life; and materials relating
                      to state and local history, especially
                      Fremont and the Sandusky Valley, and to
                      existing special collections: the
                      Frohman Theatre Collection, a Great Lakes
                      collection, and a collection on William
                      Dean Howells.

Address: 1337 Hayes Avenue
                      Fremont, OH 43420

J119. HAYES REGIONAL ARBORETUM

Collections: One specimen of each species of native
                      woody plant indigenous to the Whitewater
                      Drainage Basin of Indiana and Ohio; 1833
                      dairy barn.

Research Fields: Arboricultural; botanical; taxonomical;
                      solar energy

Address: 801 Elks Road
                      Richmond, IN 47374

J120. THE HICKORIES MUSEUM OF THE LORAIN COUNTY HISTORICAL SOCIETY

Collections: Antique pattern glass; John Monteith book
                       collection; old school suplies & antique
                       toys; genealogy; costumes; Indian;
                       agriculture; Victorian furnishings.
                       Historic buildings: 1837, The Sally
                       Bronson House; 1837-68, The Thomas W.
                       Laundon House, Elyria; 1894-95, The
                       Hickories, Elyria; 1909, The Lorain
                       Lighthouse, Lorain.

Research Fields: Genealogy and local history archives.

Address: 509 Washington Avenue
                       Elyria, OH 44035

J121. HISTORIC LANDMARKS FOUNDATION OF INDIANA

Collections: Period furnishings; paintings by early
                       Indian artists.

Research Fields: Victorian decorative arts; architecture
                       of Indiana; restoration and perservation
                       techniques; community conservation;
                       historic buildings survey.

Address: 3402 Boulevard Place
                       Indianapolis, IN 46208

J122. HISTORIC NEW HARMONY INC.

Collections: 1814-1834 house museums of the Harmonist
                       and Owen periods; geological and natural
                       science collections of the earliest
                       geological surveys.

Research Fields: Geology; archaeology; decorative arts

Address: Church & West Streets
                       New Harmony, IN 46731

J123. HISTORICAL SOCIETY OF DES PLAINES

Collections: Furnishings; items of local significance;
                       costumes; photography, pioneer tools

Research Fields: History of city of Des Plaines and Maine
                       township, Cook County, Illinois

Address: 789 Pearson
                        Des Plaines, IL   60016

J124. HUDDLESTON FARMHOUSE INN MUSEUM

   Collections: Farmhouse; outbuildings complex; farm
                        implements; Huddleston family records

   Research Fields: Architectural history; local history;
                        perservation technology

   Address: U.S. Route 40 West
                        Cambridge City, IN   47327

J125. ILLINOIS AND MICHIGAN CANAL MUSEUM

   Collections: Artifacts; pictures; documents relevant
                        to the history of the Canal; log cabin;
                        root cellar; village jail, blacksmith
                        shop; tinsmith shop; workshop; railroad
                        station; one room country school.

   Research Fields: History and genealogy.

   Address: 803 S. State Street
                        Lockport, IL   60441

J126. ILLINOIS STATE ARCHIVES SPRINGFIELD, ILLINOIS

   Collections: Records from all branches of Illinois
                        territorial and State governments, such as
                        gubernatorial correspondence; journals,
                        committee reports, and laws of the General
                        Assembly, and 5,000 cubic feet of Illinois
                        Supreme Court case files, 1820-1936. Also
                        included are records of land grants to
                        early French, British, and American
                        settlers in Illinois and all records of
                        initial Federal and State land sales in
                        Illinois; as well as materials concerning
                        the planning, financing, and construction
                        of the Illinois and Michigan Canal; the
                        organization and development of State
                        financial institutions; the establishment
                        and administration of State mental, penal,
                        and educational institutions; and the
                        planning and construction of State
                        buildings and public works.

There are also materials from all six
State constitutional conventions; territorial and State population censuses,
1818-65; schedules for Illinois of U.S.
censuses of agriculture, manufacturing,
mortality, and social statistics, 1850-80,
and population, 1880; military records of
Illinois residents' participation in the
Black Hawk, Mexican, Civil, Spanish-
American, and Korean Wars, and World Wars
I and II; and reports filed with the
Secretary of State and the Auditor of
Public Accounts by banks, savings and loan
associations, and profit and non-profit
corporations. The Archives Division also
holds all unpublished material and
research data gathered by the Illinois
Historical Records Survey of the Work
Projects Administration.

Research Fields: Illinois State and local government;
                     archives of permanent legal,
                     administrative, or research value.

Address: Illinois State Archives
                     Springfield, IL 62706

J127. ILLINOIS STATE HISTORICAL LIBRARY

Collections: The Library has an estimated four million
                     manuscript items, consisting of 200 large
                     collections and over 2,000 small ones.
                     The collections relate to all phases of
                     state history, with most of the items
                     dating from 1818, the year of statehood.
                     Outstanding are holdings relating to
                     Abraham Lincoln and his contemporaries;
                     papers of political leaders, including
                     U.S. Senators and Representatives,
                     governors, legislators, and other state
                     officials; and military collections
                     pertaining to the Black Hawk War and the
                     Civil War. Records of education,
                     religious, business, labor, and social
                     groups are also held.

Research Fields: Illinois, the Midwest, and Abraham
                     Lincoln.

Address: Old State Capitol Building
                     Springfield, IL 62706

J128. INDIANA DEPARTMENT OF NATURAL RESOURCES, DIVISION OF
       MUSEUMS AND MEMORIALS

       Collections: Period furnishings; art; artifacts;
                               natural history specimens; primary source
                               material.

       Research Fields: Indiana natural and cultural history

       Address: 202 N. Alabama Street
                               Indianapolis, IN 46204

J129. INDIANA DUNES NATIONAL LAKESHORE

       Collections: Cultural prehistoric collection; fur
                               trade items; 19th century farming and
                               settlement; natural history; herbarium.
                               Historic structures: 19th century, Bailly
                               Homestead; 19th century, Chelberg Farm;
                               1933, World's Fair Houses.

       Research Fields: Air and water quality; plant and animal
                               ecology.

       Address: 1100 N. Nineral Springs Road
                               Porter, IN 46304

J130. INDIANA HISTORICAL SOCIETY

       Collections: Library of historical books, maps,
                               pictures, broadsides, pamphlets and bound
                               volumes relating to the area of Indiana
                               and the Old Northwest available for use by
                               any responsible researcher on premises.

       Research Fields: Indiana history

       Address: 315 W. Ohio Street
                               Room 350
                               Indianapolis, IN 46202

J131. INDIANA STATE LIBRARY

       Collections: Personal papers and other private
                               materials relating to Indiana, including
                               diaries, correspondence, account books,
                               business and financial records,
                               non-current records of State and local
                               institutions and organizations, a few

manuscript maps and charts, photographs,
oral history tapes and transcripts, and a
few video tapes. Subjects represented are
pioneer settlements and trade with
Indians, the War of 1812, the Mexican War,
the Civil War, politics, social life, and
economic conditions.

Research Fields: All categories of non-government
materials pertaining to Indiana and its
people, with the exception of
architectural engineering and technical
drawings, church records, and genealogical
data.

Address: 140 North Senate Avenue
Indianapolis, IN 46204

J132. INDIANA STATE MUSEUM

Collections: State natural history; Indiana history;
archaeology; botany; zoology; geology;
decorative arts; art and art history of
Indiana, arts and crafts; Indian;
paleontology; art collections by Hoosier
Artists.

Research Fields: Exhibit preparation and accession
purposes; archaeology, geology,
pre-history; history; education.

Address: 202 N. Alabama Street
Indianapolis, IN 46204

J133. INDIANA UNIVERSITY ART MUSEUM

Collections: Ancient Egyptian, Greek, Roman sculpture;
vases; jewelry, and glass; 14th through
20th century European and American
paintings, sculpture, prints, drawings,
decorative arts; African, Oceanian, pre-
Columbian, Japanese, Chinese, S.E. Asian
paintings, sculpture, prints, ceramics,
decorative arts.

Research Fields: Archaeology; numismatics; ancient art

Address: Indiana University
Bloomington, IN 47405

J134. INDIANA UNIVERSITY DEPARTMENT OF FOLKLORE

Collections: Over 30,000 field collections, in
                    typewritten or manuscript form, collected
                    primarily in Indiana, Michigan, Ohio, and
                    Kentucky, providing information on
                    folklore genres and folklore data. In
                    addition to these collections, the
                    Archives also has a large slide and tape
                    collection and copies of dissertations and
                    theses completed in the Folklore
                    Institute.

Research Fields: Folklore and history

Address: 504 North Fess
                    Bloomington, IN 47401

J135. INDIANA UNIVERSITY LIBRARIES

Collections: Over 770 collections covering a wide
                    variety of subjects and most geographical
                    regions of the world; particular emphasis
                    has been placed on 19th and 20th century
                    British and American literature, Latin
                    American history and culture before
                    independence, Indiana history and letters,
                    and U.S. history and politics. Included
                    are diaries, scrapbooks, correspondence,
                    art materials, records of publishing
                    firms, and photographs.

Research Fields: Modern British, French, German, and
                    American literature; Indiana history and
                    letters; and publishing and book selling
                    records. Will also accept materials
                    relevant to general library holdings
                    and/or to University curriculum.

Address: 7th and Jordan
                    Bloomington, IN 47401

J136. INDIANA UNIVERSITY MUSEUM

Collections: 8,000 negatives of the Rodman Wannamaker
                    collections of American Indian photographs
                    taken by Joseph Dixon from 1908 to 1926,
                    and 2,000 photographs covering Indiana and
                    Midwest history.

Research Fields: Photographs of American Indians and of
                    Indiana history subjects; ethnographic

photographs from throughout the world and photographs depicting the history of the Midwest.

Address: Student Building
                    Bloomington, IN 47401

J137. INDIANA UNIVERSITY ORAL HISTORY RESEARCH PROJECT

Collections: 353 oral history interviews, including transcripts, concentrating on 20th century Indiana, and more specifically, the history of local communities, state politics, industry, the legal profession, Indiana University, and experiences in World War I. Interviews not related to Indiana include the black press, environmental groups, and biographies of several public figures.

Research Fields: Oral history recordings concerning any aspect of Indiana's history, with emphasis on the period since 1945.

Address: 405 North Park Avenue
                    Bloomington, IN 47401

J138. INDIANAPOLIS MUSEUM OF ART

Collections: European and American paintings; contemporary art; oriental art; ethnographic art; Clowes Fund Collection; J.M.W. Turner Collection; the W.J. Holliday Collection.

Research Fields: Art and decorative arts history

Address: 1200 W. 38th Street
                    Indianapolis, IN 46208

J139. INTERNATIONAL MUSEUM OF PHOTOGRAPHY AT GEORGE EASTMAN HOUSE

Collections: Materials documenting the history of photography. There are extensive collections of 19th century daguerreotypes, tintypes, and Kodak snapshots; many later photographs; 1,200 letters, diaries, and other manuscripts; and 25 audio recordings of symposia and of interviews with photographers.

Research Fields: Historical photographs relating to the
                    history of aesthetics of photography.

Address: 900 East Avenue
                    Rochester, NY 14607

J140. KALAMAZOO COLLEGE LIBRARY

Collections: Materials relating to the College,
                    1832-1933; the Michigan Baptist State
                    Convention Collection, 1825-1906,
                    letters, pastoral reports, record books of
                    the Convention, and journals and daybooks
                    of missionaries and circuit riders in
                    western Michigan; and correspondence,
                    diaries, manuscript magazine articles, and
                    other papers, 1930-63, such as those of
                    Maynard Owen Williams, chief of the
                    foreign staff of National Geographic
                    Magazine.

Research Fields: College records and Michigan Baptist
                    history

Address: College and Baptist Room
                    Thompson and Academy Streets
                    Kalamazoo, MI 49007

J141. KALAMAZOO PUBLIC LIBRARY

Collections: Records of local churches; area school
                    district minutes; Public Library
                    historical materials; papers of local
                    organizations, such as the Woman's
                    Christian Temperance Union, the Child
                    Welfare League, and the Kalamazoo County
                    Agricultural Society; and letters dealing
                    with the establishment of a woman's
                    professorship at the University of
                    Michigan. There are also several hundred
                    glass negatives (1870-1910) of Kalamazoo
                    people, buildings, and industries; most
                    are identified although not all have
                    prints for examination.

Research Fields: Kalamazoo city, township and county items;
                    personal, club, and governmental items.

Address: 315 South Rose Street
                    Kalamazoo, MI 49006

J142. KALAMAZOO PUBLIC MUSEUM

Collections: Anthropology; history; glass; Egyptology;
                    oriental objects.

Research Fields: State and local history; costume and
                    textiles; history of photography.

Address: 315 S. Rose Street
                    Kalamazoo, MI 49007

J143. KAMPSVILLE ARCHEOLOGICAL MUSEUM

Collections: Archaeological materials describing
                    cultures dating back to 800 BC;
                    reconstructed prehistoric Indian village.

Research Fields: Archaeology research

Address: Highway 100
                    Kampsville, IL 62053

J144. LANDMARK SOCIETY OF WESTERN NEW YORK, INC.

Collections: A collection of photographs, slides,
                    building files, survey books, and
                    drawings, relating to architecture,
                    chiefly in New York State, Rochester, and
                    Monroe County. Included are drawings
                    sponsored by the Historic American
                    Buildings Survey, as well as drawings by
                    Walter Cassebeer and Claude Bragdon.

Research Fields: Architecture, preservation, the
                    decorative arts, and local history in
                    western New York.

Address: 130 Spring Street
                    Rochester, NY 14608

J145. MCKINLEY MUSEUM OF HISTORY, SCIENCE & INDUSTRY

Collections: Health; archives; astronomy; glass;
                    physical science; Streets of Yesteryear;
                    Foucault Pendulum; historic vehicles;
                    canal boat replicas; dolls; toys;
                    Dueber-Hampden watches.

Research Fields: Health education; astronomy; history;
                    science and industry; street of shops.

Address: 749 Hazlett Avenue
                        Canton, OH 44701

J146. MIAMI PURCHASE ASSOCIATION

Collections: Notes, photographs, and research reports
                        concerning historic buildings and
                        neighborhoods in Cincinnati and
                        southwestern Ohio.

Research Fields: Architecture, archaeology, and historic
                        preservation in southwestern Ohio.

Address: 812 Dayton Street
                        Cincinnati, OH 45214

J147. MICHIGAN DEPARTMENT OF STATE

Collections: State of Michigan Archives, including
                        records of the Executive Office, and the
                        offices of the Secretary of State,
                        Attorney General, Auditor General, as
                        well as other departments, commissions,
                        and special legislative study committees.
                        There are also local government records,
                        including county, city, and township
                        materials. Special collections include
                        the personal papers of individuals
                        prominent in Michigan government, as well
                        as maps and visual documents.

Research Fields: State and local public records; private
                        materials which pertain to the State and
                        its government; photographs and maps.

Address: State Archives Unit
                        3405 North Logan Street
                        Lansing, MI 48918

J148. MICHIGAN STATE UNIVERSITY ARCHIVES AND HISTORICAL
      COLLECTIONS

Collections: Holdings of the Historical Collections
                        include a variety of materials relating
                        to individuals, families, businesses, and
                        other organizations, primarily in
                        Michigan in the 19th and 20th centuries.
                        Some 40 groups of Civil War letters are
                        available, as are Biblical and liturgical
                        texts, dating from 1470 to 1927. The

University Archives consists of University records and private papers of individuals connected with the University, including documentation of the university's involvement in overseas educational programs. The Land Grant Research Collections consist mainly of microfilm copies of the papers of the members of Congress and others connected with the land grant movement.

Pictorial records consist of over 30,000 items, many of them relating to campus life and activities of Michigan State University. The Oral History Collection contains materials on University history and a set of interviews relating to lumbering in Michigan.

Research Fields: University records of legal, administrative or historical value; personal papers of the officials, faculty, and alumni of the University, and others; materials relating to such University interests as rural life, engineering, human ecology, the liberal arts, natural science, social science, education, business, communication arts, and human, osteopathic, and veterinary medicine; and research materials on the origins and development of the land-grant philosophy of education.

Address: East Lansing, MI 48824

J149. MIDWEST MUSEUM OF AMERICAN ART

Collections: American Impressionists, Regionalists, Abstract Expression Illustrators; Chicago & Pop Art; prints, drawings, sculpture, photography; works by Albert Bierstadt, Childe Hassam, Robert Reid, Charles Hawthorne, Maurice Prendergast, Ernest Lawson, John Singer Guston, Andrew Wyeth, Grandma Moses, Grant Wood, Thomas Hart Benton.

Research Fields: American folk painting & American Art Movements.

Address: 429 S. Main Street
Elkhart, IN 46515

J150. MOODY BIBLE INSTITUTE

Collections: A manuscript collection of 1,000
                      pieces, comprised mainly of letters of
                      Dwight L. Moody, R.A. Torrey, and James
                      M. Gray. There are also 200 biographical
                      files concerning persons affiliated with
                      the Institute, an extensive photograph
                      collection, and documents relating to the
                      founding of the Institute.

Research Fields: Dwight L. Moody and presidents of the
                      Moody Bible Institute, and the history
                      of the Institute.

Address: 820 North LaSalle Street
                      Chicago, IL   60610

J151. MORTON ARBORETUM

Collections: Botany; horticulture; entomology;
                      herbarium; prairie preservation
                      project.

Research Fields: Botany; entomology; horticulture;
                      pathology; taxonomy, aboriculture.

Address: Route 53
                      Lisle, IL   60532

J152. MUSEUM AT THE BILLY GRAHAM CENTER

Collections: Materials related to the 18th, 19th
                      and 20th century church; emphasis on
                      Evangelism.

Research Fields: American church history; emphasis on
                      Evangalism Revival and missions.

Address: 500 E. Seminary
                      Wheaton, IL   60187

J153. THE MUSEUM, MICHIGAN STATE UNIVERSITY

Collections: Great Lakes history; archaeology;
                      paleontology; folklife; live mammals;
                      agriculture; popular culture.

Research Fields: Vertebrate zoology; vertebrate
                    paleontology; anthropology; folklife;
                    popular culture.

Address: West Circle Drive
                    East Lansing, MI   48824

J154. MUSEUM OF CONTEMPORARY ART

Collections: 20th century painting; sculpture;
                    graphics; photography; mixed media;
                    artist's conceptual works; sound
                    installation.

Research Fields: Modern art

Address: 237 E. Ontario Street
                    Chicago, IL   60611

J155. MUSEUM OF SCIENCE AND INDUSTRY

Collections: Scientific visitor-participation
                    exhibits depicting principles, tech-
                    nological applications and social impli-
                    cations in fields of agriculture,
                    transportation, communications;
                    chemicals; steelmaking; petroleum;
                    photography; aerospace; medicine; natural
                    gas; electricity; nuclear energy; pub-
                    lishing; food; chemistry; physics; and
                    many other fields. Locomotive drawings;
                    documentary materials on the Chicago
                    Century of Progress Exposition (1933-34)
                    and the Chicago Railroad Fair (1950),
                    consisting of architectural blueprints,
                    correspondence, and other material;
                    records of the Huegely Mill of Nashville,
                    as well as ledgers, orders, and corres-
                    pondence reflecting wheat prices and
                    methods of production; and glass slides
                    relating to the history of the Museum of
                    Science and Industry, other science
                    museums, international expositions and
                    various scientific and technical fields
                    (1926-37).

Research Fields: History of science; history of
                    technology.

Address: 57th Street and Lake Shore Drive
                    Chicago, IL   60637

J156. NATIONAL ARCHIVES AND RECORDS SERVICE

Collections: Records of field offices of Federal
                      agencies in Illinois, Indiana, Michigan,
                      Minnesota (except U.S. Court records),
                      Ohio, and Wisconsin. Included are
                      records of the U.S. Circuit and District
                      Courts, the Bureau of Indian Affairs
                      (primarily Wisconsin), and the Army
                      Corps of Engineers.

Research Fields: Federal records within the geographic
                      area of interest of this Federal
                      Archives and Records Center.

Address: 7358 South Pulaski Road
                      Chicago, IL 60629

J157. NATIONAL WOMAN'S CHRISTIAN TEMPERANCE UNION

Collections: Materials from the United States and
                      many other countries, regarding
                      intemperance and related social
                      problems; manuscripts of U.S. and
                      foreign temperance leaders, most notably
                      Frances E. Willard; annual minutes of
                      the National Woman's Christian
                      Temperance Union and other temperance
                      organizations in most of the fifty
                      states; and other temperance
                      organization materials.

Research Fields: Alcohol, narcotics, and tobacco, and
                      documentation of the Prohibition and
                      temperance movements.

Address: 1730 Chicago Avenue
                      Evanston, IL 60201

J158. NEW HARMONY WORKINGMEN'S INSTITUTE

Collections: Papers relating mainly to the New
                      Harmony Community of Equality and to the
                      town of New Harmony. Included are
                      records of organizations; correspondence;
                      diaries and travel accounts from Europe,
                      1805-13, the West Indies, and the United
                      States, 1816-17; and papers of
                      individuals relating to the educational,
                      political and social ideas of the early
                      19th century.

Research Fields: New Harmony and Posey County, IN

Address: Tavern and West Streets
                       New Harmony, IN

J159. THE NORTHERN INDIANA HISTORICAL SOCIETY

Collections: Pioneer items; tools; primitives;
                       china; pottery; glass; mementoes of
                       early South Bend, St. Joseph County;
                       military artifacts; photo collection.

Research Fields: Ethnic contributions to local area;
                       pioneer era; industry; transportation.

Address: 112 S. Lafayette Blvd.
                       South Bend, IN 46601

J160. OBERLIN COLLEGE

Collections: Records relating to Oberlin College and
                       the town of Oberlin. Included are
                       materials on movements with which
                       Oberlin has been associated, such as
                       missions, the antislavery movement, and
                       temperance. There are also personal
                       papers of faculty, graduates, and other
                       Oberlin related individuals; municipal
                       government records of the town of
                       Oberlin; and photographs of the College
                       and the town.

Research Fields: Oberlin College and the town of
                       Oberlin

Address: 420 Mudd Learning Center
                       Oberlin, OH 44074

J161. OHIO HISTORICAL CENTER

Collections: Historical objects, paintings, decor-
                       ative arts, drawings, prints, craft tools
                       and products, textiles, costumes, glass
                       of Ohio and Midwest; pre-Columbian Indian
                       artifacts and art objects; prehistoric
                       archaeology of Midwest; natural history;
                       invertebrates, insects, fish, reptiles,
                       birds, mammals, minerals; industry;
                       military.

Research Fields: Industrial; military; labor; business;
                      politics; archaeology.

Address: Interstate 71 and 17th Avenue
                      Columbus, OH 43211

J162. THE OHIO HISTORICAL SOCIETY

Collections: A collection of manuscripts, state
                      government records, local government
                      records, and audio-visual materials
                      relating to Ohio. Included are the
                      papers of prominent individuals such as
                      Warren G. Harding and Paul Laurence
                      Dunbar, and of institutions such as the
                      Anti-Saloon League of America. The
                      Society is also the official State
                      archives and holds county and municipal
                      records for central Ohio.

Research Fields: Ohio history in general, including
                      archival material, with special emphasis
                      on women's history, black history, and
                      labor history.

Address: I-71 and 17th Avenue
                      Columbus, OH 43211

J163. OLD ECONOMY

Collections: Archives of the Harmony Society, includ-
                      ing religious, business, and personal
                      records, music, correspondence, accounts,
                      legal documents, maps, plans, and other
                      materials concerning the society's
                      activities in Wuertemberg (Germany),
                      Pennsylvania, and Indiana.

Research Fields: Harmony Society

Address: 14th and Church Streets
                      Ambridge, PA 15003

J164. ORIENTAL INSTITUTE MUSEUM, UNIVERSITY OF CHICAGO

Collections: Art and archaeology of the Ancient Near
                      East, Egypt, Assyria, Syria, Cyprus,
                      Palestine, Anatolia, Nubia, Iran, Early
                      Christian, Islamic material.

Research Fields: Ancient Near Eastern archaeology and
                      history, sculpture, decorative arts;
                      Ancient Near Eastern languages; Islamic
                      languages and civilization.

Address: 1155 E. 58th Street
                      Chicago, IL   60637

J165. PENNSYLVANIA HISTORICAL AND MUSEUM COMMISSION

Collections: Primarily records of the executive,
                      legislative, and judicial branches of
                      state and provincial government. Major
                      record groups include records from most
                      departments, boards, and commissions of
                      the executive branch, and records of
                      Pennsylvania's proprietary and
                      Revolutionary War governments. 257
                      manuscript groups contain the records and
                      papers of prominent individuals and
                      families, business concerns, and numerous
                      social, cultural, political, and military
                      organizations, relating to almost every
                      aspect of Pennsylvania history. Included
                      among these records are special
                      collections of maps, posters, postcards,
                      photographs, and motion picture films.

Research Fields: The Commonwealth of Pennsylvania, with
                      particular emphasis on the records of
                      state government; and papers of
                      Pennsylvania governors and other state
                      officials.

Address: Third and Foster Streets
                      William Penn Memorial Museum and Archives
                      Building
                      Harrisburg, PA   17120

J166. POLISH MUSEUM OF AMERICA

Collections: 350 originals of Polish artists;
                      costumes; religious artifacts; Polish
                      military memorabilia; memorabilia of T.
                      Kosciuszko; memorabilia of Paderewski.

Research Fields: Polish culture

Address: 984 N. Milwaukee Avenue
                      Chicago, IL   60622

J167. PRO FOOTBALL HALL OF FAME

Collections: Mementoes from the games and players
                    including equipment, photos, films;
                    material pertinent to the development of
                    pro football in the U.S.; printed game
                    accounts; files on players, games and
                    circumstances contributing to football's
                    growth; artists' work, such as
                    illustrations, photos and paintings.

Research Fields: Professional football history

Address: 2121 Harrison Avenue N.W.
                    Canton, OH 44708

J168. PUBLIC LIBRARY OF CINCINNATI AND HAMILTON COUNTY

Collections: A collection relating chiefly to Ohio
                    and inland water navigation. Included
                    are diaries of inland river captains and
                    pilots; and account books, freight books,
                    landing lists, lock books, logbooks,
                    passenger lists, wharfboat books and
                    logs, photographs, and other records of
                    steamboats, packet lines, and individual
                    boat operators. The collection also
                    includes papers of several Ohio families;
                    papers of political and artistic figures;
                    aerial photographs; and several
                    Renaissance, medieval, and Oriental
                    manuscripts.

Research Fields: Inland rivers

Address: 800 Vine Street
                    Cincinnati, OH 45202

J169. ROCHESTER MUSEUM AND SCIENCE CENTER LIBRARY

Collections: Twelve collections and additional single
                    items relating primarily to the history
                    of the Genesee area. Included are
                    records of several local business firms;
                    letters and other papers of Susan B.
                    Anthony, Freeman Johnson, and Sir William
                    Pulteney; records and papers relating to
                    the Erie and Genesee Valley canals; 19th
                    century account books; Civil War letters
                    and documents; a photograph collection
                    for the period 1900-30; and 19th century
                    police and coroner's records.

Research Fields: Manuscript and audio-visual material
                        relating to the history, natural history
                        and archaeology of the Genesee country
                        with special emphasis on Monroe County
                        and the Rochester area.

Address: 657 East Avenue
                        Rochester, NY

                        Mailing Address:
                        P.O. Box 1480
                        Rochester, NY   14603

J170. ROCHESTER PUBLIC LIBRARY

Collections: A collection of material relating to the
                        history of Rochester and Monroe County,
                        largely from the 19th century. Included
                        are letters, diaries, and journals of
                        early pioneers, account books, a few
                        literary manuscripts, other unpublished
                        manuscripts, manuscript maps, photo-
                        graphs, municipal documents, association
                        records, and genealogical source data.

Research Fields: Western New York

Address: 115 South Avenue
                        Rochester, NY   14604

J171. ROCHESTER UNIVERSITY ORAL HISTORY PROJECT

Collections: Transcripts of interviews with people
                        who have been involved in the labor
                        movement in the Chicago area. A small
                        number of interviews are with people who
                        have immigrated to Chicago or who are
                        involved in the labor movement in other
                        areas.

Research Fields: Labor history; women in the labor
                        movement; and immigration history; family
                        history and Afro-American history.

Address: 430 South Michigan Avenue
                        Chicago, IL   60605

J172. ELIZABETH SAGE HISTORIC COSTUME COLLECTION

Collections: 19th and 20th century Western European &
                    American clothing accessories; ethnic
                    clothing; household textiles.

Research Fields: 19th and 20th century fashions;
                    systematic methods of categorizing &
                    identification of clothing items.

Address: 203 Wylie Hall
                    Indiana University
                    Bloomington, IN 47405

J173. MAURICE SPERTUS MUSEUM OF JUDAICA

Collections: Archives; archaeology; art library;
                    decorative arts; Jewish ceremonial arts;
                    ethnology; folklore; slide library.

Research Fields: Judaica and pertinent decorative arts

Address: 618 S. Michigan Avenue
                    Chicago, IL 60605

J174. SPERTUS COLLEGE OF JUDAICA

Collections: A collection tracing the growth of the
                    Chicago Jewish community, including
                    records of synagogues and of philan-
                    thropic, cultural, social service, and
                    religious organizations, and papers of
                    individuals who contributed to the
                    development of the community.

Research Fields: History of the Chicago Jewish community

Address: 618 South Michigan Avenue
                    Chicago, IL 60605

J175. STATE UNIVERSITY OF NEW YORK

Collections: Items relating chiefly to American artist
                    Charles Burchfield but also containing
                    items relating to other artists from
                    western New York State. Burchfield
                    materials include his writings, note-
                    books, letters, and slides of him and his
                    studio. Notebooks of artist and

teacher George William Eggers also are
represented.

Research Fields: Items pertaining to Charles Burchfield
                     and to outstanding western New York State
                     artists, including architects, sculptors,
                     photographers, and craftspeople; art
                     organizations, movements, critics,
                     collectors, dealers, and schools, both
                     contemporary and historical, in the eight
                     western New York counties.

Address: 1300 Elmwood Avenue
                     Buffalo, NY   14222

J176. STATE UNIVERSITY OF NEW YORK

Collections: A collection relating primarily to
                     Chautauqua County, NY. Included are the
                     Fredonia Academy and Fredonia Normal
                     School cornerstone materials; composer
                     Robert Marvel's manuscript scores;
                     diaries; journals; business account books
                     and ledgers; other music scores; literary
                     manuscripts; aerial photographs of
                     Chautauqua County; other photographs and
                     maps; and oral history tapes relating to
                     the history of the College and to
                     one-room school rural education in
                     Chautauqua County.

Research Fields: Local history, relating to Chautauqua,
                     Cattaragus and Allegany counties in New
                     York State; music materials.

Address: Reed Library
                     Fredonia, NY   14963

J177. STATE UNIVERSITY OF NEW YORK

Collections: Collections relating chiefly to the
                     history of the Genesee River Valley in
                     New York State. Among the materials are
                     the papers of the Wadsworth family,
                     pioneer settlers of the Valley;
                     philanthropist William Pryor Letchworth;
                     architectural historian Carl Schmidt; and
                     the archives of the College.

Research Fields: History of the Genesee Valley, the State
                     University of New York College at
                     Geneseo, and local families.

Address: Milne Library
                      Genesco, NY 14454

J178. SWEDISH AMERICAN HISTORICAL SOCIETY, INC.

Collections: Books; periodicals; manuscripts;
                      microfilm; oral history.

Research Fields: Archives; religion; education;
                      journalism; fine arts; government;
                      science; business; industry from 1840 to
                      present day of Swedes in the United
                      States.

Address: 5125 N. Spaulding Avenue
                      Chicago, IL 60625

J179. SWEDISH AMERICAN MUSEUM ASSOCIATION OF CHICAGO

Collections: Paintings, tools and artifacts describing
                      the emigration of the Swedish people to
                      the United States; special displays
                      featuring famous Swedes in this country;
                      furniture and woodcarvings by Swedish
                      Americans.

Research Fields: Swedish pioneer life; contributions of
                      Swedes to development of America.

Address: 5248 Clark Street
                      Chicago, IL 60640

J180. THE TIME MUSEUM

Collections: 2,500 timepieces dating from 2800 B.C. to
                      present, displaying the chronological
                      development of timekeeping devices.

Research Fields: History of horology

Address: 7801 E. State Street
                      Rockford, IL 61125

J181. TOLEDO-LUCAS COUNTY PUBLIC LIBRARY

Collections: Personal papers, organization records,
                      and other materials, relating chiefly to
                      the development of the Toledo area.

Collections focus on pioneer history, the War of 1912, the Civil War, and 19th and early 20th century urban development. Progressive reform materials, including the papers of Samuel "Golden Rule" Jones, are of special interest. 3,000 photographs and some 19th century manuscript maps document urban growth. About 35 oral history interviews relate to social ethnic, industrial, and black history of the Maumee Valley area.

Research Fields: Toledo and Lucas County history, 1815-, and regional Ohio history.

Address: 325 Michigan Street
                    Toledo, OH 43624

J182. UNIVERSITY OF AKRON

Collections: Papers of individual psychologists and the records of journals, organizations, and institutions. There are also photographs, films, audio tapes, early tests, and oral histories, all relating to psychology in America.

Research Fields: Materials relating to American psychology

Address: Archives of the History of American Psychology
                    Akron, OH 44325

J183. THE UNIVERSITY OF CHICAGO LIBRARY

Collections: Over 700 collections spanning the social and cultural history of England, 13th-20th centuries; Ireland, 17th-19th centuries; continental Europe, 18th-20th centuries; and Southeast Asia, 20th century; as well as those covering U.S. literary, social, political, and religious history. Important American topics include the Civil War era; Kentucky and settlement of the Ohio Valley; Chicago and regional history; 20th century literature and literary criticism; social amelioration and reform; philanthropy; socialism; religious history; and the history of American sociology and social research.

There are also collections dealing with
medieval and classical philology and the
history of science, especially atomic
science and physics and their social
implications.

Research Fields: 20th century European and American
                    intellectual history; South Asian
                    cultural and social history; American
                    sociology and anthropology; Czech and
                    Slovak immigration history; development
                    and social control of atomic energy; and
                    the history of The University of Chicago
                    and related institutions, boards,
                    governing bodies, and individuals.

Address: 1100 East 57th Street
                    Chicago, IL 60637

J184. UNIVERSITY OF CINCINNATI

Collections: The University of Cincinnati archives,
                    including official and administrative
                    records, as well as personal paper
                    collections; materials relating to urban
                    studies, with emphasis on 20th century
                    Cincinnati; materials in medical history,
                    with emphasis on 19th and 20th century
                    Cincinnati medical records and papers;
                    county and local government records and
                    other manuscripts and audio-visual
                    materials from an eight county area in
                    southwestern Ohio; and other materials,
                    including literary manuscripts from the
                    medieval period, as well as the 20th
                    century. Among the individuals on whom
                    collections focus are Alfred Bettman,
                    Gilbert Bettman, Martha Ransohoff, and
                    Albert Sabin.

Research Fields: Materials relating to the University of
                    Cincinnati, urban studies, medical
                    history, and county and local government,
                    and other records and manuscripts from an
                    eight county region in southwestern
                    Ohio.

Address: 610 Main Library
                    Cincinnati, OH 45221

J185. UNIVERSITY OF CINCINNATI GEOLOGY MUSEUM

       Collections: Geology; science; natural history;
                             petrology; mineralogy; paleontology;
                             outdoor museum.

       Research Fields: Related to collections

       Address: Department of Geology
                            University of Cincinnati
                            Cincinnati, OH 45221

J186. UNIVERSITY OF ILLINOIS

       Collections: Manuscript and archival materials
                             relating to the history of Illinois, the
                             Midwest, the Old Northwest, the Upper
                             Mississippi Valley, and colonial policy
                             in the Great Lakes area; Illinois
                             farming, business, organizations,
                             professions, politicians, and citizens;
                             and communitarianism in the United
                             States.

       Research Fields: Related to the collections

       Address: 1A University of Illinois Library
                            Urbana, IL 61801

J187. UNIVERSITY OF MICHIGAN

       Collections: Over 3,500 collections relating chiefly
                             to the history of Michigan and the
                             University of Michigan. Subject holdings
                             of special note include the temperance
                             and prohibition movement, America's
                             interest in the Philippine Islands, 20th
                             century American government and politics,
                             the Civil War, lumbering, church history,
                             conservation, women's history, black
                             history, pacifism and conscientious
                             objection, journalism, medicine,
                             agriculture, and the life of immigrant
                             groups in Michigan. Included are records
                             of organizations, papers of individuals,
                             and audio-visual materials.

       Research Fields: Michigan and the University of Michigan

       Address: 1150 Beal Avenue
                            Ann Arbor, MI 48109

J188. UNIVERSITY OF MICHIGAN,

ENGINEERING-TRANSPORTATION LIBRARY

Collections: Transportation history with emphasis on
                    19th century North America. There are
                    1,000 pieces of correspondence, 12,000
                    prints and photographs covering all modes
                    of transportation, 60 minute books and
                    ledgers of the Detroit United Railway
                    Lines, and 18,000 items of the personal
                    and business papers of Charles Ellet,
                    Jr., American civil engineer.

Research Fields: Transportation history, including
                    technology, travel, planning and
                    contruction, and social impact; diaries,
                    maps, photographs, engineering and
                    technical drawings, and business and
                    financial records of transport
                    industries.

Address: 312 Undergraduate Library Building
                    Ann Arbor, MI 48109

J189. UNIVERSITY OF MICHIGAN LIBRARY

DEPARTMENT OF RARE BOOKS AND SPECIAL COLLECTIONS

Collections: Over 100 collections relating chiefly to
                    literature, the theater, music, science,
                    history, economics, and protest movements
                    in the United States and Europe in the
                    19th and 20th centuries. Included are
                    personal correspondence and papers,
                    literary manuscripts, promptbooks, music
                    scores, government documents, records of
                    literary and civil rights organizations,
                    photographs, and scrapbooks.

Research Fields: 19th and 20th century theater, literary
                    and scientific topics, protest movements,
                    and historical papers of more than local
                    interest.

Address: Department of Rare Books and
                    Special Collections, Ann Arbor, MI 48109

J190. UNIVERSITY OF MICHIGAN MUSEUM OF ANTHROPOLOGY

Collections: Archaeology; ethnology; ethnobotany; zoo
                    archaeology; human osteology; geological

Research Fields: Archaeology; ethnology; geology; human
                     evolution

Address: Museum of Anthropology
                     Ann Arbor, MI   48109

J191.   UNIVERSITY OF NOTRE DAME ARCHIVES

Collections: Manuscript and archival materials, visual
                     and audible documents, and microfilms of
                     manuscript material principally from the
                     19th and 20th centuries, relating chiefly
                     to the Catholic church in the U.S. and to
                     the University of Notre Dame. Materials
                     relating to the University include office
                     files, account books and ledgers,
                     personal manuscript collections of
                     members of the faculty, photographs, oral
                     history tapes, microfilms and related
                     materials. Papers relating to the
                     Catholic church in the U.S. are divided
                     into four categories--diocesan, clerical,
                     lay and organizational--and are composed
                     of the same types of materials.

Research Fields: The University of Notre Dame and American
                     Catholicism

Address: P.O. Box 513
                     Notre Dame, IN   46556

J192.   UNIVERSITY OF NOTRE DAME LIBRARIES

Collections: Documents and autograph letters of popes,
                     cardinals, bishops and other historical
                     figures; modern autograph letters and
                     literary manuscripts of British and
                     American authors, including Catholic
                     authors in general; photographs of
                     Catholic authors; historical manuscripts
                     relating to Europe and early America; and
                     motion pictures, photographs, tape
                     recordings, microforms and phonodiscs
                     relating to international sports and
                     games and Notre Dame sports.

Research Fields: Catholic church history; British and
                     American authors, including Catholic
                     authors; Dante; the Renaissance; U.S.
                     history and culture; U.S. Presidents;
                     international sports and games; botany
                     and horology.

Address: Department of Rare Books and Special
                        Collections Notre Dame, IN 46556

J193. UNIVERSITY OF PITTSBURGH

Collections: Approximately 211 collections concen-
                        trating on the post-Civil War period,
                        primarily in Pittsburgh and western
                        Pennsylvania. Included are the personal
                        papers of political figures, labor union
                        representatives, businesspersons, politi-
                        cal and social activists, and the records
                        of companies, institutions, organi-
                        zations, societies, labor unions,
                        schools, and churches, as well as various
                        government records of the cities of
                        Allegheny and Pittsburgh and Allegheny
                        County, such as tax records, inactive
                        voters' registration cards, voting return
                        books, building permits, and birth,
                        death, and marriage records.

Research Fields: The growth and development of urban-
                        industrial society as represented by
                        Pittsburgh and western Pennsylvania.

Address: Hillman Library
                        Pittsburgh, PA 15260

J194. UNIVERSITY OF TOLEDO

Collections: Letters of American historical figures,
                        such as colonial governors, signers of
                        the Declaration of Independence,
                        Presidents, military leaders in the
                        Revolutionary War, scientists, leaders in
                        the women's rights movement, writers, and
                        black poets. Also included are the
                        archives of the University of Toledo.

Research Fields: Local history items; manuscripts of
                        political, literary, and business
                        leaders; papers of black poets; and
                        archival materials of the University of
                        Toledo.

Address: 2801 West Bancroft Street
                        Toledo, OH 43606

J195. UPPER WABASH BASIN REGIONAL RESOURCE CENTER

Collections: Herbarium with 9,200 speciments from
                       2,262 species, 723 genera; 160 families;
                       seed collection with approximately 250
                       specimens, not catalogued; animal and
                       bird skins; preserved animals; seed
                       depository.

Research Fields: Ecology; wildlife biology; aquatic
                       biology.

Address: 2303 College Avenue
                       Huntington, IN 46750

J196. LOUIS A. WARREN LINCOLN LIBRARY AND MUSEUM

Collections: Books and pamphlets, exclusively Lincoln;
                       association books; collateral
                       publications; periodicals; clippings;
                       paintings; original photographs;
                       manuscript collections.

Research Fields: Abraham Lincoln

Address: 1300 S. Clinton Street
                       Fort Wayne, IN 46801

J197. WAYNE COUNTY HISTORICAL MUSEUM

Collections: China; glass; silver, textiles;
                       children's museum; anthropology,
                       apothecary; agriculture; antiques;
                       architecture; costumes; fire-fighting
                       equipment; guns; hobbies; numismatics;
                       musical instruments; toys and dolls;
                       transportation. Historic houses: 1823,
                       Soloman Dickenson Log House; 1858,
                       Victorian home.

Research Fields: Southeast Indiana

Address: 1150 North "A" Street
                       Richmond, IN 47374

J198. WAYNE STATE UNIVERSITY

Collections: The Archives serves as the official
                       depository for the American Federation of
                       State, County and Municipal Employees,
                       American Federation of Teachers, Air Line

Pilots Association, Industrial Workers of
the World, The Newspaper Guild, United
Auto Workers, United Farm Workers, and
state and local labor organizations.
Collections include oral history and
photographs, as well as the personal
papers of union leaders and other
political and labor activists.

Research Fields: American labor history and related social
and economic reform movements; 20th
century urban America.

Address: Walter P. Reuther Library
Detroit, MI 48202

J199. WESTERN RESERVE HISTORICAL SOCIETY

Collections: Costumes; textiles; glassware; porcelain;
early aircraft; 1895-1976 automobiles;
1770-1920, twenty furnished period rooms.
Historic buildings: 1812-1850, Hale Farm
and Village Bath, with working farm and
restored buildings in a village setting;
1815, Shandy Hall, simple pioneer home in
Unionville, 1803, Loghurst, oldest house
built in Western Reserve; Canfield,
Lawnfield, home of President James A.
Garfield in Mentor. More than 1,500
collections, relating chiefly to the
exploration, growth, and development of
the state of Ohio and the Old Northwest,
with emphasis on the northeastern section
of Ohio known as the Western Reserve.
Special interest areas include Cleveland
urban, black, ethnic, and Jewish history,
and American genealogy. Also included
are collections dealing with the Civil
War, the antislavery movement, the
Shakers, and the era of the American
Revolution, as well as the personal
papers of nationally prominent men and
women who resided in northeastern Ohio.

Research Fields: U.S., Ohio, and local history especially
of northeastern Ohio.

Address: 10825 East Blvd.
Cleveland, OH 44106

J200. THE WILLARD LIBRARY OF EVANSVILLE

Collections: Manuscript and documentary materials
relating to the history of Evansville and

Vanderburgh County, IN, and adjacent areas of Indiana, Illinois, and Kentucky. Important holdings include records of Willard Library and its predecessors; materials of the Southwest Indiana Historical Society and the Vanderburgh Historical and Biographical Society; papers of author Annie Fellows Johnston, social reformer Albion Fellows Bacon, and businessman and civic leader Norman A. Shane, Sr.; scripts of radio newscasts; records of the Evansville Station of the U.S. Weather Service; and miscellaneous personal papers and city, township, and county records.

Research Fields: Individuals, companies, institutions, and events of Evansville and neighboring communities. Also the history of the tri-state region, comprised of southwestern Indiana and adjacent areas of Illinois and Kentucky.

Address: 21 First Avenue
Evansville, IN 47710

J201. WRIGHT STATE UNIVERSITY LIBRARY

Collections: Over 150 collections, including archives of Wright State University; correspondence, diaries, scrapbooks and other private papers of individuals; records of businesses and service establishments; documents from commercial, civic, social, farm and labor organizations; and photographs and maps concerning the history of aeronautics, the Miami Valley, and Ohio. Included are papers of the Wright brothers and James M. Cox; county and local government records from Montgomery, Greene, Clark, Champaign, Darke, Preble, Mercer, Shelby, Auglaize, Miami, and Logan counties; and records of 19th century agricultural equipment manufacturers and flood control projects.

Research Fields: The history of the eleven county Miami Valley area of southwestern Ohio, and materials on early aviation and aeronautics prior to World War I.

Address: Dayton, OH 45431

PROPER NAME INDEX

Abbott, Carl, B1, C1, C2, G1, I1.
Abbott, Edith, D1, I2.
Abzug, Robert H., F1.
Agocs, Carol, D3, E1.
Alberts, Robert C., C4, I3.
Alexander, June Grautin, D4, E2.
Allswang, John, E3, E4, F2, F3.
Alford, Clarence W., A1.
Anderson, David D., F4, H1, H2.
Anderson, James M., E5.
Anderson, Nels, D5.
Andrews, Wayne, I4, I5.
Angle, Paul, H3.
Angus, David I., D6, F5.
Ankenbruck, John, A2.
Armstrong, Louise, C5, D7.
Armstrong, Richard, H4.
Arndt, Karl John Richard, E6, H5.
Arnold, Eleanor, D8, G2.
Asbury, Charles, D9.
Aschenbrenner, Joyce, D10.
Asher, Robert, C6.
Atherton, Lewis, D11, H6.
Atkeson, Mary M., H7.

Babson, Steve, C7, D12, E7.
Badger, Reid, H8, I6.
Bahr, Howard M., D13, D14, E8.
Bakerman, Jane S., D15, E9, H9.
Bald, Frederick Clever, A3.
Baldwin, Leland D., A4.
Ballard, Robert M., B2.
Barclay, Norgan J., E10.
Barnes, Joseph W., C8, I7.
Barnhart, John D., C9, C10, F6.
Barrows, Robert G., D16, F7, G3.
Baskin, John, G4.
Bastian, Robert W., I8.
Bate, Phyllis A., C11.
Baughman, James L., C12.
Bauman, John F, D17, E11. F17.
Baylen, Joseph O., D18, E12.
Beale, Calvin L., C19.
Becker, Carl W., G5.
Beijbom, Ulf, D19, E13.
Bendler, E. Perry, B3, C13.

235

Findlay, James, E44.
Fish, John Hall, D58, E45, F30.
Fish, Lydia Marie, E46.
Fisher, James S., C56.
Fisk, Arthur M., A20.
Flader, Susan L., B16.
Flanagan, John T., D59, E48, H37, H38, H39, H40.
Flanagan, Maureen A., E47, F31, G22.
Flinn, Thomas A., F32.
Fogarty, Robert, E49.
Folmar, John N., C57.
Foster, R. Scott, F33.
Fox, Daniel J., B71.
Fox, Dixon Ryan, A21, F34.
Franklin, Ray, B17.
Frary, Ihna T., I33.
Frederick, John T., H41.
Fuller, Sara, A22, E50.
Fuller, Wayne E., G23, H42.
Funchion, Michael F., E51, F35.

Gallagher Smith, James P., I40.
Gandre, Donald A., C58.
Garrean, Joel, C59.
Gates, Paul W., C60, G24.
Gazell, James Albert, H43.
Gedics, A1, C61, E52.
Gehring, Wes D., G25, H44.
Geib, George W., A23.
Gerber, David A., D60, E53, E54.
Gibson, Arthur H., A45.
Ginger, Ray, A24, F36, F37, H46.
Gitlin, Todd, D61, E55.
Glass, James A., I34.
Glazer, Sidney, A25, A67, C124.
Goldman, Mark, A26, C62.
Gosnell, Harold F., F38, F39.
Goode, John Paul, B18.
Gosnell, Harold F., E56.
Gottfried, Alex, E57, F40.
Governor, Alan B., H47.
Grabnowski, John J., D62.
Graham, James Q., Sr., D63, G26.
Grant, H. Roger, C63.
Grant, William R., D64.
Gray, Ralph D., A27, A28.
Greenley, Albert H., A29.
Grey, Lennox B., H48.
Griffin, William W., E58, F41.
Groh, George W., E59, G27.
Groselose, Barbara, H49.
Gross, Barry, H50.
Gutgesell, Stephen, A30.
Gutierrez, Armando, E97.
Gutman, Herbert G., C64.

GEOGRAPHICAL INDEX

Ann Arbor, MI, B64, C106.

Benton Harbor, MI, E49.
Blue Island, IL, G34.
Boston, MA, D44, D50, E120.
Buffalo, NY, A6, A26, C62, C93, C105, C119, C122, D68, D104, E29,
    E46, E53, E95, I72.

Calumet Region (IN), A50.
Cannelton, IN, C154.
Cass County, MI, D140, E124, E125, G29, G84.
Chicago, IL, A33, A53, A64, A71, B7, B9, B10, B11, B18, B20, B35,
    B37, B49, B50, C2, C11, C15, C31, C38, C42, C50, C63, C78, C84,
    C86, C89, C98, C100, C103, C108, C137, C139, C145, C148, C152, C152A,
    C153, C163, D1, D2, D5, D10, D18, D19, D23, D24, D25, D26, D27,
    D36, D43, D44, D45, D49, D50, D51, D52, D57, D58, D61, D66, D72,
    D73, D74, D78, D79, D92, D99, D100, D102, D105, D112, D113,
    D116, D119, D124, D126, D129, D131, D132, D133, D135, D142,
    D145, E3, E4, E12, E22, E23, E24, E27, E31, E34, E42, E43, E47,
    E51, E55, E56, E57, E62, E67, E69, E70, E73, E75, E78, E85, E93,
    E96, E101, E114, E115, E116, E118, E120, E131, F2, F3, F8, F22,
    F28, F31, F35, F38, F39, F40, F44, F45, F53, F54, F57, F59, F64,
    F73, F74, F76, F79, F80, F90, F95, F104, F105, F106, F107, F108,
    F113, G1, G6, G10, G12, G13, G15, G22, G30, G32, G37, G39, G63,
    G78, G81, H3, H8, H11, H13, H14, H28, H29, H30, H31, H43, H48,
    H62, H63, H64, H70, H71, H73, H74, H78, H84, H96, H97, H101,
    H102, H103, H104, H105, H106, H107, H110, H112, H119, H120, I2,
    I4, I6, I9, I11, I12, I13, I15, I17, I18, I19, I22, I23, I24,
    I25, I27, I32, I37, I38, I39, I41, I42, I48, I49, I60, I70, I71,
    I73, I80, I81, I84, I86, I87.
Cincinnati, OH, A19, A87, C3, C49, C51, C146, C147, D55, D56, D107,
    E40, F19, F48, F71, G18, G20, G33, G43, G60, G69, G87, H17, H23,
    H32, H65, H79, H95, H111, I20, I30, I52, I67, I78, I89.
Cleveland, OH, A17, A90, C29, D62, E30, E92, G8, G50, I45, I57,
    I82.
Columbus, OH, D42, D109, D117, F78.
Crawfordsville, IN, H100.

Daisytown, PA, E11
Detroit, MI, B54, B55, B56, B71, C7, C14, C43, C46, C97, C110,
    C169, D3, D9, D12, D32, D64, D93, D96, D125, D144, E1, E7, E38,
    E74, E83, E87, E103, E104, E119, F21, F25, F46, F62, F68, F91,
    G54, G55, G73, G74, G89, G91, H4, H87, H112, I31, I40, I58.
Duquesne, PA, D41, F18.

Mail-order catalogues, C84, C138
Manuscript collections, A8, A13, A18, A20, A36, A45, A46, A66, A78,
    A83
Meat-packing industry, C159
Medicine, G62
Merchandising, C84
Merrill, see Skidmore, Owings, and Merrill
Middletown, D30, D31, E8
Mies van der Rohe, I24, I59
Mobility
    -- social, D16, D115, D136, D138, D139, G38
    -- geographical, G3, G56, G77
Modernization, A42

Natural gas industry, C13
Newspaper collections, A55

Oil industry, see petroleum industry
Owings, see Skidmore, Owings, and Merrill

Petroleum industry, C113, C150, C166
Philanthrophy, cultural, C137, D78, D102, H64, H103
Planning, see urban planning
Poetry, H34, H40, H51, H89, H112, H114--see also literature
Poles, D22, D116, D144, E10, E19, E73, E95, E96, E116, F54
Public administration, F11
Public utilities, B9
Pullman, George, C98, D26

Railroads, C2, C31, C57, C60, C63, C122, C130, C148, G1--see also
    transportation
Recreation, D143
Regionalism, A41, A58, A65, A69, A70, A71, A79, C52, D123, D124,
    H32
Roads, C71--see also transportation

Saloons, D50, D97
Settlement houses, D28, D33, D40, D44, D49, D55, D62, D100, D117,
    D137, E85, G7, G10, G81
Settlement patterns, C45
Skidmore, Owings, and Merrill, I22, I25
Slovaks, D4, E2
Social institutions, D50, D98, D105, D113, F83
Sociology, Chicago School, D57, D131, D145, F23
Steel industry, C6, C36, C53, C65, C77, C127, C160, C165
Suburbs, C2, D3, D128, G1, G6, G34, G43, G50, G51, G76, G79, I85
Swedes, D19, E13

Technology, C126, C149, D90, G42
Theatre, H50, H114
Trade expositions, C146, D27, F15, H111--see also world fairs
Transportation
    -- surface, C71
    -- water, B5, C80, C95, C109, C135, C167

Urban planning, D26, F90, I32, I38, I53, I74, I78, I79